Alan Bennett
Plays One

Alan Bennett first appeared on the stage in 1960 as one of the
authors and performers of the revue Beyond the Fringe. His
stage plays include *Forty Years On*, *Getting On*, *Habeas Corpus*,
The Old Country and *Enjoy*, and he has written many television
plays, notably *A Day Out*, *Sunset Accross the Bay*, *A Woman of
No Importance* and the series of monologues *Talking Heads*.
An adaptation of his television play, *An Englishman Abroad*
was paired with *A Question of Attribution* in the double bill
Single Spies, first produced at the National Theatre in 1988.
This was followed in 1990 by his adaptation of *The Wind in the
Willows* and in 1991 by *The Madness of George III*, both produced
at the National Theatre. *The Lady in the Van* was produced at
The Queen's Theatre in 1999.

ALAN BENNETT
Plays One

Forty Years On,
Getting On,
Habeas Corpus
and *Enjoy*

Introduced by the author

faber and faber

This collection first published in 1991
as *Forty Years On and Other Plays*
by Faber and Faber Limited
3 Queen Square London WC1N 3AU

Reissued as *Alan Bennett: Plays One* in 1996

Typeset by Wilmaset, Bikenhead, Wirral
Printed and bound in Great Britain by
Mackays of Chatham plc, Chatham, Kent

A CIP record for this book
is available from the British Library

ISBN 0-571-17745-X

6 8 10 97 5

CONTENTS

INTRODUCTION

In 1969 I had a letter from a producer in BBC Radio saying he'd fished out an old script of mine from the pool and thought it might have possibilities for a radio play. I liked the idea of a producer at Portland Place dredging up drama from a pool of old paperwork but he was six months too late, and I smugly wrote back, to point out that the play in question, *Forty Years On*, was already running in the West End.

In fairness, the version of the play put on at the Apollo in 1968 was very different from the one I'd submitted to the BBC two years before. There was no mention of Albion House, the run-down public school which is the setting for the play, nor of the Headmaster, whose retirement is the occasion for the presentation of 'Speak for England, Arthur', the play within the play. The memoirs of T. E. Lawrence and Virginia Woolf occur in the original script and the visit to the country house on the eve of the First War, but these are presented as the memoirs of Hugh and Moggie, an upper-class couple who sit out the Second World War in the basement of Claridge's. The transitions in time and the representation of memory, which are hard to bring off on the stage, are the stock-in-trade of radio, but I'm thankful now that the BBC put this first script on the discard pile, thus forcing me to rewrite it in the version eventually produced on the stage. What the letter did remind me of was the struggle there'd been finding the play a shape.

To begin with, most of the parodies in the play I'd written separately and stockpiled, hoping vaguely to put together a kind of literary revue. When I began to think in more narrative terms these parodies proved a stumbling-block, as I found I had to create characters who could conceivably have had memories of, say, the age of Oscar Wilde, Lawrence of Arabia and of Bloomsbury. Hence the Claridge's couple, Hugh and Moggie. When I subsequently hit on the (fairly obvious) idea of a school play, with the school itself a loose metaphor for England, it resolved much that had made me uneasy. It had all been too snobbish for a start, but once in the context of the school play, which guyed them just as much as it celebrated them, Hugh and Moggie and Nursie, their Nanny, became more acceptable. They're still *quite* snobbish, of course, and certainly not the common man. But to put a play within a play is to add another frame which enables one to introduce more jokes, and also more irony as references within the play find echoes outside it. Jokes like the Headmaster's 'Thirty years ago today, Tupper, the Germans marched into Poland and you're picking your nose'; ironies like Churchill announcing peace in Europe in 1945 just as the boys in the present day fling themselves into a fierce fight.

The play enshrines some terrible jokes. One way of looking at *Forty Years On* is as an elaborate life-support system for the preservation of bad jokes. 'Sandy will accompany you, disguised as a waiter. That should at least secure you the entrée.' One of the boys is called Lord. It's true that there was such a boy at Giggleswick School from whose prospectus I pinched some of the names, but he's only so called in order to furnish the Headmaster, wandering about holding his empty coffee cup, with the blasphemous exchange 'Lord, take this cup from me.' The child does so. 'Thank you, Lord.' But I like bad jokes and always have, and when an audience groans at a pun it's often only because they wish they'd thought of it first, or at any rate seen it coming in time to duck.

Besides, these bad jokes were the survivors; even worse jokes had bit the dust along the way. When the play opened in Manchester it included a piece about the first London visit of the Diaghilev ballet in 1911.

> *A boy got up as Nijinsky, dressed as the faun in* L'Après-Midi, *dances behind a gauze, while downstage the practice pianist reminisces:* Ah yes. Nijinsky. I suppose I am the only person now able to recall one of the most exciting of his ballets, the fruit of an unlikely collaboration between Nijinsky on the one hand and Sir Arthur Conan Doyle on the other. It was the only detective story in ballet and was called *The Inspectre de la Rose.* The choreography was by Fokine. It wasn't up to much. The usual Fokine rubbish.

8

Ordinarily, good taste in the person of the Lord Chamberlain would have put paid to that last joke. But this was 1968, and *Forty Years On* was one of the plays on his desk when the Lord Chamberlain's powers expired and stage censorship was abolished.

There were other jokes, equally bad but more 'satirical'. At one point Field Marshal Earl Haig strode on, in bright red gloves: 'As you all know, I have just this minute returned from the First World War. Indeed, so recently have I returned I haven't had time to wash my hands.' And much more in the same vein. The play was such a ragbag I even considered including a story about Earl Haig at Durham Cathedral. The Field Marshal was being shown round by the dean where they paused at the tomb of the Venerable Bede. Haig regarded it thoughtfully for a moment, then said: 'Of course. Bede. Now he was a woman, wasn't he?' It's a good example of scrambled memory, but the laborious explanations that I had to go into with the cast decided me against inflicting it on an audience.

Hugh and Moggie were suggested by – but not modelled on – Harold Nicolson and Vita Sackville-West. In 1968 Nicolson's diaries had just been published with his passionate account of the fight against Appeasement in the thirties and how, come the war, appeasers like Chips Channon conveniently forgot to eat their words about Germany and pretended they'd been right all along. The play is stiff with quotations. The readings from the lectern enable actual quotations to be incorporated into the structure of the play, but there are umpteen more, some lying about on the surface in mangled form and others buried in shallow graves. 'Patience is mine: I will delay saith the Lord.' 'They are rolling up the maps all over Europe. We shall not see them lit again in our lifetime.' Some quotations I have lost track of. I thought I'd invented the phrase 'snobbery with violence' to describe the school of Sapper and Buchan (and Ian Fleming, for that matter), but then I was told it had been used before, but where and in what circumstances I have forgotten.

The form of *Forty Years On* is more complicated than I would dream of attempting now. It is a play within a play in which the time-scale of the first play gradually catches up with the time-scale of the second, one cog the years 1900–39, the other 1939–45, and both within the third wheel of the present day. What doesn't seem to have worried me at the time is what kind of educational institution it is that would mount such a production. This didn't seem to worry the audience. After all, it is only a play. Or a play within a play. Or a play within that. Plenty of jokes anyway (too many, some people said), and it's hard to fail with twenty-odd schoolboys on the stage. I've a feeling they (and the set) came via a Polish play, *The Glorious Resurrection of Our Lord*, that I saw in the World Theatre Season at the Aldwych in 1967, in which choirboys sang above a screen that ran across the stage. I saw *Zigger Zagger* that year, too, with the stage a crowded football terrace, which made me realize how theatrical a spectacle is an audience watching an audience.

Because *Forty Years On* employs a large cast, and also because it is as much a revue as a play, it seldom gets performed. Schools do it from time to time, and ironically, in view of the Headmaster's strictures, sometimes find it necessary to cut the Confirmation Class. This raises the dizzy possibility of the pretend headmaster rushing onto the stage to put a stop to 'this farrago of libel, blasphemy and perversion' only to find the real headmaster hard on his heels, bent on putting a stop to him putting a stop to it.

Forty Years On had been such a happy experience that when, in 1971, I wrote my second play it was natural that Stoll Theatres, who'd put the first one on, should want to keep the winning team together. Accordingly, we had the same director, Patrick Garland, the same designer, Julia Trevelyan Oman and the management even contrived that we should begin rehearsing on the same stage, Drury Lane, and on the same day, August Bank Holiday, as three years before. In some cultures they would have slit the throat of a chicken. In view of what was to happen it would have been just as effective.

Getting On is an account of a middle-aged Labour MP, George Oliver, so self-absorbed that he remains blind to the fact that his wife is having an affair with the handyman, his mother-in-law is dying, his son is getting ready to leave home, his best friend thinks him a fool and that to everyone who comes into contact with him he is a self-esteeming joke. In 1984 one would just say, 'Oh, you mean he's *a man*,' and have done with it. But in 1971 the beast was less plain, the part harder to define, and casting the main role proved a problem. The script was turned down by half a dozen leading actors and I had begun to think there was something wrong with the play (there was: too long) when Kenneth More's name came up. Kenneth More was, to say the least, not an obvious choice. As an actor and a man he had a very conservative image and to many of my generation he was identified with one of his most famous parts, that of Douglas Bader in the film *Reach for the Sky*. It was one of the films we were making fun of in the 'Aftermyth of War' sketch in *Beyond the Fringe*.

> I had a pretty quiet war really. I was one of the Few. We were stationed down at Biggin Hill. One Sunday we got word Jerry was coming in, over Broadstairs, I think it was. We got up there quickly as we could and, you know, everything was very calm and peaceful. England lay like a green carpet below me and the war seemed worlds away. I could see Tunbridge Wells and the sun glinting on the river, and I remembered that last weekend I'd spent there with Celia that summer of '39.
>
> Suddenly Jerry was coming at me out of a bank of cloud. I let him have it, and I think I must have got him in the wing because he spiralled past me out of control. As he did so . . . I'll always remember this . . . I got a glimpse of his face, and you know . . . he smiled. Funny thing, war.

Some nights, greatly daring, I would stump stiff-legged around the stage in imitation of Douglas Bader, feelingly priggishly rewarded by the occasional hiss. Douglas Bader, that is, as played by Kenneth More, and here we were casting him as a Labour MP. It seemed folly. But was it? A veteran of many casting sessions since, I have learned how the argument goes. When all the obvious choices have been exhausted, a kind of hysteria sets in as more and more unlikely names are suggested. The process is called Casting Against the Part and it's almost a parlour game; a winning combination would be, say, Robert Morley as Andrew Aguecheek.

All of which is to do an injustice to Kenneth More, who was a fine naturalistic actor, and although he had never stepped outside his genial public stereotype, Patrick Garland and I both thought that if he could be persuaded to do so, it might remake him as an actor. The example of Olivier and Archie Rice was invoked, with high-sounding phrases like 'taking his proper place in the modern theatre'. In retrospect, it seems silly, conceited and always futile. Kenneth More had no intention of remaking himself as an actor. Why should he? His public liked him the way he was. It would be much simpler to remake the play, and this is what he did. However, all this was in the future. We had lunch, he was enthusiastic about the play, seeing it as a great opportunity, and so the production went ahead, with Mona Washbourne, Gemma Jones and Brian Cox in the other parts.

I didn't attend many of the rehearsals. I still wasn't certain that one should. The question had not arisen in *Forty Years On* since I was there anyway as a member of the cast. Practices differ. Some playwrights attend the first read-through (and sometimes *do* the first read-through), then aren't seen again until the dress rehearsal. Others are at the director's elbow every day. There is something to be said for both. When one only puts in an occasional appearance the actors tend to think of the author as the Guardian of the Text, an uncomfortable and potentially censorious presence before whom they go to pieces. On the other hand, a playwright who is at every rehearsal soon ceases to be intimidating but has to exercise a corresponding tact. The temptation to put one's oar in is strong. Actors come to a performance slowly; blind alleys have to be gone down, toes slid gingerly into water. To the playwright (the brute) the cast seem like small boys stood shivering and blowing into their hands on the side of a swimming-bath. Why don't they just dive in and strike out for the other end with strong and perfect strokes?

After all, it's perfectly obvious to the playwright how to do the play. He could do it himself if only he could act.

It seemed easiest to keep away, which is what I did. When I'm asked these days why I invariably go to rehearsals and on location with films I have some nice answer ready. But if I'm honest it's because that autumn with *Getting On* I made a wrong decision. I wrote in my diary:

> The saddest thing about this production so far is that it is getting on quite well without me. I go down to the theatre from time to time, sneaking into the auditorium without being seen in case my presence should make the actors nervous. If they do see me they ply me with questions about the text. 'Would he say this?' asks Kenneth More, pointing to an inconsistency. 'No, *he* wouldn't,' is what I ought to say, 'but *I* would.' Instead I construct a lame theory to justify the inconsistency. 'What is she doing upstairs at this time?' asks Gemma Jones. 'Why did you send her off?' Why indeed? Because I'd run out of things for her to say, probably. 'Maybe she's putting the children to bed,' is what I answer. When a play's being cast it might be as well to pick someone to play the author too for all the help he can give them.

Even with the final dress rehearsals no alarm bells rang. The play was too long, admittedly, and ought to have been cut in rehearsal or, better still, beforehand, which is another lesson to be learned: if there are to be cuts, get them over with before rehearsals begin. But there was still a fortnight's tour in Brighton when all this could be done. No panic.

Now Brighton is a dangerous place. It is the home or the haunt of many theatricals, who take an entirely human pleasure in getting in first on plays bound for the West End. They come round, proffer advice, diagnose what is wrong and suggest remedies. That is one section of the audience. The other consists (or did in 1971) of playgoers for whom the theatre has never been the same since John Osborne, and if they don't like a play they leave it in droves. Indeed, it sometimes seems that their chief pleasure in going to the theatre in Brighton is in leaving it, and leaving it as noisily as possible. In *Beyond the Fringe* the seats were going up like pistol shots throughout the performance so that, come the curtain, there were scarcely more in the audience than there were on the stage. On the other hand, *Forty Years On* had done well. Brighton was where Gielgud had got his second wind and the play came into focus. But that was familiar ground. Audiences at Brighton like what they know and know what they like and one person they did like was Kenneth More.

Until he was actually faced with an audience Kenneth More was scrupulous about playing the part as written (and sometimes overwritten). It's true, he flatly refused to say 'fuck' since it would ruin the matinees, but this didn't seem to me to be important, so long as he continued to play George Oliver as the kind of man who did say 'fuck' (the play maybe just happening to catch him on a day when he didn't). Kenny himself of course said it quite frequently in life, but that was neither here nor there. The first night in Brighton didn't go well and I was surprised (it is evidence of my own foolishness) how nervous the audience made him. Nothing in his debonair and easy-going exterior prepared one for the vulnerable actor he became that night. It was plain he had been expecting the audience to love him and when they didn't he felt lost.

That first week the Brighton audience lapped up the jokes but yawned at the bits in between. We made some cuts, but found it hard because it was now plain that Kenneth More saw the piece as a comedy while I was trying to keep it a serious play. At the beginning of the second week in Brighton, and without there having been any warning or disagreement, he called a rehearsal to cut the play to his own taste, while instructing the management not to allow me into the theatre until this had been done. The following day I found myself barred from the theatre altogether and in fact never saw the play in its entirety from that day until it closed in the West End eight months later. When it was playing at the Queen's I'd sometimes slip in to see how it was going, find he'd introduced more new lines to make his character more acceptable to the audience and come away feeling the piece had nothing to do with me at all. The younger members of the cast were fine, but there seemed to be an alliance between Kenneth More and Mona Washbourne to make it all nice and palatable, and with no ambiguity. I've always felt the play is too plotty, but it wasn't plotty enough for them. George is meant to be so self-absorbed that he has a diminished sense of the existence of others. Finding it unbearable that he should be playing a character who doesn't care that his mother-in-law may be dying, Kenny had inserted his own line: 'I'll go and see her doctor tomorrow.' I wrote in my diary at the time: 'It's as if after Tuzenbach's death in *Three Sisters* Irena were to come on and say: "I have three tickets for the 11.30 train to Moscow tomorrow. I have rented us a beautiful apartment and I already have my eye on several possible husbands." ' But not really, because, alas, it isn't *Three Sisters*. I took it all very seriously. Two more diary entries:

> It has been my experience that when directors or management start talking about the importance of the text it is because they are about to cut it. In the same way the people who talk most about the sanctity of human life are the advocates of capital punishment.

> Seeing this production of my play without having attended the rehearsals or had anything to do with it until I actually saw it on stage is like going to see a relative who has been confined in an institution. A parent in a home. A son at boarding-school. Their hair is cut differently, they are wearing strange clothes; they have a routine with which one is not familiar, other friends, other jokes. Yet the features are the same. This is still the person I know. But what have these people done? What right have they to dress him up like this, cut off his hair, put her in that shapeless garment. This is my child. My mother.

All I was complaining about was that it had been turned into 'a lovely evening in the theatre'.

There was a comic side to all this. *Getting On* is set in George Oliver's North London home and furnished in a style that was becoming generally fashionable in the early seventies. I knew the style well, having parodied it as part of a TV series in 1966 *Life in NW1*. This was a period when stripped pine was in its infancy and the customary objects of such a household – the jelly moulds, the cane carpetbeaters, the Seth Thomas clocks and Asian Pheasant plates – were not so readily available as they have since become. Attics were still unexplored, tallboys unstripped and the nightdress potential of Edwardian shrouds not yet fully exploited. My own house was of course stuffed with such objects. Rather than scour the junk shops of Brighton and Portobello Road, it seemed easier to transfer my own possessions onto the set. But I was barred from the theatre. So while a look-out was kept for the star rehearsing on the stage I smuggled in my precious *objets trouvés* at a side door.

The question will, of course, be asked: what was the director, Patrick Garland, doing during all this? It was a question that kept occurring to me at the time, when I felt betrayed by him and by the management. In retrospect I think that by concentrating on Kenneth More and leaving my feelings to take care of themselves, Patrick probably did the right thing, though I found it hard to take when it was happening. A leading actor is like a thorough-bred horse, to be coaxed and gentled into the gate. One false move and his ears are back and he's up at the other end of the paddock. With a West End opening large amounts of money are involved and where there is money there is always bad behaviour. In films, where more money is at stake, the behaviour is much worse, and the writer traditionally gets the mucky end of the stick. Nor should one ever underestimate the courage required of actors. To go out in front of a first-night audience bearing the main brunt of a new play is a small act of heroism. Actors must always have a sense that they are there to do the author's dirty work. He may have written it, but he doesn't have to go out there and *say* it. They are in the trenches, he is back at base.

In the event, the play won an *Evening Standard* Award for the Best Comedy of 1971. It had never seemed to me to be a comedy and at the ceremony I said it was like entering a marrow for the show and being given the cucumber prize. Kenneth More is dead, dying courageously and very much in the mould of the parts he liked playing. I still think that he could have been, if not a better actor than he was given credit for, certainly a more interesting one. He wasn't the simple, straightforward good-natured guy he played: he was more complicated than that. But because he wanted so much to be liked he left a large tract of his character undeveloped. Acting is a painful business and it's to do with exposure, not concealment. As it is, the play still remains uncut. It's far too long, too wordy, and probably reads better than it performs: a good part but a bad play.

The third play in this collection, *Habeas Corpus*, was written in 1973. It was an attempt to write a farce without the paraphernalia of farce, hiding places, multiple exits and and umpteen doors. Trousers fall, it is true, but in an instantaneous way as if by divine intervention. I wrote it without any idea of how it could be staged and rehearsals began with just four bentwood chairs. The big revolution occurred after two weeks rehearsal when the director, Ronald Eyre, decided we could manage with three. Remembering *Getting On* I had worked hard on the text beforehand and together we cut it to the bone before rehearsals started. The bare stage specified in the stage directions is essential to the bare text. Re-introduce the stock-in-trade of farce (as the Broadway production tried to do) and the play doesn't work. There is just enough text to carry the performers on and off, provided they don't dawdle. If they have to negotiate doors or stairs or potted plants or get anywhere except into the wings, then they will be left stranded halfway across the stage, with no line left with which to haul themselves off.

Neither *Getting On* nor *Habeas Corpus* is what Geoffrey Grigson called 'weeded of impermanence', a necessary condition apparently if a play or a poem is to outlast its time. Topical references are out. Of course plays don't become timeless simply by weeding them of timely references any more than plays become serious by weeding them of jokes. But the jokes in *Habeas Corpus* about the Permissive Society do date it and some of the other jokes make we wince. Still, *Habeas Corpus* is a favourite of mine if only because it's one of the few times I've managed not to write a naturalistic play. It's also the only one of my plays to be done regularly by amateurs. I can see why. It's cheap to put on, there are plenty of good parts, mostly out of stock – henpecked husband, frustrated wife, lecherous curate, ubiquitous char – and everyone is slightly larger than life, which helps with the acting. But it's not altogether farce. Death doesn't quite lay down his book and poor Dennis ends up doomed. The original production ended on an even blacker note, explaining what to anyone who didn't see the original production must seem a mysterious stage direction: 'Wicksteed dances alone in the spotlight until he can dance no more.' The original version of the play had no dance and ended with the quip:

> Whatever right or wrong is
> He whose lust lasts, lasts longest.

Putting music to the play was the idea of Ronald Eyre. Carl Davis recorded some rumbustious incidental music on a fair-ground organ and, hearing it, Alec Guinness wanted to add a coda to the play. In top hat and tails he begins a debonair dance number, which slowly shudders to a halt as the spotlight dwindles, a real dance of death. It was the idea of this dance that helped him to reconcile the otherwise uncongenial character of Wicksteed to his own. It was a great bonus to the play and the exact opposite of what had happened in *Getting On*, an actor adding something to the play, enlarging it to accommodate his talents. I can't imagine anyone else bringing off that dance, or how to describe it in a stage direction. I imagine most amateur productions turn it into a knees-up, which is very different but no bad way to end.

Sometime in 1989 I read in the *Guardian* that the Victorian school at Burley Woodhead in Yorkshire was to be taken down stone by stone and re-erected in Bradford Museum, where it is to be visited by, among others, patients suffering from Alzheimer's Disease, in the hope, one presumes, of jogging their memories. This school transport came handily at the end of the decade to remind me of the last play in this collection, *Enjoy*, which I wrote as the decade opened and which had predicted just that.

The title is possibly a mistake; *Endure* would probably have been better, though hardly a crowd-puller, or even, despite the implicit threat of chorus girls, *Look on the Bright Side*. Still, *Enjoy* it was and I can't change it now.

It's the story of an old couple who live in one of the last back-to-backs in Leeds. Mam's memory is failing and Dad is disabled. While he lands up in hospital, the end of the play sees Mam still happily living in the back-to-back, now lovingly reconstructed in a museum. The fact that one of the social workers who affect this transformation is their long-lost son in drag may have had something to do with the less than ecstatic reception the play received, but, that apart, the whole notion of the play was dismissed at the time as far-fetched, expressionistic even. A back-to-back in a museum! I was told in future to stick to the particularities of dialogue and the niceties of actual behaviour that I was supposed to be good at, and leave social comment to others.

Of course, there are things wrong with the play – the title certainly; the drag maybe, particularly since it persuaded some critics that I cherished a shamefaced longing to climb into twinset and pearls. James Fenton, I was told, even referred to the drag character as 'the writer'. Mr Fenton's subsequent abandonment of dramatic criticism to become the *Independent*'s correspondent in the Philippines was one of the more cheering developments in the theatre in the eighties, though when President Marcos claimed to be a much-misunderstood man, I knew how he felt.

However, if only in a spirit of 'I told you so', I noted in the course of the eighties various news items, like the reconstruction of the school at Burley Woodhead, which bore out the central thesis of the play and proved it to have been, though I say so myself, prophetic. For instance, a room was created in 1984 at Park Prewett Hospital in Basingstoke furnished as it would have been forty years ago in order to assist elderly patients in 'reminiscence therapy'. There was the exhibit, also in 1984, at the Miami Zoo of urban man in his natural habitat: a man in a sitting-room in a cage. There was the proposal, later abandoned, to reconstruct part of the Death Railway in Thailand as a tourist attraction. Most pertinent of all (and, of course, this is the cutting I have lost, so you will have to take my word for it) was the devoted reproduction in a museum somewhere in England of the last of the prefabs, with the couple who had lived in it doing a regular stint as curators.

Whether or not I got it right, I still like the laying-out scene in Act Two because it is one of the few occasions when a character of mine has done what characters in plays and novels are supposed to do, namely, taken on a life of their own. Until the two women started to lay Dad out I had thought Mr Craven was dead and his erection (on the typewriter) took me as much by surprise as it did them. It is such a farcical scene it perhaps belongs to a different play, though the setting and the atmosphere of it owe something to Peter Gill's season of D. H. Lawrence plays which I saw in the seventies at the Royal Court.

With the exception of *Habeas Corpus* all these plays are too long – well over an hour each way, which is all I can ever take in the theatre – and in performance they should be cut. As Churchill said, 'The head cannot take in more than the seat can endure.' I recently took a child to see *The Wind in the Willows*. He first of all asked how long it was likely to last, and then, 'How many are there of those things when they let you out for a bit?' 'Intervals? Just one.' 'Oh. Those are the bits I like best.'

Alan Bennett
January 1991

FORTY YEARS ON

To my mother and father

CHARACTERS

THE HEADMASTER
FRANKLIN, a housemaster
TEMPEST, a junior master
MATRON
MISS NISBITT, the Bursar's Secretary
HEAD BOY and LECTERN READER
THE ORGANIST

The Play Within the Play

FRANKLIN   plays HUGH
MATRON   plays MOGGIE
MISS NISBITT   plays NURSIE
THE HEADMASTER and TEMPEST play various parts

All other parts are played by the boys of Albion House School. These boys should be on the stage wherever possible. Even when they take no direct part in the action they should be ranged round the gallery as onlookers. Any scene shifting or stage setting should be done by them.

The first performance of *Forty Years On* was given at the Apollo
Theatre, London, on 31 October 1968. It was presented by Stoll
Productions Ltd and the cast was as follows:

HEADMASTER	John Gielgud
FRANKLIN, a Housemaster	Paul Eddington
TEMPEST, a Junior Master	Alan Bennett
MATRON	Dorothy Reynolds
MISS NISBITT, the Bursar's secretary	Nora Nicholson
THE LECTERN READER	Robert Swann
ORGANIST	Carl Davis
SKINNER	Anthony Andrews
SPOONER (Horn)	Roger Brain
CARTWRIGHT (Flute)	Andrew Branch
FOSTER	William Burleigh
WIMPENNY	Philip Chappell
WIGGLESWORTH (Trumpet)	Thomas Cockrell
TREDGOLD (Guitar)	George Fenton
CHARTERIS	Freddie Foot
LEADBETTER	Paul Guess
GILLINGS	Dickie Harris
DISHFORTH	Peter Kinley
LORD	Robert Langley
BOTTOMLEY (Alto)	Stephen Leigh
SALTER	Denis McGrath
MACILWAINE	Keith McNally
JARVIS (Treble)	Stephen Price
CRABTREE	Colin Reese
RUMBOLD	Merlin Ward
MOSS (Violin)	Neville Ware
TUPPER	Alan Warren

The play was directed by PATRICK GARLAND and designed by
JULIA TRAVELYAN OMAN. Lighting was by ROBERT ORNBO.
Music arranged and directed by CARL DAVIS.

AUTHOR'S NOTE

The text here printed differs in some small details from that first performed on the stage at the Apollo Theatre. In performance certain sections of the play were thinned down and odd lines cut in order to reduce the playing time. In the printed version these sections have been restored.

I would like to thank Collins and Co. for permission to quote from Sir Harold Nicolson's *Diaries and Letters 1930–39*, Sir Osbert Sitwell for the quotation from *Great Morning* and Mr Leonard Woolf for the quotation from *Downhill All The Way*.

ACT ONE

The Assembly Hall of Albion House, a public school on the South Downs.

The Assembly Hall is a gloomy Victorian Gothic building, with later additions, a conglomeration of periods without architectural unity. It is dingy and dark and somewhat oppressive. A gallery runs round the hall, and on the gallery stage right is an organ. Staircases lead up to the gallery stage right and stage left. At the head of the staircase stage right is a lectern and below it is a hymn board. To the rear of the stage is a War Memorial, with lists and lists of names which run the whole height of the set. This War Memorial consists of two sliding doors and behind these doors is a back-projection screen. Whenever a scene takes place in Albion House these doors remain closed as at the opening of the play. During the Claridge's scenes they are opened to reveal a photograph of the relevant period of the Second World War. During the memoirs (i.e. all scenes preceded by a reading from the lectern) the screen shows a photograph relevant to the subject of the memoir. It should be emphasized that the screen is used for decorative purposes rather than to provide information essential to the understanding of the play. I have not indicated where these doors are opened to reveal the screens or the photographs projected, except for the T. E. Lawrence Lantern Lecture and at the end of Acts One and Two.

When the curtain rises the stage is dark. We hear the sounds of school, a chapel bell, the sound of a cricket match and boys repeating by rote in class. An organ plays softly. A boy enters and switches on the lights.

Another boy enters with a hand-bell which he rings across the stage and off it, and as the sound fades away the boys of Albion House School enter singing a processional hymn. They form up at the front of the stage, followed by FRANKLIN, MATRON, TEMPEST *and* MISS NISBITT. *When they have all taken their places the* HEAD-MASTER *enters.*

HEADMASTER: Members of Albion House, past and present.
Parents and Old Boys. It does not seem so many years since
I stood in this hall on November 11, 1918, to hear the
headmaster declare a half holiday on the occasion of the
Armistice. That was my first term at Albion House as a
schoolboy, and now I am headmaster and it is my last term.
It is a sad occasion . . .
(*A jet aircraft roars overhead temporarily drowning his words,
and he waits.*)
. . . it is a sad occasion, but it is a proud occasion too. I can
see now some of the faces of my school-fellows on that
never-to-be-forgotten November morning, many of them
the sons of old boys who, proud young trees for the felling,
fell in that war. And in many a quiet English village there
stands today a cenotaph carved with their names, squire's
son rubbing shoulders with blacksmith's boy in the
magnificent equality of death. Scarce twenty summers
sufficed to weather those names before England must needs
take up arms in a Second World War.
(*Another aircraft passes.*)
(FRANKLIN *is visibly impatient during this speech.
Occasionally he blows his nose, or stares at the ceiling.*)
And now that too has passed into history. None of you boys
are old enough to remember that Second War, nor even
some of you masters. Yet I remember them both. I can still
see myself standing at that window one summer day in 1918
and listening to the rumble of the guns in Flanders.
(FRANKLIN *blows his nose loudly.*)
I stood at that window again in June 1940 to see a lone
Spitfire tackle a squadron of the Luftwaffe. Those times left
their mark on Albion House. Some of the older ones among
you will remember Bombardier Tiffin, our Corps
Commandant and Gym Instructor, lately retired. The more
observant ones among you will have noticed that one of
Bombardier Tiffin's legs was not his own. The other one,
God bless him, was lost in the Great War. Some people lost
other things, less tangible perhaps than legs but no less

worthwhile – they lost illusions, they lost hope, they lost faith. That is why . . . chewing, Charteris. That is why the twenties and thirties were such a muddled and grubby time, for lack of all the hopes and ideals that perished on the fields of France. And don't put it in your handkerchief. Hopes and ideals which, in this school, and in schools like it all over the country we have always striven to keep alive in order to be worthy of those who died. It was Baden-Powell I think –

(FRANKLIN *clears his throat.*)

– I think it was Baden-Powell who said that a Public Schoolboy must be acceptable at a dance, and invaluable in a shipwreck. But I don't think you'd be much use in either, Skinner, if you were playing with the hair of the boy in front. See me afterwards. A silent prayer.

(FRANKLIN *does not close his eyes during the prayer.*)

O God, look down upon our bodies which are made in Thine own image. Let us delight in our boy bodies that they may grow day by day into man bodies that our boy thoughts may become man thoughts and on that glorious day when manhood dawns upon us it may dawn upon us as on the clean dewy grass with birds singing in our hearts and innocence looking from our eyes. . . .

CARTWRIGHT: Amen.

HEADMASTER: I haven't finished. I haven't finished. As I was praying . . . so that day by day as our bodies grow more beautiful so too our soul life may grow more beautiful as the soul is the mirror of the body and the body the mirror of the soul.

ALL: Amen.

HEADMASTER: This school, this Albion House, this little huddle of buildings in a fold of the downs, home of a long line of English gentlemen, symbol of all that is most enduring in our hopes and traditions. Thirty years ago today, Tupper, the Germans marched into Poland and you're picking your nose. See me afterwards. We aren't a rich school, we aren't a powerful school, not any more. We don't set much store by cleverness at Albion House so we don't run away with all the prizes. We used to do, of course, in the old days and we must not forget those old days, but what we must remember is that we bequeathed our traditions to other schools, and if now they lead where we follow it is because of that. My successor is well-known to you all, in the person of Mr Franklin. . . .

(WIGGLESWORTH *cheers feebly*.)

When the Governors want your approval of their appointments, Wigglesworth, I'm sure they will ask for it. Mr Franklin has long been my senior housemaster. Now he is promoted to pride of place. Doubtless the future will see many changes. Well, perhaps that is what the future is for. We cannot stand still, even at the best of times. And now, as has always been the custom on this the last day of term, staff and boys have come together to put on the Play. Perhaps here I might say a word about Mr Fairbrother, whose jealously guarded province the play has always been. I recall with particular pleasure that first trail-blazing production of *Dear Octopus*, and last year's brave stab at *Samson Agonistes*. We shall miss him and his Delilah of that production, Miss Glenys Budd, who has contrived to delight us on innumerable occasions. Now of course she is Mrs Fairbrother. Long may they flourish amid the fleshpots of Torquay. *Ave atque vale*.

O God, bless all those who leave and take their ways into the high places of the earth that the end of leaving may be the beginning of loving, as the beginning of loving is the end of life, so that at the last seekers may become finders and finders keepers for Thy Name's Sake. Amen.

Mr Franklin has put together this term's production . . . a short fling before he is crippled with the burden of administration. He has recruited a veritable galaxy of talent. Connoisseurs of the drama, could they but spare the time from rummaging in the contents of their neighbours' ears, Jarvis, may be interested to note that I myself am to play some part in this year's proceedings. On the distaff side no

expense has been spared in procuring the services of
Matron (*cheers*), Miss Nisbitt (*groans*), and of course Mr
Tempest (*a guffaw*). Now if I could just see those boys I
had occasion to admonish we will sing the school song
together and the play will begin shortly. Skinner, Tupper.

ALL: Forty years on, when afar and asunder
    Parted are those who are singing today
    When you look back and forgetfully wonder
    What you were like in your work and your play.
    Then it may be that there will often come o'er you
    Glimpses of notes, like the catch of a song;
    Visions of boyhood shall float then before you,
    Echoes of dreamland shall bear them along.

Chorus:

    Follow up, follow up,
    Follow up, follow up, follow up
    Till the field rings again and again
    With the tramp of the twenty-two men
    Follow up, follow up.
    Forty years on, growing older and older
    Shorter in wind as in memory long
    Feeble of foot and rheumatic of shoulder
    What will it help you that once you were strong?
    God give us bases to guard or beleaguer,
    Games to play out whether earnest or fun;
    Fights for the fearless and goals for the eager,
    Twenty and thirty and forty years on!
    Follow up, follow up *etc.*

(*Chorus as above.*)

(*The boys now set the stage for the school play. Everyone should
have something definite to do, with the exception of the*
HEADMASTER. FRANKLIN *is at the centre of the activity,
organizing, interfering, setting matters to rights. The main
section to be set up is the chairs, etc., at stage left to represent
the basement of Claridge's. This should not be a literal
representation, nor a gloomy air-raid shelter. It is only
specifically referred to as Claridge's basement twice during the*

play and should not be tied down too definitely to that, but simply be the setting for HUGH, MOGGIE *and* NURSIE *during the years 1939–45. They obviously would not have been in Claridge's basement every minute of the war. The props should be simple, stylish and capable of being made by the boys themselves.*

The boys who play instruments tune them up during this section.)

FRANKLIN: I want everyone not connected with the play off the stage right away.

HEADMASTER: I thought it best to say much as I've always said at the end of term. Like it or not, Franklin, boys are conservative creatures. The tug of ritual, the hold of habit. They like it.

FRANKLIN: They love it. (*To a boy carrying something.*) You're going the right way about getting a rupture. Get under it, you silly child, get under it.

Where's Miss Nisbitt? Has anybody seen Miss Nisbitt?

(*The* HEADMASTER *is wandering about, getting in everybody's way and looking a bit lost.*)

I want everyone not in the opening scene off the stage now. Headmaster, you're not in the opening scene, are you?

HEADMASTER: No. (*But makes not attempt to go.*)

TEMPEST: Skinner, Tupper. I don't want you two sitting together. No, Tupper. You stay there. That's the whole object of the exercise. And you, young man, you want to be round here.

(TEMPEST *takes* CHARTERIS, *who is to act as prompter, by the scruff of his neck, and puts him below stairs stage right, where he remains for the duration of the play.*)

MATRON: (*To* FRANKLIN) Oh Bill, I won't be a tick. I've got to minister to one of my small charges who's been sick. It's the excitement coming on top of that mince. I'll just assess the damage and be back in a jiff. All hands to the pumps!

TEMPEST: Oh, Best of Ladies, Matron mine! How did you like our excellent Headmaster's farewell speech? Did it wring your withers?

MATRON: No. And I don't think you ought to either.

TEMPEST: O vain futile frivolous boy. Smirking. I won't have it. I won't have it. I won't have it. Go find the headmaster and ask him to beat you within an inch of your life. And say please. I can't find the music. I put it down somewhere and can't think where.

FRANKLIN: Charles, have you seen Miss Nisbitt.

TEMPEST: The last time I saw her she was *en route* for the lavatory.

FRANKLIN: What the hell is she doing there? I want her on stage. Miss Nisbitt.

(MISS NISBITT *rushes on to the stage still adjusting her dress.*)

MISS NISBITT: I'm so sorry. I just had to go to the Bursary.

FRANKLIN: Don't move an inch from this spot till the start. And look after these. They're the choir's music. And don't move. Do you understand?

MISS NISBITT: Yes, Mr Franklin.

HEADMASTER: Am I needed yet? Does anybody want me?

FRANKLIN: Oh, Wigglesworth. Maximum of fuss, minimum of performance. Take hold of the damned thing. You frame like a girl.

(*A boy should be testing microphones saying 'Testing, testing, testing. One, two, three, four, one, two, three four.' The lights flicker on and off.*)

Who's mucking about with the flaming lights? You touch that switch again, Crabtree, and I'll flay the bloody hide off you. What will I do?

CRABTREE: (*On the microphone*) Flay the bloody hide off me, sir.

FRANKLIN: Right.

HEADMASTER: And don't swear, boy. It shows a lack of vocabulary.

(MISS NISBITT *is taking advantage of the confusion to steal off.*)

FRANKLIN: Miss Nisbitt, I thought I told you to stay here.

MISS NISBITT: I was just wondering whether I ought to put on a cardigan. Do you think I'll be warm enough. July can be very treacherous. And it's better to be safe than sorry. I might get something I can't get rid of. I don't think it's unreasonable to ask. After all, I've just nicely got over a cold and I washed my hair last night. I should feel much happier. . . . (*Exits.*)

TEMPEST: . . . I wish I could put my hands on the choir's parts. (FRANKLIN *hands the music to him and* TEMPEST *exits.*)

FRANKLIN: Wigglesworth. If I might just have a word in your fair, albeit somewhat grubby ear. That is a nut. And this is a bolt. It is a long established custom that the one goes inside the other. Thus. Had your forefathers, Wigglesworth, been as stupid as you are, the human race would never have succeeded in procreating itself.

HEADMASTER: Surely *somebody* wants me?

MATRON: I do, Headmaster. I wonder if I might sit you down and paint your face.

HEADMASTER: I don't see why not, provided you exercise restraint.

(*She takes him to one side, throws a Union Jack over him from the prop basket and begins to make him up.*)

MATRON: Just a spot of five and nine, I think. And we'll try and take out your eyes a little.

HEADMASTER: I'm still not altogether happy about this, you know, Matron. I wish I'd never agreed to do it.

MATRON: You can't abandon ship at this late date, Headmaster. We're relying on you. You're absolutely essential, isn't he, Mr Franklin? Purse your lips ever so slightly, that's it.

FRANKLIN: Go easy on the Helena Rubinstein, Matron. He only wants the bare essentials.

HEADMASTER: The bits I have to do aren't so bad, but there are some bits I haven't even been allowed to see. I suppose that means it's either sex or God. It'll be that business of the School Magazine all over again. The trouble with you, Franklin, is that you have this unfortunate tendency to put ideas into the boys' heads.

FRANKLIN: I thought that was what education meant.

HEADMASTER: I never liked the word 'education'. I prefer the word 'schooling'. Still, what does it matter.

MATRON: That's the spirit.

HEADMASTER: Besides, it's never been my policy to interfere with my housemasters. I've done my best. I've maintained the forms. I've not always believed in them, but I've maintained them. When I became Headmaster –

(*There is a boy behind his chair making faces. The* HEADMASTER *peers in* MATRON's *mirror.*)

– you can't afford to do that with a face like yours, Leadbetter.

(*He is covered in a flurry of powder.*)

MATRON: You'll do. I'll just dust you off and your own mother wouldn't know you.

(*The stage should now be clear ready for the play to begin. The* HEADMASTER *again addresses the audience.*)

HEADMASTER: Are we ready? I am told that what we are to see is neither comedy nor tragedy, but a mixture of both. And that's a jolly good opportunity for you, parents included, to keep your wits about you so as to tell the one from the other. In those parts that are funny, and in those parts only, I shall expect you to laugh. And in other parts, er, the reverse. And intelligently. Remembering always that as the crackling of thorns under a pot, Cartwright, so is the laughter of a fool. For what we are about to see, may the Lord make us truly thankful.

(*He gives a final look about him and goes off. The stage is now set for the School Play. There is a pause. From somewhere off stage there is a whisper.*)

MATRON: Where's Miss Nisbitt?

FRANKLIN: Oh *hell*.

(MISS NISBITT *runs on to the empty stage, looks round in horror and then runs off as a boy ascends to the lectern and the School Play begins. The lights are down. A light on the lectern.*)

LECTERN: 'All our past proclaims the future,
Shakespeare's voice and Nelson's hand,
Milton's faith and Wordsworth's trust
In this our chosen and our chainless land.'

The Albion House Dramatic Society presents *Speak for England, Arthur*, a memoir of the life and times of two nice people in a world we have lost. (*The boys around the gallery, each carry two clip-boards. On cue they reverse the boards which spell out the title of the play* Speak for England, Arthur)
We begin a quarter of a century ago, in the basement of Claridge's Hotel, London.
HUGH, *a Member of Parliament;* MOGGIE, *his wife,* NURSIE, *her Nanny.* CHRISTOPHER, *their son.*
(*Eleven o'clock strikes on Big Ben as* HUGH (FRANKLIN), MOGGIE (MATRON), NURSIE (MISS NISBITT) *and* CHRISTOPHER (TEMPEST) *enter, coming downstairs from the gallery stage left.* HUGH *is a Tory MP, upper-class, mild, scholarly and disillusioned.* MOGGIE, *his wife, is aristocratic, eccentric, sloppily dressed, but with great presence.* NURSIE *is as all Nannies are, or were, slightly older than* HUGH *and* MOGGIE, *but seeming much older and still apt to treat them as they were when children. Sharp, vinegary, unemotional.*
CHRISTOPHER *is a young man in his early twenties.*)

HUGH: Come on, Nursie.

NURSIE: But I've left my gas-mask.

HUGH: Never mind.

MOGGIE: If we've missed it Nursie, I shall never forgive you.
(FRANKLIN, *as* HUGH, *is still wearing his gown.*)

NURSIE: (*As* MISS NISBITT) You've still got your gown on.
(FRANKLIN *tears it off and throws it offstage.*)

MOGGIE: Wars break out once, or at the most twice in a lifetime and you have to lose your gas-mask. It must be past eleven now.

HUGH: It's all right. The ultimatum's for eleven. The broadcast is after that.
(*He fiddles with* NURSIE's *portable wireless.*)

NURSIE: Now you leave it alone. I understand it. See! You keep your fingers to yourself, young man. It's not a machine you know, that you can do just what you like with.
(CHAMBERLAIN's *voice is heard, broadcasting the Declaration of War on September 3rd, 1939.*)

RADIO: I am speaking to you from the Cabinet Room at 10 Downing Street. This morning the British Ambassador in Berlin handed the German Government a final note stating that, unless we heard from them by eleven o'clock that they were prepared at once to withdraw their troops from Poland, a state of war would exist between us. I have to tell you now that no such undertaking has been received, and that consequently this country is at war with Germany. You can imagine what a bitter blow it is to me that all my long struggle to win peace has failed.

HUGH: Grovel, grovel, grovel! He's got so used to grovelling to Hitler he now feels he has to grovel to us.

MOGGIE: Do you mind! The Prime Minister's trying to speak.

NURSIE: And I'm trying to listen.

RADIO: Now may God bless you all. May he defend the right. It is the evil things we shall be fighting against, brute force, bad faith, injustice, oppression and persecution . . . and against them I am certain that right will prevail.

CHRISTOPHER: I wish I was.

(*An air raid siren goes, faintly.*)

NURSIE: What're you crying for, young lady. What's done is done. I knew there'd be tears. That Hitler has no business interfering with other people even if they are foreign.

HUGH: Well, thank God for that! What a relief!

NURSIE: There! Big blow! That's better.

HUGH: We're at war. At long last. We're at war.

CHRISTOPHER: You don't have to go though.

MOGGIE: Things won't ever be the same, you know.

CHRISTOPHER: They said that last time.

MOGGIE: And things never *were* the same last time. So it will be even less the same this time. It won't be the same world. Goodbye darling. Except that they say it will be over by Christmas.

HUGH: They said *that* last time too. I heard in the lobbies he wanted to wriggle out of it even at this stage. 'What have we got to do with Poland?' (*Shakes hands with* CHRISTOPHER) 'What have we got to do with Poland?'

MOGGIE: Poor old thing. I've always had a soft spot for him.

NURSIE: It's his mother I feel sorry for.

(CHRISTOPHER *exits left*.)

HUGH: Collapse of all my hopes, my public life, he made it sound as if he'd just lost a by-election not determined the fate of Europe. He doesn't even know what day it is. He might have made something of that.

MOGGIE: Yes, it's Sunday.

NURSIE: Fancy declaring war on a Sunday. They've no respect.

HUGH: Not *Sunday*. It's September 3rd. Cromwell's great victory over the Scots. Now let God arise and let his enemies be scattered. Only Chamberlain doesn't know that.

MOGGIE: I'm not in the least surprised. I didn't know it either.

HUGH: It's September, you see. Hitler waited until the harvest's in.

(CHRISTOPHER *re-enters left carrying a greatcoat and he changes into uniform as they talk*.)

NURSIE: Cheats never beat.

HUGH: At least this time we know what we're fighting for.

MOGGIE: We knew what we were fighting for last time.

HUGH: What?

NURSIE: What's dead long ago and Pardon took his place.

CHRISTOPHER: This time, last time, what difference does it make.

MOGGIE: We were fighting for . . . honour and . . . oh lots of things I can't remember now, but I remember that I knew quite clearly then.

HUGH: They can't have been very important if you can't remember them now.

MOGGIE: One always forgets the most important things. It's the things one can't remember that stay with you.

NURSIE: I lost goodness knows how many babies in the last war, two peers, a viscount and umpteen commoners. Scarcely a nanny among my acquaintance but didn't lose at least a couple.

HUGH: I feel more lighthearted than I've done for years.

CHRISTOPHER: (*Shouldering kit-bag*) I don't. (*Exits*.)

MOGGIE: It's the end of our world, Nursie. They are rolling up
the maps all over Europe. We shall not see them lit again in
our lifetime.

NURSIE: There's a drop on your nose, dear. Use my
handkerchief. And is that dinner down your frock. Tsk,
tsk.

HUGH: I'd better get down to the House.

NURSIE: On a Sunday?

MOGGIE: Perhaps we'll come and sit in the gallery. It'll be a bit
of history. Come along.

NURSIE: I can't go yet. There's an air raid on and I haven't got
my gas-mask. Just think. All those people to knit for.
There's not a moment to lose.

*(The area representing Claridge's is downstage left. The
changeovers from Claridge's to the memoirs should be done as
cuts, not soft fades.*

Cut to the LECTERN.

CHARTERIS, *who is also the Prompter for the School Play, sits
below the lectern. It is his job to alter the Hymn Board. He now
puts up the date of the reading – 1900.)*

LECTERN: As the bells rang out on that last day of the old
century, they did not ring out the end of one era and the
beginning of another. To enter upon the new century was
not like opening a door and crossing a threshold. The old
Queen was still alive, and when she died most of what she
stood for lived on.

And so, as the lights go up on the twentieth century we are
still in the world of Elgar and Beerbohm, the age of Oscar
Wilde.

(Enter WITHERS, *the butler, played by the* HEADMASTER,
pushing LADY DUNDOWN, *an Edwardian dowager*
(TEMPEST) *in a wheel-chair.)*

LADY D: Is there anything in the newspaper this morning,
Withers?

WITHERS: They have named another battleship after Queen
Victoria, ma'am.

LADY D: Another? She must be beginning to think there is some resemblance. I see the Dean of Windsor has been consecrated Bishop of Bombay.

WITHERS: Bombay. Hmm. If I may say so, ma'am, that seems to me to be taking Christianity a little too far.

LADY D: And where is your good lady wife on this bright summer's morning?

WITHERS: Still at death's door, I'm afraid, m'lady.

LADY D: Still? But she has been there now for the last sixteen years.

WITHERS: Yes. And I, m'lady, I have never left her bedside.

LADY D: So I see. A great mistake, if I may say so. You should remember the proverb, a watched pot never boils. Well, Withers, you must not take up any more of my valuable time. And besides, I must speak to my nephew.

WITHERS: But I cannot see him anywhere.

LADY D: A sure sign that he is in the vicinity. Gerald!

(GERALD GROSVENOR *enters in a scarlet military tunic, carrying a pith helmet with plumes.*)

GERALD: Good morning, Aunt Sedilia.

LADY D: The weather is immaterial. Gerald, do I detect a somewhat military note in your appearance? What is the reason for these warlike habiliments?

GERALD: I have been called to the Colours.

LADY D: Indeed? Whereabouts?

GERALD: South Africa.

LADY D: South Africa? I trust that will not interfere with your attendance at my dances?

GERALD: I'm afraid so.

LADY D: Tsk, tsk. How can the Zulu expect to be treated as civilized people when they declare war in the middle of the season!

GERALD: It's not the Zulu, Aunt Sedilia. It's the Boer.

LADY D: It comes to the same thing. I have never understood this liking for war. It panders to instincts already catered for within the scope of any respectable domestic establishment. Which brings me to my point. Your marriage. I have been going through my list and have hit upon the ideal person. Lady Maltby.

GERALD: Lady Maltby!

LADY D: Constance Maltby. (*She rises from wheel-chair.*) I can walk. It's just that I'm so rich I don't need to. Consider her advantages. She is in full possession of all her faculties, plus the usual complement of limbs . . . and enough in such matters, I always think, is as good as a feast.

GERALD: I have heard it said that her legs leave something to be desired.

LADY D: All legs leave *something* to be desired, do they not? That is part of their function and all of their charm. But to continue. Like all stout women she is very fat, but then, it would be inconsistent of her to be otherwise, would it not?

GERALD: Is she not connected with Trade?

LADY D: Trade? Nonsense. Her father made a fortune by introducing the corset to the Esquimaux. That is not trade. It is philanthropy.

GERALD: And she is very old fashioned besides.

LADY D: If by that you mean she dresses like her mother, yes she is. But then all women dress like their mothers, that is their tragedy. No man ever does. That is his. You have something to say?

GERALD: Yes, Aunt Sedilia. You see, I have been engaged before. Several times.

LADY D: I am aware that you have been engaged, though, if I may say so, much after the manner of a public lavatory . . . often and for very short periods.
(*The* HEADMASTER *who has been lurking off stage, now interrupts.*)

HEADMASTER: I don't think that's very funny, Tempest. If you want to make people laugh you shouldn't have to go to the lavatory to do it. And Skinner . . .

SKINNER: Yes, sir.

HEADMASTER: You may regard this as a heaven sent opportunity to draw with your fountain pen on that boy's neck, but I don't. Continue, Tempest.

TEMPEST: Er . . . I've forgotten it . . . (*To* PROMPTER) Yes, Charteris, yes.

CHARTERIS: Er . . . (*He leafs through his copy as* TEMPEST *goes over to him.*)

TEMPEST: You're not even on the right page. And what's this? *Vogue*? *Vogue*! A boy reading *Vogue*, Headmaster. You're supposed to be prompting, not reading *Vogue*. I'll *Vogue* you, young man, if you don't attend to what you're doing. (*He throws* Vogue *off the stage and finds the line on the page.*)

LADY D: You must be married next week.

GERALD: Impossible!

LADY D: Impossible! There seems to be an element of defeatism in that reply. Why, pray?

GERALD: Lady Dundown, Aunt Sedilia, I cannot marry Lady Maltby next week, because Lady Maltby is my mother.

LADY D: Well, would the week after do? I beg your pardon?

GERALD: Lady Maltby is my mother.

HEADMASTER: Disgusting! (*He exits in despair.*)

LADY D: For how long has this been the case?

GERALD: Almost as long as I can remember.

LADY D: I see. One question, Mr Grosvenor. Was your mother ever married?

GERALD: No, I must confess it, Lady Dundown, she never was.

LADY D: Splendid. My dear Gerald, wherein lies the difficulty. Your mother is a spinster, albeit not without blot. You, nameless, dishonoured, fatherless creature that you are, are unmarried. Marriage between your mother and yourself would make a decent man of you and an honest woman of her. Indeed the arrangement seems so tidy I am surprised it does not happen more often in society. Dear me. How cold it has turned. I must go in and put on another rope of pearls. The chair, Mr Grosvenor, if you please. (*Two treble voices sing 'South of the Border' or some other popular song of 1939–40.*

Lights up on Claridge's. HUGH *is sitting in his gas-mask.* MOGGIE *is reading a letter.* NURSIE *is knitting.*)

RADIO: Your gas-mask is a delicate instrument. It is not a toy.

Treat it well. Your life may depend on it. Your gas-mask should be marked clearly with your name and Identity Card number. Take it with you wherever you go. Do not let it out of your sight even when you are asleep. Practise wearing it for an hour each day until you are thoroughly accustomed to it. Failure to comply with these regulations is punishable by a fine of up to £5.

NURSIE: You've only had it on five minutes. The man said an hour.

HUGH: Doesn't do to overdo it. Little and often.

NURSIE: It's all very well for you, young man. You've got a gas-mask. I've lost mine. What if there's an alert and they catch me without it.

HUGH: You'll be smothered.

NURSIE: I don't mind that. But I don't want to be fined. I should never live it down.

MOGGIE: I wonder where Christopher is. He says he's not allowed to say, but we would know where he is if he said he was where Charles and Lena spent their honeymoon.

HUGH: Oswestry.

MOGGIE: What?

HUGH: Oswestry.

MOGGIE: Nobody ever spent their honeymoon at Oswestry. I thought it was Paris.

HUGH: The artillery go to Oswestry. Any other clues?

MOGGIE: He says he saw Napoleon's tomb this morning. That doesn't sound very much like Oswestry to me.

NURSIE: You button your lip, young lady. Careless talk costs lives.

MOGGIE: Don't be silly, Nursie, there's only us here.

NURSIE: How do you know I'm not a German parachutist?

HUGH: German parachutists don't knit, Nursie.

NURSIE: Lord Haw Haw said that the clock at Grantchester had stopped at ten to three. *And it had*. Somebody must be telling them.

MOGGIE: I do hope he's all right. Paris is such an awful fleshpot.

NURSIE: He'll be all right so long as he doesn't drink the water.

MOGGIE: We're not winning in France, are we?

HUGH: Well, if we are, the sites of the victories are getting nearer and nearer. Though why you expect me to know I can't imagine. I'm only in the Ministry of Information and we're always the last to know.

NURSIE: It must be terribly difficult retreating. Fancy having to walk backwards all that way!

HUGH: There's one thing. The weather is as perfect as it always is when the world is quaking. I remember just about this time of year in 1914 Father saying much the same to Edmund Gosse. He agreed and said it had been just the same in 1870.

MOGGIE: They used to have really piping hot days. In 1911 during the Home Rule crisis it was 97 degrees. Ninety-seven!

NURSIE: It was too hot. It was too fine to last at the beginning of this century. Fine before seven, rain before eleven, that's what I say. Lend me your gas-mask. I can do a bit of practice just in case.

(CHARTERIS *alters the hymn board to* 1906.)

LECTERN: In those days it seemed the sun would always shine.

NURSIE: Queen's Weather we used to call it, when the old Queen was still alive. And that was how it was all those years before the war.

MOGGIE: Then in 1914 it begins to rain and all through the war and after it never stops.

HEADMASTER: The war and everything that comes after grey and wet and misty and nasty.

HUGH: Never a fine day in the trenches was there.

NURSIE: Rain on Armistice Day.

MOGGIE: Rain on the queues that wait for the Dole.

HUGH: Rain on the wet tarmac as they search the empty sky waiting for an old man with a piece of paper.

HEADMASTER: But over the smooth green lawns of the Edwardian era, the sun seemed always to shine, like one's last summer term at school that memory has turned

44

all to gold.

(TEMPEST *as a* MAX BEERBOHM *figure, sits at a garden table with a straw hat and cane. As he speaks one of the boys moves round him playing the violin like a café violinist. But he should be playing one of the lush, nostalgic themes from Elgar's Violin Concerto.*)

TEMPEST: Berkshire and Hampshire, Leicester and Rutland, those were the Edwardian counties. One breath of their pine-laden air and I am through the door in the wall, back in the land of lost content. I am a young man on a summer afternoon at Melton or Belvoir, sitting in the garden with my life before me and the whole vale dumb in the heat. Is it my fancy? Did I ever take tea on those matchless lawns? Did apricots ripen against old walls and the great horn still sound at sunset? One boat on the wan, listless waters of the lake and nothing stirring in Europe for years and years and years.

HUGH: That's not how it was. That's only how he thinks it was. Really it was wars and rumours of wars just like any other time.

TEMPEST: It was what Disraeli called 'The sustained splendour of a stately life'.

HUGH: And Harold Nicolson 'that jaded lobster, the Edwardian era'. Switch it off, Nursie.

TEMPEST: How hard it is now to recall what it was like, that self-contained world of the Big House in those far-off days when the century was young and we were young with the century.

HUGH: Those houses where we stayed . . . Grabbett, Lumber, Clout and Boot Lacy, their very names are a litany of a world we have lost.

NURSIE: Is it too much to ask to be able to listen to my own wireless without you gallivanting on.

TEMPEST: One would lie in one's bed on a morning, half awake, listening to the sounds of the Great House coming to life around one. First about five, the soft closing of a door and a slow shuffling tread. . . .

HUGH: Edward VII going back to his own room.

TEMPEST: Ah, what sights those walls had seen. Here, here is Sargent's portrait of the Lavery Sisters.

HUGH: And here, oh here, is Landseer's portrait of the Andrews Sisters. (*He switches off the wireless.*) Do you remember, my dear, those endless evenings of our Scottish summers the glens glowing in golden light and in the breeze the gentle tossing of the cabers.

MOGGIE: If you want to talk in here, go outside and do it.

HUGH: Already in the kitchens the day is far advanced and Mrs Buttocks the cook had been hard at work bedevilling the breakfast kidneys. Ah, those country house breakfasts. God, I remember those, the merry conversation of bacon sizzling in the pan; the chattering of a trio of succulent kidneys.

MOGGIE: Kedgeree, cold partridge.

HUGH: The warm fragrance of crisp brown rolls, and over all the heavenly benison of coffee. Are D's two ounces or four?

MOGGIE: What?

HUGH: Points. The sweet ration. D's and E's. I was just reading my ration book. Lytton Strachey once said that in a perfect world one ought to read Sir Thomas Browne sitting between the paws of the Sphinx. Conversely I think it very fitting that I should be reading my ration book in the basement of Claridge's.

NURSIE: D's are two and E's are four.

HUGH: Damn. I've only got two D's to last me a whole month.

NURSIE: You're not going to wheedle any out of me, young man, that's for sure.

(CHARTERIS *alters the hymn board to 1908 as a treble voice sings the hymn 'Now the Day is Over'.*)

HUGH'S VOICE: When I was ill as a child at the turn of the century, I would have a night light burning in a green saucer of water right through into the morning and behind the scrap screen a bed would be set up for Nanny Gibbins. Very late as it seemed to me then, though downstairs the dancing would just be beginning, Nanny Gibbins came to bed.

(NANNY GIBBINS *is played by* MATRON, *and is a much more intimidating presence than* NURSIE. *At first only a voice behind the screen, she casts a monstrous shadow on the wall as she unbuckles her black bombazine armour and talks to the little boy in the bed.*)

BOY: What time is it, Nanny?

NANNY: Time you were asleep, young man.

BOY: What time is that?

NANNY: Time you had a watch. Time you learned to say please. Time you knew better. Go to sleep.

BOY: What are you doing, Nanny?

NANNY: I'm doing what I'm doing. Go to sleep.

BOY: Nanny!

NANNY: What?

BOY: I've got a pain in my leg.

NANNY: Do you wonder you've got pains in your legs when you don't do your business. Well, next time you'll sit there till you do. Forgotten to fold your vest, young man. I can't turn my back for two minutes. And clean on this afternoon.

BOY: I feel sick.

NANNY: Do you wonder you feel sick sitting on them hot pipes. How many more times must I tell you, you sit on them pipes you'll catch piles.

BOY: What are piles?

NANNY: You mind your own business. Piles is piles, and you'll know soon enough when you catch them because your insides'll drop out and you'll die and then where will you be? Lie down, sitting up at this time of night.

BOY: What time is it?

NANNY: Time for Bedfordshire. Time you had your bottom smacked.

BOY: Can I have an apple?

NANNY: No, you can't. Apples at this time of night. Apples don't grow on trees you know. (*She has a drink from a bottle.*)

BOY: What's that?

NANNY: That's Nanny's medicine.

BOY: What for?

NANNY: It's for Nanny's leg. Nanny's got a bone in her leg.

BOY: Can I have some for my leg?

NANNY: No, you can't. Going out without your wellies on, do
you wonder you get pains in your legs. You go out without
your wellies on, you'll go blind. That's why St Paul went
blind. Went out on the Damascus Road without his wellies
on. See, did I say no? Lie down this minute. If I have
another muff out of you there'll be ructions. Give us a kiss.
Kisses make babies grow. Night, night, sleep tight. God
bless and go to sleep or the policeman'll come and cut your
little tail off.

RADIO: The hour has come when we are to be put to the test, as
the innocent people of Holland and Belgium and France are
being tested already. And with our united strength and with
unshakeable courage fight and work until this wild beast
that has sprung out of his lair upon us shall be finally
disarmed and overthrown.

(SKINNER *and* TUPPER *are pulling faces, mocking the note of
rather ludicrous ferocity with which Chamberlain delivers this
speech.* FRANKLIN, *who is listening to the speech as* HUGH,
catches sight of them, strides across and hits SKINNER.)

FRANKLIN: This may be ancient history to you, Skinner, but to
your mother and father it spelled life and death.

RADIO: In those circumstances my duty was plain. I sought an
audience of the King this evening and tendered to him my
resignation, which His Majesty was pleased to accept.

HUGH: Never be Prime Minister at the start of a war, Nursie.

NURSIE: Hmm. Some of us have got better things to do. Good
riddance to bad rubbish, that's what I say. Here, you're not
doing anything for the war effort, wind this. (*She hands him
a hank of wool to hold.*)

HUGH: It's always the same. Asquith, the Younger Pitt, their
hearts not in it. The man who's led you into it isn't the one
to lead you out of it.

(MOGGIE *enters in WVS uniform.*)

48

MOGGIE: Chamberlain, Chamberlain, fly away home, your house is on fire and your children all gone. Still I always had a soft spot for him. And what has Churchill done? He's just a trouble maker. Why couldn't they have Halifax? (HUGH *fiddles with the wireless and turns it to Happidrome, a wartime radio programme, and the music plays under the dialogue.*)

NURSIE: How many more times do I have to tell you, don't play with that wireless. See! I've just put a new accumulator in and it's got to last me for the duration.

MOGGIE: I heard a joke in the canteen today. What did Hitler say when he fell through the bed?

NURSIE: I don't know. What did Hitler say when he fell through the bed?

MOGGIE: At last I'm in Po-land.

(*The* HEADMASTER *strides on to the stage and stands in wordless accusation looking at* MATRON.)

HEADMASTER: I must apologize to all parents.

BOYS: (*In chorus*)
    Willy, Willy, Harry Stee
    Harry Dick John Harry Three
    One two three Neds
    Richard two
    Henries four five and six
    Then who?
    Tudor Henries seven and eight
    Edward Mary and Elizabeth
    James, Two Charles', James again
    William and Mary, Anne the plain
    Four Georges from Hanover
    William Four Victoria.

SCHOOLMASTER (TEMPEST): And who came after Queen Victoria? Rumbold.

RUMBOLD: I don't know sir.

SCHOOLMASTER: Someone once said, Rumbold, that education is what is left when you have forgotten all you have ever learned. You appear to be trying to circumvent the process

49

by learning as little as possible. Wigglesworth?

WIGGLESWORTH: Edward, sir.

SCHOOLMASTER: Edward what?

WIGGLESWORTH: Edward VII, sir.

SCHOOLMASTER: And who came after Edward VII . . . *they all did*. And what do we know of Edward VII. Who haven't I asked? Rumbold? Nothing. He knew nothing of Queen Victoria. He knows nothing of Edward VII. You are a stupid boy, Rumbold, but by God you're a consistent one. Anybody?

WIGGLESWORTH: He was fat, sir.

SCHOOLMASTER: No, Wigglesworth, Edward VII was not fat. He was *very* fat. Not all the art and device of the tailor could disguise the fact that Edward VII was an enormously fat man. Cosseted and indeed corseted from a very early age. . . . Are you taking this down? . . . he grew almost by a process of geometrical progression as year succeeded year. Pleat, ruche and gusset him how they would he yet remained enormous, how enormous we can see from our wall map of Edward VII. Whence came this vast and ever-broadening girth? It was not heredity for at eighty-one his mother Queen Victoria was very small for her age. One reason behind his fatness and behind the fatness of his behind – that's not funny, Wigglesworth – was that he ate perhaps more than four times as much as the majority of his subjects. For some this was a boon in disguise for each year upon the anniversary of his birth he was weighed in potatoes which were then fried and distributed to the lower classes. His fatness affected his health. A loyal subject wrote in to suggest he attach balloons to his elbows to take the weight off his legs.

(*For some time there has been the sound of distant singing, apparently of a psalm, it grows louder and louder until the words are discernible sung in tipsy, hearty voices to the tune and metre of a psalm.*)

BOYS: As I was walking down the street, I saw a house on fire,
    And at the window's first storey, a face, a human face

Crying Help, Help, I am on fire.
We said, Jump, you silly bastard
Because we have a blanket.
He jumped, hit the deck and broke his stupid neck,
Because we had no blanket.
Laugh, how we laughed,
The tears ran down our trouser legs
I haven't laughed so much since Grandma died
And Aunty Mabel caught her left titty in the mangle
And whitewashed the ceiling.
Sinners, miserable sinners.

TEMPEST: What is all this din, Charteris? Is it in the script?

CHARTERIS: No, sir. It's the rugger team.

TEMPEST: Is it?

(FRANKLIN *walks purposefully across the stage towards the rear.*)

FRANKLIN: Go on, man. Don't stop for God's sake.

HEADMASTER: Franklin. Franklin. What is happening. Tempest, what is this hiatus in the proceedings?

TEMPEST: Mr Franklin's gone out to try and stop the singing, Headmaster.

HEADMASTER: Stop it? Do you mean to say it's not part of the entertainment?

TEMPEST: Oh no. It's entirely spontaneous.

HEADMASTER: Spontaneous? Then it must be stopped at once. Go out there and stop it.

TEMPEST: Me, sir? Wild horses on their bended knees would not get me out there.

(*Enter* FRANKLIN, *dragging* TREDGOLD, *the beefy Captain of Games, by his collar.*)

FRANKLIN: Come on, you grubby barbarian.

HEADMASTER: Now then, Franklin, who's been acting the giddy goat? You, Tredgold. You should know better than this, Tredgold . . . a school prefect, captain of games, father a governor of the school. Oh, Tredgold, you disappoint me.

TREDGOLD: I do apologize, sir, but it's the rugger team just back from Stowe . . . we licked them, sir, 17 : 6.

HEADMASTER: O, dismal youth, with your boots knocking about your neck, it's all very well to apologize . . . 17 : 6! O, Tredgold, well done! Well done! Take your hand off Tredgold's collar, Franklin, School prefect, captain of games, father a governor of the school . . . doesn't need you hanging on to his collar. I think a short prayer might not come amiss. O God. Let us give thanks for the warm embrace of the sun and the chaste kiss of the rain, thanking Thee as we match our splendid young limbs against each other in the rough and the tumble of our games together, so that at the last, rain-washed, sun-gilded, heaven-bent, we may repose upon Thine eternal changelessness and thus at the last when we are called to go whither we know not hence, we may see God . . . you won't find him down there, Tupper . . . and bask in the presence of His glory from henceforth unto henceforth. Amen. Seventeen six. Amen. Amen.

TREDGOLD: I think they'd appreciate it, sir, if you spoke to them.

HEADMASTER: Do you think so. Certainly, certainly, I'll speak to them at once. Seventeen six!

FRANKLIN: Tredgold, you privileged great lout, kindly inform your little Male Voice Choir, that if I ever get my hands on them they'll be singing several octaves higher.

(FRANKLIN, TREDGOLD *and the* HEADMASTER *exit.*)

TEMPEST: This is all very vexing.

WIGGLESWORTH: Can't we go out and join them, sir?

TEMPEST: Certainly not. Get back in your places. And stop messing about.

WIGGLESWORTH: Aw, sir. Come on. It's only the play, sir.

TEMPEST: Only the play! Only the play! Wigglesworth. Fumbling, uncertain, pathetic though our attempts may be, we are here engaged in the highest activity known to man, which is not, Wigglesworth, rugby football. We are about the business of art. There have always been people like you, Wigglesworth, down the ages, people who say: Oh, it's only the play. It was doubtless a fifteenth-century Florentine Wigglesworth who came up to da Vinci and said, Why don't you make her laugh on the other side of her face, Leonardo. Oh, Picasso, she's got eyes in the back of her head. Oh, Dostoievsky, you do look on the dark side. You mindless twirp. Here we are trying to salvage something from the Wreck of Time and you say it's only the play. (*The rugger team now come in at the rear and embark on another song. They come forward to the front of the stage, passing a rugger ball among themselves, feinting passes to the audience. All the boys gradually join in the song, the first verse of which is sung by the team alone, the second as a treble solo and the last by the whole school with organ accompaniment.*)

BOYS: (*To the tune of 'The Church's One Foundation'*)

The dogs they had a party
They came from near and far
And some dogs came by aeroplane
And some dogs came by car
They came into the courtroom
And signed the visitors' book
And each dog took his arsehole
And hung it on a hook.

The dogs they all were seated
Each mother's son and sire
When a dirty little mongrel
Got up and shouted Fire!
The dogs they were in a panic
They had no time to look
And each dog took his arsehole
From off the nearest hook.

The dogs they were so angry
For it was very sore
To wear another's arsehole
You never wore before
And that it is the reason

53

Why a dog will leave its bone
To sniff another arsehole
In the hope it is his own.

FRANKLIN: Get out of my sight, the lot of you, before I strangle you in your own bootlaces.

HEADMASTER: Tredgold, keep them under wraps, old chap. Take them behind the fives courts where they can sing to their hearts' content.

I'd better say at this juncture, Franklin, that I'm not entirely pleased with the way things are going.

FRANKLIN: I refuse to be held responsible for a coachload of drunken louts who . . .

HEADMASTER: I wasn't referring to that. Boy nature filling its lungs and shouting forth its full throated praise of physical prowess, no harm in that. I was eighteen myself once.

FRANKLIN: I should want witnesses of that.

HEADMASTER: No. There's an element of mockery here I don't like. I don't mind your tongue being in your cheek, but I suspect your heart is there with it.

FRANKLIN: You can't expect to agree with everything. One generation treading on the toes of its predecessors. That is what tradition means.

HEADMASTER: I am still Headmaster. Do not try to tell me what tradition means. You shouldn't be doing that, MacIlwain. Nail-biting is the act of a beast. Anyway, get on. Where are all your actors? It's all a bit too slip-shod. They ought to be here. We shouldn't have to hang about waiting. Whose turn is it now?

FRANKLIN: Yours, Headmaster.

HEADMASTER: Precisely and where is . . . mine? Mine? Of course it is. Clear the stage then. Clear the stage. I can't start with you dogging my every footstep.

(CHARTERIS *alters the hymn board to 1909.*)

LECTERN: T. E. Lawrence sets out for Mesopotamia, 1909. He had a spare shirt, and stockings, a camera and a borrowed map. He was twenty-one. And he was going ostensibly to search for material for a thesis on Crusader Castles. It was

54

the start of a longer search. There is a certain strain in the English, delicate, fastidious, self-despising, which draws some of them to the Arabs, drives them to adopt their code of chivalry, courtesy, and cruelty, and thus obtain the franchise of the desert. Such people are tough, awkward and they are not modest. Masculine women and feminine men, they count the appetite a sin and the flesh a luxury. They strip themselves to the bone. They become soldiers, explorers and indefatigable travellers. But these are just names and excuses and in their various disguises they are all pilgrims.

HEADMASTER: (*Slide 1. Portrait of T. E. Lawrence*) T. E. Lawrence, the man and the myth. Which is man and which is myth? Is this fact or is it lies? What is truth and what is fable? Where is Ruth and where is Mabel? To some of these questions I hope to be able to provide the answer. No one who knew T. E. Lawrence as I did, scarcely at all, could fail but to be deeply impressed by him. It is given to few men to become as he did, a legend in his own lifetime, and it was in pursuit of that legend that I first sought him out in June of 1933 at his cottage at Clouds Hill in Dorset. (*Slide 2. Picture of Clouds Hill.*)

It was a simple cottage but I thought I detected Lawrence's hand in the rough white-washed wall, the stout paved doorstep and the rough oak door, upon which I knocked, lightly. It was opened by a small, rather unprepossessing figure slight of frame, fair-haired and with the ruddy gleaming face of a schoolboy. It was a schoolboy. I had come to the wrong house.

(*Slide 3. Desert picture. Upside down.*)

Some of us are a little old to stand on our heads, Crabtree. Thank you.

I knew of Lawrence of course from his exploits in Syria, where he had been attached, though none too deeply, to British Expeditionary Force. Speaking fluent Sanskrit he and his Arab body servant, an unmade Bedouin of great beauty, had wreaked havoc among the Turkish levies.

55

Aurens the Arabs called him for they are unable to
pronounce their L's as distinct from the Chinese who can
pronounce little else.

It is interesting, though fruitless, to speculate that had fate
taken him to China he would have been known as Lollens.
However, that is by the way.

(*Slide 4. Picture of an Eastern person.*)

It was at this time he was taken for a Circassian eunuch by
the infamous Sheikh Hans and subjected to unspeakable
privations, the mark of which he bore for the rest of his life,
and which bored everyone else thereafter.

(*Slide 5. T. E. Lawrence in Arab dress.*)

Shaw, or Ross as Lawrence then called himself, returned
from the East in 1919. Shyness had always been a disease
with him, and it was shyness and a longing for anonymity
that made him disguise himself. Clad in the magnificent
white silk robes of an Arab prince, with in his belt the short
curved, gold sword of the Ashraf descendants of the
Prophet, he hoped to pass unnoticed through London.
Alas, he was mistaken. 'Who am I?' he would cry
despairingly. 'You are Lawrence of Arabia' passers-by
would stop him and say, 'And I claim my five pounds'. For
a while he sought refuge in academic seclusion as a fellow of
All Souls in Oxford.

(*Slide 6. T. E. Lawrence at All Souls in Oxford.*)

Here he could mix on equal terms with some of the greatest
men of his age, but, as Robert Graves has noted, he could
not bear to be touched, so that even to rub shoulders with
the great filled him with deep loathing.

(*Slide 7. A smiling picture of T. E. Lawrence.*)

One hesitates to talk of Lawrence and his body, though the
two were inseparable. He feared his body as a savage fears
the night. His body was a wild beast to be tamed and cowed
into submission, and when I first knew him it had been
beaten and tanned to the texture of an old whip. There have
been those, as there always are those, who have said that
there was something feminine about his make-up, but his

was always so discreet.

But can one ever forget him, those china blue eyes, that boyish, almost girlish figure and that silly, silly giggle. The boys at his school had called him Tee Hee Lawrence, and always at the back of his hand or the back of his mind there was that ready snigger.

When I became headmaster the first boy I ever expelled was for reading the works of Lawrence. This morning I receive in my post a letter from the Oxford and Cambridge Matriculation Board telling me that the works of Lawrence are next year's set texts. I just can't keep up.

FRANKLIN: D. H. not T. E.

HEADMASTER: Oh, these literary fellows, they're all the same.

RADIO: (*A broadcast of Robb Wilton's monologue beginning 'The day war broke out, my missus said to me . . .' This is interrupted by an announcement*) We are interrupting this broadcast for a message of national importance. At three o'clock this afternoon the Admiralty issued the following appeal: 'All yachtsmen and owners of sea-going craft in the neighbourhood of the Channel Ports are asked to report to their respective harbour masters without delay. Ships should be sea-worthy and capable of immediate active service.' That is the end of the announcement.

(HUGH *is holding a telegram*.)

HUGH: But he's missing, Nursie.

NURSIE: Missing? Missing? That's him all over. Never there when he's wanted, that boy. He'll turn up.

HUGH: They said at the War Office somebody saw him still on the beach when the last boats were leaving.

MOGGIE: There must have been hundreds left. I don't know how any got away at all. He never would push himself forward.

NURSIE: He was a dawdler. Everything done at the last minute. He'd be late for his own funeral.

MOGGIE: I can't bear not knowing one way or another.

NURSIE: Exactly. Anybody with a bit of consideration would have sent a postcard. There must be plenty of those, it's a

57

seaside place. Here, hold this wool for me. It'll occupy your mind.

MOGGIE: I've been down at Victoria all day serving tea. I kept asking and asking. Poor lambs. They had to be turned out of the carriages they were so tired.

HUGH: I saw some of them in the Park when I was walking to the Ministry. Hundreds of them just laid out on the grass in their stockinged feet. There was one boat-load landed right on the Commons steps. I only hope some of the Munichers were there to see that. I've put his name on the list in *The Times*. We shall just have to wait.

MOGGIE: It's all waiting so far, this war. Waiting for the bombs, waiting for the troops. Is it ever going to start?

NURSIE: Patience is mine, I will delay saith the Lord.

(CHARTERIS *alters the hymn-board to 1913.*)

LECTERN: March, 1913. Lady Ottoline Morrell walks with Bertrand Russell on Primrose Hill.

Sometime in that year of 1913 I walked with Bertie Russell through Regent's Park to Primrose Hill. It was on this hill that the Prince Regent had once thought to put that Pavilion he eventually built at Brighton, and it was here that Wells had pictured the final apocalyptic scene of the War of the Worlds. But it was very peaceful when we walked there: sheep and lambs grazed among the trees and in the distance the solid splendour of St Pauls rose above the smoke of the city.

(LADY OTTOLINE MORRELL *is played by* SKINNER *and* TUPPER, *the one playing the top half, the other the bottom. These two halves are not in sync. and when she sits down, her legs keep crossing and uncrossing, independently of what her top half is doing. She is garishly dressed, in a bright orange wig, many coloured costume and orange stockings which are fully revealed when she crosses her legs.* FRANKLIN *plays* RUSSELL.)

OTTOLINE: Oh, Bertie.

RUSSELL: Yes, Ottoline.

OTTOLINE: I had an accident yesterday. One of my breasts

popped out of my frock.

RUSSELL: Oh? Which one?

(*The voice of the* HEADMASTER *offstage.*)

HEADMASTER: Franklin, do my ears play me false. Come here this minute.

OTTOLINE: It was while I was playing bridge with Queen Alexandra. Fortunately I was playing my cards very close to my chest so no one noticed.

RUSSELL: I don't think you have ever appreciated, Ottoline, the saving qualities of elastic.

OTTOLINE: Do you ever have the same problem?

RUSSELL: Mutatis mutandis, no. But then I have led a very sheltered life. I had no contact with my own body until the spring of 1887, when I suddenly found my feet. I deduced the rest logically.

HEADMASTER: (*Offstage*) Franklin!

RUSSELL: Ottoline!

OTTOLINE: Yes, Bertie?

RUSSELL: I would like to take the earliest opportunity of seducing you. Would half-past seven on Thursday the 4th suit you?

HEADMASTER: (*Coming down the stairs*) Go away, you boys, you're not to listen to this. This is one of the bits you were keeping to yourself, I never had any inkling of it.

(*The* BOYS *clear the gallery in a great hurry.*)

FRANKLIN: I'm sure you can't object to them poking fun at Bertrand Russell.

HEADMASTER: Get up, you treacherous pedant. (*He gropes up the skirt.*) What have we got here? (*He lifts the skirt and calls up it.*) Who's up there? Come down this minute.

(*The figure splits into her component parts.* SKINNER *emerges clad in a long pair of orange tights, high-heeled black shoes and a red satin underskirt which covers the top half of his body.*)

(*To* TUPPER.) I might have known you'd have been at the bottom of it.

SKINNER: No. He was the top, sir. I was the bottom.

HEADMASTER: Don't try me, sir. I am not a fool. I am *not a* fool. What I am objecting to is the use, absolutely without qualification, of the word, breast.

FRANKLIN: I'm sure the boys may have come across the word.

HEADMASTER: They may indeed. They may even be aware of its implications. But it is not merely the boys we have to consider. We are in mixed company.

MATRON: I don't mind a bit, Headmaster.

HEADMASTER: I wasn't meaning you, Matron. Of course you're not shocked by it. You've had medical training. I have my sister Nancy in the audience.

TEMPEST: Well, she's got a bust like a roll-top desk.

FRANKLIN: Headmaster, I think you must face facts. We have it on excellent authority that this lady was rather slip-shod in her personal appearance.

HEADMASTER: So you make a pantomime horse out of her.

FRANKLIN: It's in Stephen Spender's autobiography which I read with the Arts Sixth last term. He actually saw her breast pop right out of her frock. It was on top of a bus. I can give you the page reference.

HEADMASTER: And the number of the bus too, I suppose. What Mr Spender saw is his own business. I would merely say that if everyone who caught an unlooked-for glimpse of the female bosom chose to publish it in book form, civilization would very shortly grind to a halt. Don't misunderstand me. I know the times are changing. I am trying to be as liberal as I can. But there is a time and a place for everything.

FRANKLIN: And might one be permitted to ask the time and place for a breast?

HEADMASTER: Certainly. It is in the mouth of an infant of six months and under. There must have been other features about this woman, this Emmeline Squirrell, apart from the fissiparous nature of her décolletage.

SKINNER: Tupper and I were just about to pluck your heartstrings, weren't we, Tupper?

TUPPER: Yes, sir.

HEADMASTER: If there are any heartstrings to be plucked round here, gentlemen, I will be the one to pluck them. Do you understand?

SKINNER:
TUPPER: } Yes, sir. Yes, sir.

HEADMASTER: Go straight on. We'll have all this out in the interval.

(HUGH *is listening to a radio bulletin giving statistics of air losses during the Battle of Britain.*)

NURSIE: You're putting on weight down at that depot, young lady. It's exercise you want, not standing about in a canteen all day.

MOGGIE: You just mind your p's and q's, or I shall write and tell them about your gas-mask. It's just going to be like the last one, taking all the brightest and best.

NURSIE: Matter with you? Cat got your tongue? He says we shall have to fight in the ditches. Ditches indeed. He doesn't have my legs.

MOGGIE: You're not much older than he is.

NURSIE: Yes, but he hasn't had you two to cope with all his life.

(HUGH *switches off wireless.*)

HUGH: I met one of them tonight, down at the House. A very gallant young man. Everything that a hero should be. Handsome, laughing, careless of his life. Rather a bore, and at heart, I suppose, a bit of a Fascist.

MOGGIE: That's a foul thing to say.

HUGH: I just felt he'd have been happier talking to his counterpart in the Luftwaffe than to an ageing prop in the Ministry of Information. It was Aesop, the eagle talking to the mole.

MOGGIE: There weren't really airmen last time, were there, not to speak of.

HUGH: It's just like a house game at school. The people having a good time on the field while one stood shivering on the touchline, having to cheer.

MOGGIE: You do talk bloody nonsense, sometimes.

NURSIE: Just because you're in the WVS doesn't mean you're allowed to swear.

HUGH: One day people will think that it was just a war like all the others.

NURSIE: Takes two to make a quarrel.

MOGGIE: Don't talk such rubbish. Just like any other. Not this time. It's not like last time.

HUGH: Not this time. It's always not this time.

MOGGIE: I haven't time to argue. I'm on late turn. I don't wonder you get depressed, you smoke too much.

(CHARTERIS *alters the hymn board to 1914.*)

LECTERN: June, 1914. Osbert Sitwell visits a Palmist. Nearly all my brother officers of my own age had been two or three months earlier in that year of 1914 to see a celebrated palmist of the period, whom, I remember, it was said, with what justification I am unaware, Winston Churchill used to consult. My friends, of course, used to visit her in the hope of being told that their love affairs would prosper, when they would marry or the direction in which their later careers would develop. In each instance it appears the cheiromant had begun to read their fortunes, when in sudden bewilderment, she had thrown the outstretched hand from her, crying 'I don't understand it. It's the same thing again. After two or three months the line of life stops short and I can read nothing.' To each individual to whom it was said this seemed merely an excuse she had improvised for her failure: but when I was told by four or five persons of the same experience I wondered what it could portend. But nothing could happen . . . nothing. (*Osbert Sitwell. 'Great Morning'.*)

BOYS: (*In chorus offstage*)

They shall not grow old, as we that are left grow old:
Age shall not weary them, nor the years condemn.
At the going down of the sun and in the morning
We will remember them.

TEMPEST: Remember them because they had in a measure rich and abundant the quality of grace . . . grace of body, grace of manner, grace of movement. It was an awfully careless grace, bred out of money and leisure and the assurance they

62

gave. And I do not suppose it would find much favour
today.

FRANKLIN: Edward Horner, Raymond Asquith, Shaw-Stewart
and the Grenfells . . . they were not passionately concerned
with the shortcomings of the world. It was still too rich and
enthralling a place for them to find much fault with it, 'that
great free world in which comity prevailed'.

(As FRANKLIN *has mentioned their names, the faces of
Edward Horner, Raymond Asquith, and their fellows have
appeared on the B.P. screen.*)

HEADMASTER: Like a hundred or so young men of my
acquaintance I had spent the evening of August 3rd, 1914,
dutifully dancing to Mr Casani's band at Dorchester House.
Dutifully because it was the end of the season and the
weather sultry. I was bored and longed to be in Scotland.
'We're cutting,' said Edward Horner as we came up from
the supper-room. He had had a fancy to hear the
nightingales down at Kimber, and soon he, Julian and Billy
Grenfell, Patrick Shaw-Stewart and myself were in the
Grenfell motor shooting down Park Lane. It occurred to me
as we passed the Achilles Statue that one of the partners on
my card whom I'd cut was Princess Lichnowsky, the wife
of the German ambassador. But I would call the next day
and apologize.

And so through that short summer night we motored down
the white roads into Kent.

We have forgotten since how strong and fresh and pure was
in those days the first sensation of speed. But ours was the
generation to discover it. Our parents did not know it. Our
children . . . such of us who survived to have them . . .
took it for granted. In that open car, running down to
Kimber at thirty miles an hour, it was as if we had been
made sensible of the very force of life itself.

We walked up through Kimber Park to find the house
locked and shuttered for the summer. But the latch of the
nursery window was broken, as it always had been for as
long as I could remember, and we broke into the silent

63

house. Here still were all the pictures I remembered from the countless Kimber holidays of my childhood. The Arming of the King, The Piper of Dreams, A Little Child Shall Lead Them, For He Had Spoken Lightly Of A Woman's Name.

And then through the house, Patrick breaking back the tall shutters as we went, furniture sheeted, drugget down, chandeliers done up in bags, and moonlight like frost about the room. On an impulse I pulled back the white porcelain handle of the bell by a fireplace and heard, far away across the court in the deserted kitchen, a faint answering ring. We filed up the staircase, to the galleries and the state rooms, and through the bright chestnut varnish of the night nursery to the housekeeper's door where I had not been since I was a child and all the house was my province. It opened on to the maid's corridor, a narrow strip of carpet running away over the wide uneven boards under the ribs of the house, still close and heavy with the afternoon heat.

(*Back projection of the turrets and towers of a great country house against a midsummer sky. As this photograph appears, we see four of the boys, dressed in white tie and tails, lounging on the gallery in front of the screen like the subjects of the* HEADMASTER's *memoir.*)

We climbed out onto the leads among the turrets and towers and the green copper cupola. I remember the weather vane's shrill singing in the breeze, the lanyard slapping the mast as Julian Grenfell broke the square medieval flag above the dark house. I would like to think that up there on the leads at Kimber, where within months I should stand to hear the guns in France, I would like to think that on that summer night in 1914 the shiver I felt was one of foreboding. But if I shivered I fear it was only because it was the hour before dawn and cold up there on the roof. And if I felt a shadow come across the moment, it was only because, young, rich, and as I see now, happy, I could afford melancholy. For another day, another ball had ended and life had not yielded up its secret. 'This time,' I always thought as I tied my tie. 'Perhaps this time.' But there would be other nights and time yet, I thought.

And so we waited on that short midsummer night and a deer barked and our footsteps were dull on the leads. And then as the light seeped back into the sky, suddenly, just before dawn, we heard the nightingales.

(*As the nightingales sing, above them we hear the rumble of the Flanders guns and the lights go up slowly to reveal the boys, grouped on the stairs in their cadet corps uniforms, the doomed youth of the 1914–18 War.*

Full light.

MATRON *bangs down a crate of milk at the side of the stage.*)

MATRON: There's milk for those who want it. Line up by forms. Lower forms first.

(*The* BOYS *break formation and begin to chatter and come down the steps as the curtain falls.*)

CURTAIN

It is the interval of the School Play. On the open stage, the staff and boys are standing about talking. Boys are drinking milk, sitting up on the galleries with their legs dangling through or lounging about the Claridge's set. One boy has a jug of coffee, another a plate of biscuits.

MATRON: Headmaster, can I replenish you?

HEADMASTER: Just a modicum, Matron, thank you.

MATRON: You'll be shedding a few quiet tears tonight, Headmaster, handing over the ship after so long.

HEADMASTER: Retirement offers its own challenge, Matron. A chance to take up the slack of the mind, savour the rich broth of a lifetime's experience. Of course I'm not going far. I want to be within striking distance of the boys . . . biting your nails, Leadbetter? Have you no moral sense at all?

MATRON: I don't know what Mr Franklin will do without you.

HEADMASTER: Don't you? The first thing he will do is abolish corporal punishment, the second thing he'll do is abolish compulsory games. And the third thing he'll do is abolish the cadet corps. Those are the three things liberal schoolmasters always do, Matron, the first opportunity they get. They think it makes the sensitive boys happy. In my experience sensitive boys are never happy anyway, so what is the point. Excuse me. (*He has seen two boys who have donned gas-masks and are larking about with them, running at each other like bulls. He suddenly comes between them and peers in through the talc.*) Skinner! Tupper! (SKINNER *and* TUPPER *are not in fact the boys in the gas-masks, but are up to no good in the gallery where, hearing their names, they stand up guiltily.*)

SKINNER:
TUPPER: } Here, sir!

(*The* HEADMASTER *is nonplussed.*)

HEADMASTER: No. No. I know those ears. Filthy!
Wigglesworth. Cartwright. You can just stay like that the
pair of you, until I tell you to take them off.
Somewhere, somehow, somebody is smoking. It's you boy,
isn't it?

CHARTERIS: No, sir.

HEADMASTER: No, sir? You mean, yes, sir.

CHARTERIS: No, sir.

HEADMASTER: (*Picking him up and shaking him*) Don't bully me,
sir. Smoking stunts the growth. Oh, it's you, Matron.

MATRON: (*Offering him a cigarette*) Do you indulge in this
appalling habit?

HEADMASTER: No. Certainly not.

MATRON: Quite right. Wish I didn't. Bit of a change from
Fairbrother, all this. A far cry from *Dear Octopus*.

HEADMASTER: It is. It is. I suppose it's for the best.

MATRON: I'm sure it is.

HEADMASTER: I wish I were.

MATRON: Ah, the lusty Wimpenny. What's the ginger nut
situation like?

HEADMASTER: If you're going to take the radical step and throw
Dodie Smith out of the window, warts and all, as it were,
you've got to have something to put in her place.

MATRON: We had got into a rut though.

HEADMASTER: Perhaps. But the advantage with ruts, Matron, is
that when one is in them one knows exactly where one is.

RUMBOLD: Matron!

MATRON: Oh, Christmas. Dishforth is being sick again. I must
be about my errands of mercy. Get his head between his
knees. Not *your* knees, Rumbold.

MISS NISBITT: I wonder, are there any windows open. It's
terribly hot. All these boys take up far more oxygen than
they should. Mr Franklin, I wonder if you've nothing
better to do, could you open one of the windows?

FRANKLIN: Why don't you take that thick cardigan off?

MISS NISBITT: If I did that, I shouldn't feel the benefit.

TEMPEST: One of the fundamental principles upon which

human society is based, Wimpenny, is that people do not comb their hair over the ginger nuts.

WIMPENNY: They're digestives, sir.

TEMPEST: You'll be digestives too if I catch you. Desist.

MISS NISBITT: Do you think anybody would be offended if I opened a button of my blouse?

TEMPEST: Have a care, Miss Nisbitt, lest you unleash forces you are powerless to control. Matron, you dark horse. Who would ever have suspected that beneath that starched front lay such histrionic talent.

MATRON: Oh go on with you.

TEMPEST: You're wasted among your liniments and your embrocation, Molly. Fate intended you for something better. As it did me, I think.

MATRON: Tell you something that struck a chord in this old heart, that business on Primrose Hill. Gosh yes. Some of the brightest pages in life's book were written up there, you know, during the war in 36 Ack Ack Battery. I somehow seemed to come into my own round about then. The thing was, we were doing an absolutely essential job and enjoying it like hell. The battery commander was one Ron Prentiss. Sweet soul. Sweet soul, but so cheeky. I got quite silly about him. Me! Like a little fox terrier he was. I don't know, before the war boys were always put off by my fat legs. Came the war, nobody seemed to care whether you had fat legs or not. I suppose like everything else fat legs get swallowed up in the larger issue. Those tense days in the summer of 1940 when we really thought the Hun would be here any minute. He really helped me to discover myself, did Ron. Widened my horizons terribly. It was under his auspices I had my first cigarette. Then in slack periods when we weren't busy drawing a bead on the Foe we'd adjourn to the local hostelry for a festive gin and tonic. Golly it was nice.

TEMPEST: War is a strange alchemist.

MATRON: Hey ho!

(FRANKLIN *comes across the* TWO BOYS *standing waiting in*

their gas-masks.)

FRANKLIN: And what may I ask are you two comedians doing? If you don't get those gas-masks off in three seconds flat, you'll be wearing them all night.

Sorry, Headmaster, did I balk you of your prey.

HEADMASTER: Would it be impossibly naïve and old-fashioned of me to ask what it is you are trying to accomplish in this impudent charade?

FRANKLIN: You could say that we are trying to shed the burden of the past.

HEADMASTER: Shed it? Why must we shed it? Why not shoulder it? Memories are not shackles, Franklin, they are garlands.

FRANKLIN: We're too tied to the past. We want to be free to look to the future. The future comes before the past.

HEADMASTER: Nonsense. The future comes after the past. Otherwise it couldn't be the future. Mind you, I liked that last bit, the bit that I read. Was it true?

FRANKLIN: Truth is a matter of opinion, really, isn't it, Headmaster?

HEADMASTER: Did they actually go down there to that country house?

FRANKLIN: No.

HEADMASTER: Oh, so it was a lie.

FRANKLIN: It was a lie in the true sense of the word.

HEADMASTER: You still like to sail a bit close to the knuckle, don't you? It won't be for much longer. It's very easy to be daring and outspoken, Franklin, but once you're at the helm the impetus will pass. Authority is a leaden cope. You will be left behind, however daring and outspoken you are. You will be left behind, just as I have been left behind. Though when you have fallen as far behind as I have, you become a character. The mists of time lend one a certain romance. One thing at least I can say. While I have been Headmaster, Albion House has always been a going concern. Whether that will continue I am not sure. It depends on you, Franklin. But I am not sure of anything

69

nowadays. I am lost. I am adrift. Everywhere one looks, decadence. I saw a bishop with a moustache the other day.

FRANKLIN: It had to come.

Molly, see if you can get the Old Man out of the way for the first bit or he'll be breezing on to the stage again.

MATRON: Headmaster, I wonder if you'd come up to the San and have a look at Dishforth. Not a pleasant sight at the best of times, but he's a bit on the pasty side.

HEADMASTER: Can I be spared?

FRANKLIN: I think we'll just about manage.

HEADMASTER: Very well, if all the parents are back in their seats I'll just inaugurate the proceedings. If I don't say a prayer nobody else will. Lord, take this cup from me. Thank you, Lord.

LORD: You're welcome.

HEADMASTER: Don't be cheeky.

O God, who has given unto each one of us a part to play in this great drama we call life, help us so to sustain our roles that when the lights of life go down and the last curtain falls we may put off the motley of self and the raiment of sin and take our place at last in that great chorus line of saints ever more praising Thee around the glassy sea.

BOY: Hear, hear.

HEADMASTER: It is customary, Wimpenny, to say Amen at the end of prayers, not hear hear. That is heresy, and also, impudence.

And remember, this is the School play. You are not here to enjoy yourselves.

FRANKLIN: Still less, each other. Skinner, Tupper.

(CHARTERIS *alters the hymn board to 1918.*
Boys enter and garland the War Memorial with wreaths.
The SCHOOLMASTER *stands before the War Memorial as we hear the rumble of guns.*)

LECTERN: 'The splendour falls on castle walls
And snowy summits, old in story:
The long light shakes across the lakes,
And the wild cataract leaps in glory.'

70

BOYS: (*Offstage*)
    'Blow, bugle, blow, set the wild echoes flying
    Blow bugle; answer, echoes, dying, dying, dying –
(*A horn call offstage.*)
BOYS: (*On stage*)
    'O love, they die in yon rich sky,
    They faint on hill or field or river:
    Our echoes roll from soul to soul,
    And grow for ever and for ever.'
(*Another horn call as the rumble of guns grows louder.*)
SCHOOLMASTER: What are you eating, boy?
MACILWAINE: A sweet, sir.
HEADMASTER: Do you hear that, boy?
MACILWAINE: Yes, sir.
SCHOOLMASTER: And do you know what it is?
MACILWAINE: Yes, sir. It's the guns in Flanders, sir.
SCHOOLMASTER: Precisely. Young men are not busy laying
    down their lives in Flanders simply that you may eat
    sweets, particularly in my lesson. Always we must be
    worthy. Worthy of those who die. It is for us that they are
    going down into the river and they are watching us from the
    farther bank. How can we be worthy? We can make a start
    by not eating sweets in class and we can follow it up,
    Foster, by not passing notes to the boy in front.
FOSTER: Will it be over before it's our turn, sir?
SCHOOLMASTER: That depends on you, Foster. The army is not
    yet so depleted in numbers that it will take someone who
    cannot master Latin gerundives. Take this down.
'If the ten million dead of the 1914–18 War were to march
in column of fours into the gates of death, they would take
eighty days and eighty nights to pass through, and for eight
days and eight nights the marchers would be the British
dead.' In the light of that information, I want you to
calculate (1) the width of the gates of death to the nearest
centimetre and (2) the speed in miles per hour at which the
column was marching.
(*The Rugger hearties again are heard singing to the tune of 'For*

those in Peril on the Sea'.)

RUGGER HEARTIES:

It nearly broke the family's heart
When Lady Jane became a tart
But blood is blood and race is race
And so to save the family's face
They bought a most secluded beat
The shady side of Jermyn Street.

(TREDGOLD *walks round the gallery singing the second verse
against the more distant sound of the other hearties. Towards the
end of the verse the* HEADMASTER *appears and stalks him.*)

RUGGER HEARTIES:

For six months she was doing well
With a most exclusive clientele
And it was rumoured without malice
She had a regular from the Palace.
And so before the sun had set
She'd shagged her way right through Debrett.

HEADMASTER: That's quite enough, you boys. Quite enough.

(*The third verse is only partially heard and tails off into the
distance.*)

RUGGER HEARTIES:

It was not to the family's fancy
When Lord de Vere became a Nancy
And so in order to protect him
They had tattooed upon his rectum:
The working class must travel steerage.
This passage is reserved for peerage.

(HUGH *and* MOGGIE *are dancing to the music of Carol
Gibbons.* NURSIE *is watching.*)

MOGGIE: A woman at the canteen said that her son, who's in the
Ministry of Food, says that it's common knowledge that
Hitler died six months ago. Only it's being hushed up.

HUGH: *The Times* Correspondent says that air raids are having a
serious effect on bridge.

MOGGIE: Lyndoe in the *People* says they won't invade until
Venus is under Capricorn.

HUGH: When's that?

MOGGIE: 1947.

HUGH: A man has been arrested in Epsom for signalling to German planes with a lighted cigarette.

MOGGIE: Apparently they've tried one invasion already. They say that —

MOGGIE: } (*Together*) The Channel was white with bodies.
HUGH:

MOGGIE: They say that some of the Luftwaffe pilots who've been shot down were wearing lipstick and rouge.

HUGH: A German agent has reported that London is now so demoralized that titled ladies are relieving themselves in Hyde Park.

NURSIE: And there was a nun on my bus today paid her fare with a man's hand.

(NURSIE *puts various plates on a tray.*)

What's the matter with that bit?

HUGH: It's burnt.

NURSIE: 'Course it's burnt. It's to make your hair curl. And you haven't eaten your cabbage. Cabbage is bottled sunshine.

HUGH: I walked through Bloomsbury this morning. It's really caught it this time. Glass on the pavements thick as autumn leaves in Vallombrosa.

MOGGIE: Better the devil you know. If Hitler hadn't done it, London University would.

HUGH: Half Tavistock Square is down, odd houses knocked out here and there like teeth. Just a mirror hanging high up on a wall where once was 52. And somebody's coat on a peg in an attic.

MOGGIE: They were appealing down at the Canteen for us to ask soldiers in for a bath.

NURSIE: I wouldn't fancy that. They might be dirty.

(CHARTERIS *alters the hymn board to 1922.*)

LECTERN: Leonard Woolf and the Beginnings of Bloomsbury: 'In March, 1922, we started the Memoir Club and on March 6th we met in Gordon Square, dined together, and listened to or read our memoirs. The original thirteen members of the Memoir Club identical with the original thirteen members of Old Bloomsbury, were all intimate friends and it was agreed we should be absolutely frank in what we wrote and read.' (*Leonard Woolf*. Downhill All The Way.)

TEMPEST: In the twenties and subsequent thirties the pinnacle of every young man's literary ambition was to be invited to one of Virginia Woolf's Sunday morning soirées. These were invariably held at her home, No. 52 Tavistock Square, where I was a frequent visitor for I was distantly related to the Woolf family through some Alsatian cousins. The door of No. 52 was invariably opened by the maid, George, a friend of Lytton Strachey's who would show one upstairs. I can see that room now, full of talk and smoke and people. And what extraordinary people they were. Eliot was there, Auden, Spender and Isherwood, the old faithfuls and young hopefuls, but always there was someone one never quite expected to see. I saw A. E. Housman there once, lured down from Cambridge by Dadie Rylands and the prospect of All-In Wrestling at Finsbury Park.

There by the window talking to Leonard and Virginia were the Berlins, Irving and Isaiah. And then there was Virginia herself elegant and quizzical, those great nostrils quivering and the sunlight playing over her long pale face. She never used cosmetics, except to powder her nose. But then she had her father's nose. She was talking of her contemporaries, how she had spoken last week with Hemingway and how Ernest had said, When I reach for my gun, I hear the word culture. How easy it seemed for them, she thought and how hard it was for her. For she must always be asking, What is Life like. Life is like . . . Life is just . . . a bowl of cherries . . . was that it? No, for someone else had said that, and besides it was false to the whole nature of reality. Some of her books disappointed, vitiated by her intense feminism. Virginia was never a suffragette, for she subscribed to the theory that the pen was mightier than the sword and I once saw Evelyn Waugh

74

reel under a savage blow from her Parker 51. Of all the honours that fell upon Virginia's head, none, I think, pleased her more than the *Evening Standard* Award for the Tallest Woman Writer of 1927, an award she took by a neck from Elizabeth Bowen. And rightly, I think, for she was in a very real sense the tallest writer I have ever known. Which is not to say that her stories were tall. They were not. They were short. But she did stand head and shoulders above her contemporaries, and sometimes of course, much more so. Dylan Thomas for instance, a man of great literary stature, only came up to her waist. And sometimes not even to there. If I think of Virginia now it is as she was when I last saw her in the spring of 1938 outside the changing rooms in the London Library. There she stood, all flushed and hot after a hard day's reading. Impulsively perhaps I went up to her and seized her hand. 'It's Mrs Woolf, isn't it?' 'Is it?' she said and looked at me out of those large limpid eyes. 'Is it? I often wonder,' and she wandered away.

HEADMASTER: Highbrow layabouts, that's who they were. I have no time for them at all. The silly way of talking they had. How simply *too* extraordinary they used to say about the most humdrum occurrence. If you blew your nose it was exquisitely civilized. Darwins and Huxleys and Stephens and Stracheys, all living in one another's pockets and marrying each other. And they were all socialists. Why is it always the intelligent people who are socialists?
(*Two* BOYS *sing one verse of the song 'Little Sir Echo'.*
MOGGIE *is bandaging* NURSIE's *arm, according to instructions from a St John's Ambulance Brigade book.*)

MOGGIE: Hold your arm *up*, Nursie. It's supposed to be broken.

NURSIE: But it hurts.

MOGGIE: It would hurt if it was broken Keep still.

NURSIE: What is it for?

MOGGIE: My nursing course.

NURSIE: Nursing course! In my day nurses had better things to do than bandage their nannies.

(HUGH *is reading a letter.*)

HUGH: Christopher says 'The country is rather like Aldershot, all sand and pine trees and what bit I can see of it very uninviting, so I shan't miss the walks.'

MOGGIE: He won't like being a prisoner of war.

HUGH: 'I don't mind being a prisoner of war. It's not half as bad as school really and the food slightly better. There are seven old Marlburians in my hut . . .
(MOGGIE *smiles happily.*)
. . . which is rather a bore. They display to the full a disgusting capacity for making the best of a bad job. Tell Nursie I'm wearing her socks.'

MOGGIE: He's wearing your socks, Nursie.

NURSIE: I could have knitted half-a-dozen pairs while I've been stuck here being bandaged. There's no call to throttle me.

HUGH: 'A disturbingly high proportion of my fellows appears to welcome incarceration as a longed-for opportunity to dress up as chorus girls. Meanwhile the rest burrow fruitlessly under the foundations. Given half a chance the English revert with sickening alacrity to their schooldays. Those bracing phrases I thought to have heard the last of when my headmaster's door closed behind me ring out new minted on the alien air of Silesia . . . pulling one's weight, letting the side down, putting a face on it. However, I find I am kept quite busy lying on my bed all day, sleeping. And also reading, an activity which is regarded as mildly eccentric. Would you please send me any copies of this *Horizon* magazine you come across. Much love. Christopher.'

MOGGIE: Of course, he's joking, isn't he?

NURSIE: Joking indeed and him a prisoner of war. He ought to be ashamed of himself. There's a time and a place for everything.

MOGGIE: It does seem a very cheerful letter. He doesn't seem to mind quite as much as he might do. Does he mention the bestiality of the Germans at all?

HUGH: Not in so many words.

MOGGIE: But it's there between the lines, don't you think. I wish he'd tell us.

NURSIE: If wishes were horses beggars could ride.

MOGGIE: You don't think . . . you don't think they forced him to write at gunpoint like P. G. Wodehouse, do you. Just to undermine our morale?

(CHARTERIS *alters the hymn board to 1929.*)

HEADMASTER: (*Reads from the lectern*) May, 1929. The Death of Lord Rosebery. 'On the evening of May 20th, 1929, Lord Rosebery sank into a coma and in the early hours of the morning of May 21st, with his son and Lady Leconfield by his bed he died. He had given instructions that a record of the Eton Boating Song was to be played as he died, and this wish was actually carried out, although it is doubtful if he heard the haunting music, redolent of hot summer afternoons, the quiet laughter of friends and the golden days of his young manhood.'

(BOYS *sing the 'Eton Boating Song' under the lectern reading.*)

SCHOOLMASTER: Now you're sure you've got the Catechism all buttoned up, Foster?

FOSTER: I'm still a bit hazy about the Trinity, sir.

SCHOOLMASTER: Three in one, one in three, perfectly straightforward. Any doubts about that see your maths master.

FOSTER: Yes, sir.

SCHOOLMASTER: Well, Foster, here at St Onan's I usually try to make my last Confirmation Class rather more of a personal chat than a theological thing. Now Foster . . . look, we've been through the 39 Articles together, we know each other pretty well, I don't want to go on calling you Foster. What's your nickname? What do your friends call you?

FOSTER: Nitbags, sir.

SCHOOLMASTER: Well, Foster, what I want to tackle now is this problem of your body. Now your body is laid out on fairly simple straightforward lines, isn't it? You've got your two arms, and your two legs, here's that valiant worker the heart and his two stout cronies the lungs. It's all pretty straightforward.

FOSTER: Yes, sir.

SCHOOLMASTER: And here we come to the crux. You're not embarrassed about this are you, Foster. There's no need to be embarrassed about it. You're a bright observant sort of lad, you've probably noticed when you've been slipping into your togs or getting into your little jim-jams, that when you get down here things aren't straightforward at all?

FOSTER: Yes, sir.

SCHOOLMASTER: Good, good. And I suppose you must have wondered how it is that God, who by and large made such a splendid job of the rest of your little body, made such a bosh shot at that particular bit?

FOSTER: Yes, sir.

SCHOOLMASTER: Well, I agree with you. But God, whatever else He is, and of course He is everything else, is not a fool. It's not pretty, but it was put there for a purpose. Point taken, Foster?

FOSTER: Yes, sir.

SCHOOLMASTER: Good, well I think that clears up any doubts you might have had on that particular subject. Just one moment, Foster. I know you're a bit of a scallywag . . . anything I say to you will probably just go up one trouser leg and down the other. But remember this. That particular piece of apparatus we've been exploring is called your private parts. And they're called that for a reason. It's not that they're anything to be ashamed of. They're not . . . though they're not anything to be proud of either. They are private because they are yours and yours alone.

(*He moves his chair nearer the boy's.*)

And you should keep them to yourself.

(*And nearer still.*)

If anyone else touches you there that person is wicked.

(*He places his hand on* FOSTER's *knee.*)

No matter who it is, you should say to him that belongs to me. It is my property. You have no business to touch it.

FOSTER: That belongs to me and you have no business to touch it.

SCHOOLMASTER: Doesn't apply to me, Foster. (*Hitting him.*) Doesn't apply to me.

HEADMASTER: This has gone too far. Tempest, not another word shall you utter. Franklin. I am going to put my foot down. You, boy, get off the stage before you are irredeemably corrupted. Do you defy me, sir. Off. Franklin. Where are you. Don't sulk. Oh, you've gone too far this time. Tempest!

TEMPEST: Don't blame me, Headmaster. I'm an executant merely.

HEADMASTER: If you're not on the stage by the time I count three, Franklin. . . .

(FRANKLIN *stands up. He has been on the stage all the time.*)

FRANKLIN: Sir.

HEADMASTER: Don't you sir me, sir. What do you mean by it?

FRANKLIN: What is it this time, exactly?

HEADMASTER: This . . . this farrago of libel, blasphemy and perversion. Make no mistake about it, Franklin: God is not mocked. And even if He is, I'm not. Fouling the nest, the lot of you. You, Matron. A fellow of the St John's Ambulance Brigade! You disappoint me.

MISS NISBITT: (*Still in her* NURSIE *character*) I think somebody got out of the wrong side of the . . .

HEADMASTER: Miss Nisbitt. Don't let this brief parole from the Bursary go to your head. Tomorrow you will once more be chained to your typewriter.

FRANKLIN: What is it exactly that you are objecting to, Headmaster?

HEADMASTER: This . . . this confirmation class . . . this defamation class. Ha ha.

MATRON: Ha ha.

HEADMASTER: It's not funny, Matron.

TEMPEST: I'm sure it wasn't anything like yours, Headmaster.

HEADMASTER: Not like mine? Of course it was like mine. It *was* mine.

TEMPEST: But the boys and I improvised it together.

HEADMASTER: Improvised? Improvised? It is word for word as

I have been delivering it these forty years. Improvised indeed! Cribbed and ridiculed. No wonder you discouraged me from the rehearsals. I suppose that is where all this improvising as you call it went on. Well, I won't have it. I'm all in favour of free expression, provided it's kept rigidly under control.

MATRON: It's only entertainment, sir, when all's said and done.

HEADMASTER: All is by no means said and done and it is not entertainment. Do I look entertained? And look at my sister, Nancy. Fast asleep. At least I think it's sleep. It may be deep shock.

FRANKLIN: Have you ever thought, Headmaster, that your standards might perhaps be a little out of date?

HEADMASTER: Of course they're out of date. Standards always are out of date. That is what makes them standards. I am as broad minded as the next man . . .

(*The next man is* MATRON.)

. . . but I have heard matters discussed here which ought never to be mentioned, except in the privacy of one's own bathroom, and even then in hushed tones. This is Albion House, not Liberty Hall.

MATRON: I think you ought to sit down, Headmaster.

HEADMASTER: Yes, I think I had. On my last day as Headmaster. You might have waited, Franklin.

MATRON: Shall I undo your collar?

HEADMASTER: You'll undo nothing. You've undone quite enough as it is. All these years I have been at Albion House, years which have seen the decline of authority, the decay of standards, the slow collapse of all I hold most dear. And now this. Mark my words, when a society has to resort to the lavatory for its humour, the writing is on the wall.

FRANKLIN: You are a different generation, Headmaster.

HEADMASTER: So are you, Franklin. However daring and outspoken you are, to the boys you are a master, and all your swearing and your smut, your silk handkerchiefs and your suede shoes can't alter that. We're in the same boat, Franklin, you and I. Now what was going to be next?

(*He consults his programme.*) Ah, yes. Sapper! That sounds a bit better.

FRANKLIN: Perhaps you'd like to read this next bit, Headmaster. It's more up your street.

HEADMASTER: Yes . . . yes . . . this is more like it: this is the twenties and thirties, isn't it . . . the difference is, you'd read it with your tongue in your cheek . . . just because there were hundreds of thousands of unemployed doesn't mean there weren't some of us trying to lead upright decent lives.

MISS NISBITT: I remember I had some lovely holidays in St Leonards.

HEADMASTER: That is a page of memory I'm quite ready to leave unturned. And let's have no more of it. Simply because I am the Headmaster does not mean I am a complete fool.

(CHARTERIS *alters the hymn board to 1936.*)

(*At lectern.*) Whatsoever things are true, whatsoever things are pure, whatsoever is best in England I take to be the Breed. That exclusive club, whose members are the very pith and sinew of this island. You may run across them in the Long Room at Lord's, or dining alone at White's. Once met you will always know them, for their hand is firm and their eye is clear and on those rare occasions when they speak it is well to listen for they choose their words dangerously well. They hold themselves on trust for God and for the Nation, and they will never fail her for the Breed never dies.

FRANKLIN: No. The Breed never dies. Sapper, Buchan, Dornford Yates, practitioners in that school of Snobbery with Violence that runs like a thread of good-class tweed through twentieth-century literature. Novels for the discontented, for ex-officers who profess and call themselves majors long after the war is over and sink their savings in barren smallholdings out beyond the by-pass where the ribbon development ends. A few hens, a pig, a scrawny wife who plays single-handed patience in their converted railway carriage and dreams of Andover and freedom with the man who comes alternate Thursdays with the Calor Gas. It had seemed such a nice little going on in 1919. Novels full of the lost meals of childhood, new baked scones and fresh churned butter, novels of a Europe where history is still a human process, and thrones rise and fall at the behest of international villains.

A BOY: (*Sings*) Hark the Herald Angels sing,
Mrs Simpson pinched our King
Now she knocks on Edward's door
She's been married twice before.

(FRANKLIN, *who plays* LEITHEN, *has donned an overcoat and motoring goggles.* TEMPEST, *who plays* HANNAY, *is in plus fours.*)

LEITHEN: You've got some first-class Holbeins.

HANNAY: Ned.

LEITHEN: Yes?

HANNAY: I asked you here for a purpose.

LEITHEN: Yes.

HANNAY: Do you remember the last time I saw you?

LEITHEN: Intimately. It was at a little thing called Mons.

HANNAY: Since then I seem to have lost your spoor.

LEITHEN: I came through the war more or less intact. I lost an arm here, an ear there, but I was all right, a damn sight better off than a few million other poor devils anyway.
Then I got back home and there were these Weary Willies and Tired Tims in their hand-woven ties, writing gibberish they called poetry saying we'd all been wasting our time. I couldn't see it myself. If we'd done nothing by 1918 at least we'd saved the follow-on.

SANDY CLANROYDEN (*lectern reader*): Ned. Did you ever hear of a man called George Ampersand?

LEITHEN: Bostonian philanthropist and friend of kings! Who hasn't?

SANDY: I had some talk with Mr Baldwin this morning. I never saw a man more worried.

HANNAY: Of late, Ned, there have been a succession of small disasters, oh trifling in themselves . . . a Foreign

Secretary's sudden attack of dysentery at the funeral of
George V, an American ambassador found strangled in his
own gym-slip, and in Sudetenland, most mysterious of all,
a Laughing Leper who destroys whole villages with his
infectious giggles.

SANDY: The tide is flowing fast against monarchy in Europe.
Scarcely a week passes but a throne falls. Mr Baldwin
thinks it may be our turn next.

LEITHEN: Who is behind it all this time?

HANNAY: Who? That poses something of a problem. To the
good people of the neighbourhood he is a white-haired old
man with a nervous habit of moving his lips as he talks. To
the members of a not unfamiliar London club he is our
second most successful theologian. But the world knows
him as . . . George Ampersand.

LEITHEN: Ampersand. Good God.

HANNAY: (*Handing him snapshots*) He is surrounded by some of
the worst villains in Europe. Irma, his wife. Nature played
a cruel trick upon her by giving her a waxed moustache.
Sandro, his valet. A cripple of the worst sort, and
consumptive into the bargain.

LEITHEN: Is he sane?

SANDY: Sane? He is brilliantly sane. The second sanest in
Europe. But like all sane men he has at one time or another
crossed that thin bridge that separates lunacy from insanity.
And this last week the pace has quickened. Else explain
why a highly respected Archbishop of Canterbury, an
international hairdresser and a very famous king all decide
to take simultaneous holidays on the Black Sea.

HANNAY: Take a look at this snapshot. It's of a simultaneous
holiday on the Black Sea.

LEITHEN: But that's . . .

HANNAY: Exactly. A young man not entirely unconnected with
the English throne.

LEITHEN: Who is she?

SANDY: She's beautiful, isn't she. An American. Women are
queer cattle at the best of times but she's like no other

woman I've ever known. She has all the slim grace of a boy
and all the delicacy of a young colt.

LEITHEN: It's a rare combination. Who's this?

HANNAY: Completely Unscrupulos, the Greek shipping
magnate.

LEITHEN: He's got himself into a pretty rum set. And yet he
looks happy.

HANNAY: That's what Mr Baldwin doesn't like about it. During
the past few months certain reports have been appearing in
what for want of a better word the Americans call their
newspapers.

LEITHEN: About her?

HANNAY: Yes.

LEITHEN: And him?

HANNAY: Yes.

LEITHEN: But . . . I don't understand . . . where lies the
difficulty? If he loves her . . .

HANNAY: I don't think you understand. She is what we in the
Church of England called a divorced woman.

LEITHEN: God! It's filthy!

HANNAY: A divorced woman on the throne of the house of
Windsor would be a pretty big feather in the cap of that
bunch of rootless intellectuals, alien Jews and international
pederasts who call themselves the Labour Party.

LEITHEN: Your talk is like a fierce cordial.

SANDY: As yet the British public knows nothing. Mr Baldwin is
relying on us to see they remain in that blissful state.

LEITHEN: I like the keen thrust of your mind, but where does
friend Ampersand fit into all this?

HANNAY: That is what I want you to find out. Sandy will
accompany you disguised as a waiter. That should at least
secure you the entrée. But be careful. And on no account
let His Majesty know that you are meddling in this affair. A
sport called Shakespeare summed it up: There's a divinity
that doth hedge a king. Rough hew it how you will.

(*Two boys sing one verse of the song, 'Hey, Little Hen'*.)

NURSIE: You make a better door than a window.

MOGGIE: You ought to be still for a minute. You've never stopped since it started.

NURSIE: It'll be time enough to sit still when we get to the duration.

MOGGIE: What're you doing?

NURSIE: I'm doing what Mr Beveridge says we're going to have to do, adapting myself to changing circumstances. I'm sewing a button on your mink coat.

(*Enter* HUGH.)

HUGH: The invasion's started.

NURSIE: Queen Anne's dead.

HUGH: I've just seen Winston announcing it in the House, face as white as a sheet.

MOGGIE: Do you know, I thought the canteen had been busy. I thought my baking must be improving. It's going to be all right, isn't it?

HUGH: Better ask the Americans. They've got as much to do with it as we have. You'd never have guessed, listening to them cheering in the House today, that these were the same men who marched year by year, into the lobbies behind Baldwin and Chamberlain.

MOGGIE: You want to be thankful they came to their senses in time.

HUGH: I wish I thought they had. One of my colleagues actually stood up in his constituency the other day and said that if only Hitler had indulged in the fine sport of fox-hunting Europe would not be in the condition it's in today.

MOGGIE: I suppose some of the men in the barges this morning were fox-hunters.

HUGH: All of them no doubt reading over the St Crispin speech. And I suppose I am one of the gentlemen of England now abed.

NURSIE: Why is it called *D*-Day particularly?

HUGH: I wish I thought we were all fighting for the same England. I thought when it started this war would see the end of the business-men, the property developers, the mulberry-faced gentlemen with carnations in their

85

button-holes, the men who didn't want this war. As the end draws nearer you see they're still there. Ranged behind Churchill now are the very men who kept him out of office all through the thirties. And they will destroy him yet, because it is their England he is fighting for . . . the England of Halifax who went hunting with Goering, the England of Kingsley Wood who wouldn't bomb Krupps because it was private property, the England of Geoffrey Dawson altering the despatches from Berlin. We shall win this war, but when it ends there will have to be a reckoning. Then they will go down, and they will drag Churchill with them. And us too. That is the England of The Breed. They were saying down at the House that there've been some peculiar rocket planes falling in Kent. But it's all very secret.

(CHARTERIS *alters the hymn board to 1938.*)

LECTERN: September 1938. Harold Nicolson and the Announcement of Munich. 'It was twelve minutes after four. Chamberlain had been speaking for exactly an hour. I noticed that a sheet of Foreign Office paper was being passed rapidly along the Government bench. Sir John Simon interrupted the Prime Minister and there was a momentary hush. He adjusted his pince-nez and read the document that had been handed to him. "Herr Hitler", he said, "has just agreed to postpone his mobilization for twenty-four hours and to meet me in conference with Signor Mussolini and Monsieur Daladier at Munich." For a second the House was hushed in absolute silence. And then the whole House burst into a roar of cheering, since they knew this might mean peace. That was the end of the Prime Minister's speech and when he sat down the whole House rose as a man to pay tribute to his achievement. I remained seated. Liddall, the Conservative member for Lincoln behind me, hisses out "Stand up, you brute." '

(Harold Nicolson, *Diaries and Letters 1930–39*)
(*The stage becomes a court room.*
The JUDGE *is the* HEADMASTER *in a full bottom wig,*

TEMPEST *the* COUNSEL *and* FRANKLIN, CHAMBERLAIN.)
(*Drum roll.*)

JUDGE: The Court of History is now in session. Put up the prisoner.

COUNSEL: You are Neville Joseph Chamberlain, formerly of No. 10 Downing Street . . .
(MR CHAMBERLAIN *should be in Homburg hat and carrying his umbrella, and still waving his scrap of paper.*)

JUDGE: One moment, one moment. Everybody knows who the prisoner is, but who are you?

COUNSEL: Counsel for the Defence, m'lud. The solicitors appearing for the defendant are Messrs Wealthy, Witty and Wise. I am Witty, m'lud.

JUDGE: That will be for me to judge. However, before we proceed further I must warn you, Mr Chamberlain, that this court is not a court of justice, it is a court of history. And in this court we judge solely by appearances. And I don't like yours. Why are you wearing that ridiculous wing-collar?

CHAMBERLAIN: It was the fashion when I was alive, m'lud.

JUDGE: Fashion? Fashion? Slavish adherence to fashion is hardly one of the qualities one looks for in a Prime Minister. It is the fashion nowadays to wear long hair, but I don't. You've got off to a very bad start, Mr Chamberlain. Proceed.

COUNSEL: Mr Chamberlain. You are charged that on the night of September 30th, 1938, you did indecently expose yourself at the windows of your home, No. 10 Downing Street, clad only in a scrap of paper and shouting 'Peace With Honour', 'Peace with Honour'. How say you, guilty or not guilty?

CHAMBERLAIN: I'm not sure.

JUDGE: Mr Chamberlain. You are either guilty or not guilty. That is something you must decide for yourself. The Court cannot decide it for you.

CHAMBERLAIN: I thought that was what courts were for.

JUDGE: Don't be impertinent or I shall have you smacked on

the back of your legs. I shall now proceed to the sentence. (*Drum roll.*)

COUNSEL: But the evidence, m'lud.

JUDGE: The prisoner has come here for sentence. Let us get that out of the way before we hear the evidence. First things first.

COUNSEL: It's usual to have the evidence first, m'lud.

JUDGE: Don't try and tie me up in legal mumbo jumbo. I know the trial procedure backwards.

COUNSEL: On a point of law, m'lud, the defendant has his umbrella in the dock.

JUDGE: So he does. Are you expècting rain, Mr Chamberlain?

CHAMBERLAIN: No, m'lud.

JUDGE: Because I must warn you that in this court rain does not fall on the just and on the unjust but solely and indeed heavily upon the latter. Proceed.

COUNSEL: The charge arises out of a visit made by the accused to Munich to see Herr Hitler in the autumn of 1938.

CHAMBERLAIN: By aeroplane.

COUNSEL: What has that got to do with it?

CHAMBERLAIN: I went by aeroplane. I was sixty-nine. I had never flown in my life before. I was the first Prime Minister ever to fly.

COUNSEL: That may be the substance of a small footnote in the history of aeronautics but it is of no relevance to the court of history. What was your occupation at the time the offence was committed?

CHAMBERLAIN: Prime Minister and Leader of the Conservative Party.

COUNSEL: Prime Minister *and* Leader of the Conservative Party. You were doing two jobs?

CHAMBERLAIN: There was very little distinction between them.

COUNSEL: There was very little distinction between them. That was partly the trouble, wasn't it?

JUDGE: Oh, you're excelling yourself, Mr Witty. You'll have to do better than this, Mr Chamberlain.

COUNSEL: Let us look at Herr Hitler. You are not blind, your eyesight is not defective . . . it must have been perfectly obvious Herr Hitler wore a moustache.

CHAMBERLAIN: Yes, I did notice that.

COUNSEL: You did notice it, I see. You did not, I take it, recall that Kaiser Wilhelm, one of the prime causes of the First War, also had a moustache?

CHAMBERLAIN: Yes.

COUNSEL: Mr Chamberlain, do you learn nothing from history?

JUDGE: You're getting into your stride, Mr Witty. You're going to have to pull something out of the bag very soon, Mr Chamberlain.

COUNSEL: Getting back to Herr Hitler. It must have been obvious to anyone that he was a patent scallywag.

CHAMBERLAIN: He was not a gentleman certainly, but he was very fond of dogs.

COUNSEL: For sovereign states to conclude agreements on the basis of a mutual fondness for dogs seems to me to be barking up the wrong tree.

CHAMBERLAIN: But it was what the people wanted.

COUNSEL: The law of history is not a law of supply and demand, Mr Chamberlain.

CHAMBERLAIN: They were dancing in the streets.

COUNSEL: Dancing in the streets, what has that got to do with it. The purpose of international relations is not simply to enable the idle populace to take to the streets and do the fox-trot.

JUDGE: What is the fox-trot?

(COUNSEL seizes MISS NISBITT, *and they dance as the boys sing a snatch of 'Boom, why did my heart go boom?'*)

JUDGE: Thank you, Mr Chamberlain. You seem to me if I may say so . . . and since I am the Judge I may say so . . . a man of the most frivolous mind.

CHAMBERLAIN: Beg pardon.

JUDGE: You forget, this is a court of history and we do not repeat ourselves.

COUNSEL: What consequences had this crime? Did it not lead to the rape of Czechoslovakia?

JUDGE: Oh, goody! A witness! Is Czechoslovakia in the court?
(MISS NISBITT *enters, draped in a sash, representing*
CZECHOSLOVAKIA.)
Ah, charming, charming. You say you were raped, my
dear?

CZECHOSLOVAKIA: Yes, m'lud.

JUDGE: You surprise me. Proceed.

COUNSEL: I'm going to ask you for evidence of identification.
Can you see the guilty party in the court?

CZECHOSLOVAKIA: Yes. (*She points at the* AUDIENCE.)

JUDGE: No, my dear. That is the jury. And it is one of the most
cherished maxims of English law that the jury shall be
innocent until they can be proved guilty. Members of the
jury, you are not here to exchange holiday snapshots.
Kindly attend to the proceedings. Try again, my dear.
(CZECHOSLOVAKIA *points.*)
No. That is Counsel for the Defence. But you're getting
warm. Shall I give you a clue?

CZECHOSLOVAKIA: Please.
(*The* JUDGE *points at* CHAMBERLAIN.)

CZECHOSLOVAKIA: That's him over there. (*She points.*)

JUDGE: Thank you very much, my dear. I trust it won't happen
again.

COUNSEL: You have heard the evidence of Czechoslovakia. Do
you still have no regrets?

CHAMBERLAIN: I thought Appeasement was the better course.

JUDGE: Mr Witty. If I could interpose. A point that has been
puzzling me, and if the jury could drag themselves away
from their powder compacts, it would probably be puzzling
them too. You are counsel for the defence, are you not?

COUNSEL: I have that honour, m'lud.

JUDGE: And yet as counsel for the defence, you spend your time
attacking your client.

COUNSEL: But attack *is* the best form of defence, m'lud.

JUDGE: I underestimated you, Mr Witty.

COUNSEL: My case rests, m'lud.

JUDGE: Good. Good. Now we come to the pith and gist of the

proceedings, the sentence. Members of the jury, I want you to consider the following question. Was Mr Neville Chamberlain a mixed blessing? Or was he an unmixed evil? Write on one side of the question only. Neville Joseph Chamberlain, have you anything to say before I pass sentence upon you?

CHAMBERLAIN: I was a very ordinary man, m'lud.

JUDGE: You are not here for offending against the Law of Averages. Anything else?

CHAMBERLAIN: I did die shortly after leaving office.

JUDGE: Mr Chamberlain. It is given to most of us to die at some time or other in our lives. It is no excuse. And keep your mouth shut when you're talking to me. Any extenuating circumstances?

COUNSEL: The accused was born in Birmingham, m'lud.

JUDGE: So are a great many people. It is no excuse. Prisoner at the Bar. You have been found guilty in the court of history and by full process of time and I have no alternative but to give you a very short sentence, so short indeed that there are only two words in it. Perpetual ignominy.

CHAMBERLAIN: But that sentence is impossible: there's no verb in it.

JUDGE: The verb is understood. Take him down.

(CHARTERIS *alters the hymn board to 1939*.)

LECTERN: Mr Chamberlain still hesitates. At 7.30 that Saturday evening, as the German armies thundered towards Warsaw, the Prime Minister appeared in the Commons. The chamber was packed. Members on all sides of the House expected at long last to be told of an ultimatum. When Chamberlain stood up, it was to talk of a conference. If the Germans would agree to withdraw their troops, the question of Poland could be settled through diplomatic channels. There was no word of the ultimatum. Two MPs were sick. Amery and Duff Cooper were red-faced and speechless with fury. Chamberlain sat down without a cheer. The Chief Whip feared physical violence. And when

Arthur Greenwood, the acting Labour Leader rose to
speak, Amery shouted from the Conservative benches:
'Speak for England, Arthur!'

CHOIR: (*To the tune of 'The Church's One Foundation'*)
> O Speak for England, Arthur,
> For twenty years of shame,
> They wriggled out at Munich
> They'll wriggle out again.
> We're pledged to fight for Poland
> The time for talking's past
> He can take that scrap of paper
> And stick it up his arse.

COUNTER VOICES:
> Lord Halifax is ready
> To take off for Berlin
> And if he gives them Danzig
> We just might save our skin
> Why should we do the fighting
> The Jews will stand to gain
> We are the ones who'll suffer
> If England fights again.

FULL CHOIR:
> There is no peace with honour.
> There is no other way.
> There is no faith in Chamberlain,
> The dog has had his day.
> O Speak for England, Arthur!
> The night of shame is done.
> O Speak for England, Arthur!
> Soon Churchill's day will come.

(*The* HEADMASTER *now reviews many of those personalities
who have cropped up in the play and as he does so their
photographs appear on the screen, to form a kind of portrait
gallery of the years* 1900–40.)

HEADMASTER: And at the start of another war Max Beerbohm,
an old man and a legend before the First War started,
comes home from the villino at Rapallo, and Somerset

Maugham in a crowded tramp steamer from Vichy France,
home to an England where Cyril Connolly is founding
Horizon and there are lunchtime concerts in the National
Gallery and nightly in the basement of Claridge's and the
Savoy the saving remnant of the Old England sits out the
Blitz. But by now their ranks are thinning. In May, 1936,
T. E. Lawrence, swerving to avoid a couple of
errand-boys . . . where are they now . . . plunges his motor
bike over a hedge. At Tunbridge Wells, a month before
Hitler enters Austria, Ottoline Morrell dies. Little Buchan,
a mere eight stone twelve pounds falls down with a heart
attack in a Montreal bathroom in 1940. And Virginia
Woolf, filling her pockets with stones, walks into the River
Ouse on 28th March 1941, with her hat still firmly on her
head. Eddie Marsh, friend and patron of the First War
poets, flits from country house to country house, an
awkward guest, apt often to forget the war and eat the
entire family bacon ration at one go. And all through the
war, Mrs Keppel, the mistress of Edward VII, puts up the
black-out at the windows of Watlington Park and dreams of
the great days in the distance enchanted and that strange
storeyed world before 1914.

*(Churchill's voice is heard broadcasting to the crowds in
Whitehall on May 8, 1945.*

*'This is your victory, victory of the cause of freedom in every
land. In all our long history we have never seen a greater day
than this. God bless you all.'*

*The stage is filled with flags, but they are rather worn and dingy
flags, stained and brown, and full of holes, like the flags which
have hung too long in the chancels of churches. The boys wave
smaller versions of similar flags. But as Churchill's broadcast is
marking the beginning of peace in Europe, the boys have broken
out of the play to have a scuffle on their own account. They
ignore the broadcast, the flags, the school play and are
completely absorbed in the fight. One of the boys repelling an
attacker shouts 'Fascist'.*

FRANKLIN *enters as* HUGH *and they are recalled to their duties*

and dance the Hokey Cokey.
The sounds of VE Day subside, as MOGGIE *and* HUGH *and*
NURSIE *prepare to leave the shelter.*)

HUGH: Well. That's the end of that. On the whole, I suppose, a
very pointful war.

(*Enter* CHRISTOPHER *in civilian clothes.*)

MOGGIE: Yes, I said it would be. And here's Christopher back.
Hello, dear. The circle's complete – just like old times.

HUGH: Let's hope so, anyway.

NURSIE: I never did find that gas-mask.

HUGH: And you thought it would be all over by Christmas.

MOGGIE: They said that last time. Now have we got everything.
Rugs, bottles, wireless. I think that's everything.

HUGH: Everything that matters anyway. We'll soon know if
we've lost anything.

MOGGIE: Christopher?

CHRISTOPHER: I'm not sure I brought anything.

MOGGIE: All that fuss and I don't seem to care any more.

NURSIE: Don't care was made to care
Don't care was hung
Don't care was put in a pot
And boiled till he was done.

BOY: (*Reads from the lectern*)
A child in the nursery crying,
A boy in the cricket field, out,
A youth for a fantasy sighing,
A man with a fit of the gout.
Some sense of experience wasted,
Of counsel misunderstood,
Of pleasure bitter when tasted,
And of pain that did him no good.
The sum of a life expended,
A pearl in the pig trough cast,
A comedy played and ended
And what has it come to at last?
The dead man propped on a pillow,
The journey taken alone,

94

The tomb with an urn and a willow,
And a lie carved deep in the stone.

(*From 'Lines Written in Dejection' by G. J. Whyte-Melville*.)
(*During this poem the* BOYS *hum 'Forty Years On' as*
FRANKLIN, TEMPEST, MATRON *and* MISS NISBITT *put off
their costumes and resume their roles as the staff of Albion
House School. The* HEADMASTER *enters without his gown, a
cup of tea in his hand.* CHARTERIS *alters the hymn board to
1968.*)

HEADMASTER: In our crass-builded, glass-bloated, green-belted
world Sunday is for washing the car, tinned peaches and
Carnation milk.

FRANKLIN: A sergeant's world it is now, the world of the lay-by
and the civic improvement scheme.

HEADMASTER: Country is park and shore is marina, spare time
is leisure and more, year by year. We have become a battery
people, a people of under-privileged hearts fed on pap in
darkness, bred out of all taste and season to savour the
shoddy splendours of the new civility.
The hedges come down from the silent fields. The lease is
out on the corner site. A butterfly is an event.

TEMPEST: Were we closer to the ground as children or is the
grass emptier now?

MISS NISBITT: Tidy the old into the tall flats. Desolation at
fourteen storeys becomes a view.

MATRON: Who now dies at home? Who sees death? We sicken
and fade in a hospital ward, and dying is for doctors with a
phone call to the family.

HEADMASTER: Once we had a romantic and old-fashioned
conception of honour, of patriotism, chivalry and duty. But
it was a duty which didn't have much to do with justice,
with social justice anyway. And in default of that justice
and in pursuit of it, that was how the great words came to
be cancelled out. The crowd has found the door into the
secret garden. Now they will tear up the flowers by the
roots, strip the borders and strew them with paper and
broken bottles.

95

LECTERN: To let. A valuable site at the cross-roads of the world. At present on offer to European clients. Outlying portions of the estate already disposed of to sitting tenants. Of some historical and period interest. Some alterations and improvements necessary.

(*The* HEADMASTER *shakes hands with* FRANKLIN. *He takes one last look at the school and takes his leave, as* FRANKLIN *brings the* BOYS *to their feet and they sing, with full organ accompaniment and descant, the first verse of the Doxology, 'All People That On Earth Do Dwell'.*)

CURTAIN

GETTING ON

To Keith

CHARACTERS

GEORGE OLIVER, MP
GEOFF PRICE
POLLY OLIVER
BRIAN LOWTHER, MP
ENID BAKER
ANDY OLIVER
MRS BRODRIBB

Voices off:
Two children, a boy of eight, a girl of four

The play is set in London.
The time is the present.

Getting On opened at the Queen's Theatre on 14 October 1971. The cast was as follows:

GEORGE OLIVER, MP	Kenneth More
POLLY OLIVER	Gemma Jones
BRIAN LOWTHER, MP	Brian Cox
ENID BAKER	Mona Washbourne
GEOFF PRICE	Sebastian Graham-Jones
ANDY OLIVER	Keith Skinner
MRS BRODRIBB	Edna Doré

Directed by Patrick Garland
Designed by Julia Trevelyan Oman
Lighting by Joe Davis

AUTHOR'S NOTE

The text here printed differs in some respects from that first presented at the Queen's Theatre. That version had been clumsily cut without my presence or permission and some small additions made: the jokes were largely left intact while the serious content of the play suffered.

I have removed the additions and largely restored the cuts. This makes the text overlong. But in the event of further productions I would ask that the play be cut with an eye to its seriousness as well as its humour. Otherwise it becomes a complacent light comedy with sad and sentimental moments.

The play was originally entitled *A Serious Man*.

ACT ONE

The play is set in the basement or the ground floor of an Edwardian house, of which the kitchen and living-room run into one another. The kitchen is at the rear of the stage. The outside door is upstage and there is another door downstage which goes upstairs. Also downstage left is a large Victorian overmantel mirror, which George frequently addresses. There is much white paint, and the house has an airy good feeling to it . . . not cluttered Victoriana. Nevertheless, there are a lot of objects around, furniture, glasses, pictures. A collage of children's drawings on the wall, photographs, Mr Heath, Private Eye covers. A red election rosette, haphazard, not artistic. A string of onions, a pan stand, some stripped pine. But not new looking. Fairly worn. It shouldn't look particularly smart or trendy.

There is a child crying upstairs.

GEORGE OLIVER, MP *enters.*

He is a man of about forty, rather glamorous once, now a bit florid, worn, running to fat. He wears quite good clothes, but they don't hang well on him. He smokes cheroots.

His voice, originally northern, is now a pretty nondescript educated voice, but his accent thickens when angry or passionate. He is a deeply misanthropic man, hence his jokes.

GEORGE: If I were to be taken and pinioned for hours at a time in a shuddering, jerking box of steel and glass, lights flashed in my eyes, fumes blown up my nose and gas pumped into my lungs, if this were to be done by the Chinese, then I should be the subject of stern leaders in *The Times* and the righteous anger of the *Daily Express*. Yet I submit to this treatment of my own free will. I do it every week and it's called driving down to London. Hello.
(*During this speech* GEOFF *has entered from the stairs door, and hangs about behind him.* GEOFF *is nineteen, handsome in a Pre-Raphaelite way and very thin.*)
I thought you were Polly.

GEOFF: (*Who looks at himself as if not entirely certain he isn't*)
N-o-o.

GEORGE: Who are you? No. Don't tell me. You could be one of
several people. You aren't the man from the central
heating, or the man who comes to mend the washing
machine. Both almost daily visitors. Perhaps you are
another unemployed actor. Several leading lights in the
National Theatre have not been ashamed to plunge their
feather dusters through our accumulated possessions. Indeed, that is one of the reasons I don't go to the theatre: it's
hard to believe in Pastor Manders when you knew him first
as a somewhat below average window cleaner. And if not an
actor, what?

GEOFF: The marble, I . . .

GEORGE: A supply teacher perhaps. My son has bitten Miss
Gainsborough's leg again? Or from the Portobello Road
with a new addition to our already definitive collection of
stripped pine?

GEOFF: I brought the marble.

GEORGE: Marble?

GEOFF: They were clearing out this old bakery in Kentish Town
and Polly . . . your wife . . . thought the slabs would come
in useful, somewhere.

GEORGE: Somewhere. Look around this room . . . I'm sorry, I
don't know your name.

GEOFF: Geoff.

GEORGE: Look around this room, Geoff. Can you see anywhere
where marble might come in useful? Do you see any surface
not adequately covered, anywhere in fact where marble
might come in handy?

GEOFF: Not off-hand, no.

GEORGE: No. And the only reason I can think of why my wife
should be picking up the odd marble slab is that with her
customary foresight and economy she thinks it will come in
handy for a good gravestone for me.

GEOFF: I don't think so.

GEORGE: Is she upstairs?

GEOFF: She's just putting the children to sleep.

GEORGE: Humanely, I hope. Oh, shut up. I've caught this mood of relentless facetiousness from the car radio. Have you noticed that the BBC keeps its silliest programmes, and its jokiest announcers, for those times in the morning and evening when people are on their way to and from *work*. It's very significant. Why should the BBC choose those times to cover the land in a pall of fatuity? What is it about work that we have to be hurried to and from it by drivelling idiots? I tell you what I think, I think it's an indication of profound malaise in the social structure.

GEOFF: I'd never thought of that.

GEORGE: Is that tea you're making?

GEOFF: Yes.

GEORGE: That's not the teapot. There's the teapot.

GEOFF: Yes. Sorry.

GEORGE: That is an appliance for forcing beef tea down the noses of unsuspecting invalids. It hasn't quite found its place yet.

GEOFF: It's nice. You've got lots of nice things.

GEORGE: We have so many things that by the law of averages some of them must be nice.

(POLLY *enters by the stairs door left. She is thirtyish, attractive, perceptibly younger than* GEORGE. *Harassed. Scatterbrained, or deliberately giving that impression, but not stupid. She is carrying a pile of children's clothes, or one or two of the children's paintings. She should always be doing something about the house, finding odd jobs to do. She never wastes a minute.*)

POLLY: It *is* you. James said it was you and I said it was time he went to sleep.

CHILD'S VOICE: Dad. Dad. Dad.

(*She shouts up the stairs.*)

POLLY: No, it isn't George. It's the television.

CHILD'S VOICE: Will you come up and see me?

POLLY: No, I can't. Not now. Read your reading book. This is George, my husband. This is Geoff . . . I never asked your other name.

GEOFF: Price.

POLLY: Price. By rights it's an old-fashioned inhaler. I can't think what to do with it.

GEOFF: Flowers?

POLLY: Flowers, I suppose, but I always think that's a bit of a defeat. James has been using it as a rocket launcher. I suppose it will come in somewhere. Sit down, Geoff.

GEOFF: Can't I help?

POLLY: I'll see to it. How were the dark satanic mills?

GEORGE: Rather nice today. I saw Nelly and Sam who send their regards. The Town Hall do was bloody. I said my piece for Granada. And I saw a falcon on the motorway. (*To* GEOFF.) Sit down, sit down, for goodness' sake.

POLLY: Are you wanting anything to eat? We had ours with the children.

GEORGE: No. I ate on the motorway. At the 'Grid n'Griddle'. I had ham n'eggs. And now I've got 'ndigestion. Oh, and I ran into McMasters.

POLLY: In Manchester? Which cup would you like?

GEOFF: I'm easy. Any.

POLLY: Would you like A View of Lowestoft, a Masonic mug from Salford, or The Revd E. S. Clough, Twenty-Five Years at Scotney Road Chapel, Pudsey?

GEOFF: Yes, that one.

GEORGE: There's not much to choose except that one's chipped, one's cracked and the other you can't get your finger through the handle.

POLLY: Scones. They're home-made.

GEOFF: If I lived here I should get fat.

GEORGE: He said I could go back to Oxford any time I wanted.

POLLY: That's nice to know, anyway. Lovely and thin, George used to be, just like you.

GEORGE: I don't think I was ever quite as thin as that.

POLLY: I wouldn't care about you getting fatter if you were getting jollier. People are thinner now, aren't they. Young people. Younger people, I mean. It's the right foods.

GEORGE: We never had any oranges during the war. You won't remember the war, of course.

GEOFF: No.

GEORGE: People don't seem to, nowadays. I don't suppose you were even born when it ended.

GEOFF: No. Not by a long way.

POLLY: It's funny. One meets more and more people who weren't. There didn't used to be any, and now one meets them all the time.

GEORGE: I remember the end of the war. In fact I remember the actual war.

GEOFF: That must be great.

GEORGE: Yes, it is.

(*Pause.*)

GEOFF: Did you fight at all?

GEORGE: No. I wasn't old enough.

GEOFF: It must be awful to have, you know, your earliest memories . . . you know, sort of seared by it.

GEORGE: Yes. I was evacuated to Harrogate . . . and that was a bit . . . searing. Were you . . . seared at all, Polly?

(POLLY *pointedly ignores him.*)

More tea, Geoff?

GEOFF: It's the German side of it that interests me.

GEORGE: We weren't so much interested in the Germans as bitterly opposed to them.

GEOFF: I collect one or two things . . . badges, things like that.

POLLY: Really? I'll keep my eyes open. I often see odd bits of things when I'm on my travels. I'm not sure we don't have a bit of shrapnel upstairs. A buzz bomb fell near us at Stanmore. Would you be interested in that?

(*A horn sounds outside.*)

GEOFF: That would be marvellous.

POLLY: It's just a jagged bit of metal really, but it would be nice if someone had it who really appreciated it . . . for what it is. I've never been able to find a use for it.

(*A horn sounds again, more angrily.*)

GEORGE: All right, all right. I'm double parked. You can't even

park outside your own house.
(*He goes out by the street door.*)

POLLY: George is an MP.

GEOFF: What sort?

POLLY: Guess.

GEOFF: Cons . . .

POLLY: No.

GEOFF: Sorry.

POLLY: I'm not offended.

GEOFF: It's just that . . . he has . . . a look about him . . .

POLLY: That's not party, that's politics. He's been up in his constituency holding a surgery. Where people come and tell him their troubles.
(GEORGE *returns*.)

GEOFF: What sort of thing? Troubles?

GEORGE: He'd got miles of room.

POLLY: All sorts.

GEORGE: The council's demolishing their houses, the Ministry's withholding their pensions, benefits, compensation, ejection. The load of bitterness and despair people hump about with them you'd be amazed.

POLLY: It's a very poor constituency. He was lucky to get it . . . I mean . . .

GEORGE: Not really. Poor. At least not many. It's the ones who've gone to the wall. I had a woman in today who believes that her husband, an unemployed fitter, is having an affair with the Queen. And that the Household Cavalry had her under constant watch.

POLLY: Why the Household Cavalry?

GEORGE: Why the Queen?

POLLY: Poor soul. What did you say?

GEORGE: We agreed that the best thing for me to do was to ask the Duke of Edinburgh to have a quiet word with Her Majesty and when she'd gone I had a quiet word with the Mental Health Officer. Poor bugger. Then there was an enormous. West Indian woman who said the people next door kept poisoning her cat and the police wouldn't listen to her. I didn't do anything about that at all.

POLLY: There ought to be some way of stopping them wasting your time.

GEORGE: That's why they land up with me, because nobody else has been prepared to waste their time. They just get passed on. They can't get into the army, they can't get out of the army, the wife's gone off with the kids, the kids have gone into a home, a policeman's hit them over the head. Then some people come just because it's free and they want to talk to somebody and they know it's their right. I'm quite sure there are seventy-year-old ladies who line up at the ante-natal clinic because they'd feel cheated if they didn't.

(GEOFF *is a good listener and laughs at all* GEORGE's *more obvious jokes.*)

The words Member of Parliament still have prestige though, extraordinary. One phone call and officials are scuttling about all over the place.

GEOFF: That's great.

GEORGE: There are still people who stink, did you know that? They sit there on the other side of the table in Sam's airless little office and they stink of muck and squalor and filth and despair. They're just clinging on to the bare face of life. Sorry. Shop.

POLLY: I'm just trying to think what else there is to do. Is electricity in your line, because there's the landing light. I ought to have asked Captain Oates to do it.

GEOFF: Who?

POLLY: Captain Oates. We call him, anyway. He was an electrician who came to do the bathroom. One day he went off saying, 'I'm just going out. I may be quite a time.' And he never came back. So George christened him Captain Oates.

(GEOFF *is perplexed and silent.*)

Sorry. Captain Oates was someone who went with Captain Scott.

(GEOFF *smiles, but is still uncomprehending.*)

The first man to . . .

GEORGE: The first Englishman—

POLLY: The first Englishman to get to the North –

GEORGE: South.

POLLY: South Pole. This Captain Oates was with him. He had a bad leg or something, and was holding them up so one night he went out of the tent saying, 'I'm just going outside. I may be some time.' When really they all knew he wasn't going to come back.

GEOFF: Oh.

(*He tries to force a laugh.*)

GEORGE: Though it's my belief he may have been going for a particularly long slash.

POLLY: Anyway, that's why we called the plumber Captain Oates.

GEOFF: I thought you said it was the electrician.

POLLY: It was.

(*Pause.*)

GEOFF: You must think I'm thick.

GEORGE: No. It's just a fact. You know it or you don't.

GEOFF: You both know it, though.

GEORGE: So? It's like knowing about cars or the times of trains. Facts. Nothing to do with intelligence. Of course I'm not saying you're not thick. Only that that doesn't prove it. I could well do without knowing about Captain Oates. Useless facts swilling about the brain. Could all be drained off and I should be none the wiser. Or none the stupider.

(*A crash and crying from upstairs.*)

Look out, I can hear Thompson and Bywaters. Our two children at present on licence from Strangeways. James seven . . .

POLLY: Eight.

GEORGE: And Elizabeth, three?

(POLLY *creeps to the door and listens.*)

POLLY: Go to sleep, love. No, he's not. You're not to come down.

(*Sounds of children coming downstairs.* GEORGE *goes to the door and flings it open.*)

GEORGE: No, young man. Back you go. You've no business to be out of bed. Up, up, up.

(GEORGE *goes upstairs*.)

POLLY: They are demons. Have you got a flat?

GEOFF: Sort of.

POLLY: Do you live with someone. I mean not live with 'live with', I mean –

GEOFF: Yes. In Notting Hill. We have this house. It's owned by some anarchists. I suppose it's a sort of commune really . . . we're always borrowing each other's butter anyway.

(POLLY *should be active throughout this, clearing up tea things, backwards and forwards between the kitchen and living-room, so that sometimes she misses his comments and he hers*.)

We started off trying to set up a small anarchist community but people wouldn't obey the rules.

POLLY: I suppose you think we're very corrupt.

GEOFF: No. Are you?

POLLY: All this . . . property, possessions. Politics.

GEOFF: Not this sort of stuff. This isn't really possessions, is it?

POLLY: Isn't it?

GEOFF: No. Most people wouldn't want this sort of stuff, anyway. Do I make you nervous?

POLLY: What? No. No.

(*But he does*. GEORGE *comes down*.)

GEORGE: He wants a banana and she wants a cup of tea. How many sugars?

POLLY: It varies.

GEORGE: How many sugars?

(*Unidentifiable shout*.)

Seven! Seven.

POLLY: How did you take up . . . sort of . . . doing nothing?

GEOFF: I wasn't much good at school. I got rheumatic fever when I was ten, and I got behindhand. I went to a special school for a bit.

(GEORGE *is now going upstairs again with the tea*.)

Then I kept being off school and never really got the hang of it again.

(POLLY *is in the kitchen*.)

There was a group of us. We just used to sit at the back of
the class and wank.

POLLY: Was it a comprehensive school then?

GEOFF: And I reckoned I could do that just as well at home. I
went round Art School for a bit, but I didn't reckon that
much either. Are you Sagittarius?

POLLY: Me? Why? I always forget. December 14. I generally
have to look it up.

GEOFF: (*Nodding*) Sagittarius.

POLLY: How do you know?

GEOFF: Vibes, I suppose.

POLLY: It's dogs and sport, isn't it, Sagittarius? Not really me.

GEOFF: I sussed this Libra bird on the Tube last week and she'd
never opened her mouth.

POLLY: What's George then, if you're so good at guessing?

GEOFF: Leo.

POLLY: What are you? July 30. Yes, he is. You are Leo, aren't
you? Fancy Geoff knowing that.

GEORGE: It's rubbish.

GEOFF: It isn't, you know.

(*They are about to start and argue, but* GEOFF *thinks better of
it.*)

Where is this plug?

POLLY: In the cistern cupboard. Mind you don't get a shock.

(*He opens the stairs door,* GEORGE *hears the kids coming and
pushes him aside.*)

GEORGE: All right, it's very nice of you to bring the cup down,
thank you. But, James, if I catch you out of bed once more
there'll be no Jugoslavia. Right? 'Suffer the little children to
come unto me.' You might know Jesus wasn't married.

(GEOFF *goes upstairs.*)

He says you didn't read with him.

POLLY: There wasn't time. Besides I don't understand this new
system. There I am going C-A-T and they don't do it like
that any more.

GEORGE: Will you hear my words?

POLLY: What for?

GEORGE: That television. Here. . . . Skip the first bit, I'm
going to rewrite that . . . burble, burble, burble . . . ours is
still a society in which we throw people into the dustbin,
some sooner, some later. We chuck some people in at
fifteen, we chuck others in at sixty-five. Our society is one
that produces a colossal amount of rubbish. Litter, junk,
waste. Yes?

POLLY: The leftovers.

GEORGE: The leftovers. And in among the leftovers are
people. We waste people. The best society – I think a
socialist society – is one in which fewest people are
wasted.

POLLY: Elizabeth's bottom's cleared up a treat.

(GEORGE *should be only half saying the speech, and altering it
as he goes through, while* POLLY *doesn't give it much attention
either.*)

GEORGE: Somehow society must be kept open, open at every
level so that there are always options . . .

(GEORGE *sits down – and winces.*)

Oh, sod it, what have I sat on?

(*He fetches out a crumpled, brightly painted construction.*)

POLLY: It's The Ark. James was very proud of it.

GEORGE: Egg boxes. Always egg boxes. Miss Gainsborough has
pushed the potentialities of egg boxes beyond man's wildest
dreams. I reckon she must be getting a retainer from the
Egg Marketing Board.

POLLY: It's true. All schools are the same.

GEORGE: What I want to know is when they take the crucial
step from egg boxes to differential calculus. I believe that
some people are better than others, better not because
they're cleverer or more cultivated or God knows – (*He
laughs*) – because they're better off, but –

POLLY: Are you going to do that?

GEORGE: What?

(POLLY *imitates his mid-sentence laugh.*)

I might. Why?

POLLY: Oh, nothing.

(GEORGE *is nonplussed. He repeats the sequence without laughing.*)
You didn't laugh.

GEORGE: You said . . .

POLLY: No. I liked it.

GEORGE: It's a kind of grace, I think. The chosen few. If you can't produce such people because I'm not sure they're born not made, if you can't produce them, then what you can do, and this is where socialism comes in, what you can do, is to show such people to themselves, to link them up.

POLLY: I don't think Miss Gainsborough takes much notice of James. When I spoke to her last week she had to think before she even knew who he was.

GEORGE: Not surprising if there are thirty-odd kids in the class. Anyway what does it matter? He is thick. We have got ourselves a thick child.

POLLY: Why should he be thick. I was a bright girl.

GEORGE: Heredity isn't a law of the land. If one only knew beforehand what one's children were going to be like. One ought to be able to see a trailer.
'Pause before you enter here
Lest from this womb a child appear.
Matchless he in face and skin
Fair of hair and clean of limb
But let not your mind your senses rob,
For he will be a stupid slob.'

POLLY: You laugh. If Andy were my son . . .

GEORGE: Ah, but Andy is not your son, and Andy, thank God, has brains. Brains and beauty, the only untaxable inheritance. He never had any special treatment and look at him. An advertisement for the comprehensive system, brighter than ever I was and beautiful with it. I don't suppose you've seen him?

POLLY: He was in at tea-time, just for a minute.

GEORGE: Even now touching up some respectable girl in the Classic, Baker Street.

POLLY: So we can't just abandon him.

GEORGE: Andy?

POLLY: James.

(*Pause.*)

I think he ought to go to Freshfields.

GEORGE: He is not going to Freshfields.

(*They have plainly had this conversation before.*)

Saunders Road, even with Miss Gainsborough is a very . . .

POLLY: I'm not having his whole life sacrificed to your principles . . .

GEORGE: His whole life. The kid is seven.

POLLY: Eight. You don't even know how old your own child is. Mozart was practically dead by the time he was his age. And why is it always the kids who suffer for the principle? Why is it, it's when it comes to schooling we always have to run up the Red Flag. Education with socialists, it's like sex, all right so long as you don't have to pay for it.

GEORGE: I am not having him educated with a load of shrill-voiced Tory boys to buy him advancement which at the moment his talents do not appear to merit.

POLLY: Merit. How can you talk about merit. At seven.

GEORGE: Eight. I don't know what you're bothering about. The first sound he learns to imitate is that of a police klaxon. He is capable of detecting the subtlest distinction in bodywork and performance. At the moment all indications are that we have brought into the world a tiny used car dealer.

POLLY: You see, even about something like this, you can't be serious. It's jokes, isn't it. Scoring. You are condemning him to . . .

GEORGE: (*Irritated by* POLLY's *intrusion*) I know what I'm condemning him to better than you do. I mean I had a state education.

POLLY: State education? You?

GEORGE: I went to a grammar school. (*Exits.*)

POLLY: Grammar school! Founded about 400 BC and wearing long blue frocks, some grammar school!

(*The lights change to indicate the time has changed. Possibly a child cries again upstairs as the stage is dark.* GEORGE *enters with* BRIAN LOWTHER, MP, *better dressed, better spoken but otherwise little different from* GEORGE.)

BRIAN: I was expecting another three o'clock do tonight. (*Yawns.*) I reckon you must all be losing heart.

GEORGE: What I don't understand about you, Brian . . . what's the matter?

BRIAN: I think I must have . . . (*He lifts his shoe.*)

GEORGE: Yes, you have. It's that bloody dalmatian.

BRIAN: Better hop outside and get rid of it. (*Steps outside.*)

GEORGE: It's always here that's what gets me.

Why is it always us? Why does it always have to do its No. 2's at No. 17?

BRIAN: It doesn't happen in Australia. Did you know that? When I went on that extremely boring parliamentary mission to that God-forsaken . . .

(*He comes back.*)

. . . albeit, let it be said Commonwealth country, the thing that impressed me most, lifeguards apart, was the sweetness of the streets.

GEORGE: I reckon it's sussed we're the only Socialists in the street. Question that dog closely and you'll find it reads the *Daily Express.* If I ever catch it dropping its nasty canine britches round here again I'll kick it into the middle of next week. And her as well, Mrs Frederick Brodribb.

BRIAN: Ah ah. She sounds like a supporter of the Conservative and Unionist Party. That's right. Shove the kettle on. I'm exhausted by that gruelling confrontation.

GEORGE: You're so sensible in many respects but when you actually get down to it, you're just as bad as the rest of them.

BRIAN: That's right.

GEORGE: I mean. Let's be clear what we are talking about. We are talking about the kind of class you can see any day of the week, shambling through Leeds or Nottingham, or Sheffield, shepherded by some broken-down, underpaid, defeated old man of forty-five. The class despises him. The passers-by pity him. He is the secondary school-teacher walking his charges to the baths, traipsing them through art galleries, trying not to see as they shove people off the pavement and make grabs at each other's balls.

BRIAN: I don't think you can blame that on Mrs Thatcher.

GEORGE: And on the other side we have a nice little crocodile of grey-flannelled boys with little pink caps and high middle-class voices going home to *Children's Hour* and *Ballet Shoes* and Noel Streatfeild. Which is very nice. Except that these others, they're going home to get their own teas in Peabody Buildings. They're going home to margarine adverts and the *TV Times*, and some of them, quite certainly, a fuck. At thirteen.

BRIAN: Bully for them.

GEORGE: All right. I know I'm being boring. That's quintessential Toryism. Any trace of passion or concern, they say you're being boring.

BRIAN: All right. I went to public school, of course. But looking back on it I think it may have been Borstal. I was taught by a succession of teachers all of whom seemed to have lost one or other of their limbs. It was cold, the food was disgusting, there was a great deal of what seemed to me entirely unnecessary running about and the sanitation was such as to make me a lifelong convert to constipation. And I would not send my worst enemy to public school. BUT if there are parents who are prepared to spend money on educating their children in such places . . . I am not going to stop them any more than I would stop them spending their money on power boats or go-kart racing or any other sophisticated way of throwing money down the drain. It's a question of freedom.

GEORGE: It is not a question of freedom, it's a question of justice.

(POLLY *comes downstairs, still carrying a pile of children's clothes, and wearing, as the simplest method of carrying it, a space helmet.*

BRIAN *kisses her, and she sniffs at him appreciatively.*)

POLLY: I was hoping he'd bring you back.

GEORGE: That flaming dog has messed on our steps again. It's the one species I wouldn't mind seeing vanish from the face of the earth. I wish they were like the White Rhino – six of them left in the Serengeti National Park, and all males. Do you know what dogs are? They're those beer-sodden soccer fans piling out of coaches in a lay-by, yanking out their cocks without a blush and pissing against the wall thirty-nine in a row. I can't stand it.

POLLY: Question is whether you hate the coach party because they're like the dogs or hate the dogs because they're like the coach party.

GEORGE: I hate them all. Where did you get that suit from?

BRIAN: It's old. I got it when I was in the army. Chester, I think.

GEORGE: Why don't my suits look like that?

BRIAN: Taste.

GEORGE: Not taste. Nothing that implies one cares. It looks like it's grown on you, that suit. I want something like that, bred in the bone, without anybody thinking I've paused before the mirror and *chosen* it. I want an honest suit of good broadcloth . . . whatever that is. I want to look like Sir Kenneth Clark or a well-to-do solicitor in a Scottish town or the head of an Oxford college. Such a suit as Montaigne might have worn, had he lived, or Marcus Aurelius.

BRIAN: And something wrong, that's the mark of real distinction: the tie too loosely knotted, a bit of dinner down the waistcoat.

POLLY: He's got that anyway.

BRIAN: You should go to my tailor.

GEORGE: There you are, you see. My tailor, my doctor, my dentist. Your servants. With me it's the tailor, the doctor, the dentist. They're not mine. And I'm not theirs. Oh, God, if it were only clothes though. Look at this dry pink plate of a face. Why didn't God give me a face on which the skin hangs in genial brown folds, the mouth is firm . . . but kindly . . . and with long large ears. Nearly every man of distinction has long ears.

(POLLY *and* BRIAN *involuntarily finger theirs*.)

BRIAN: In short you want them to look like one of us and be like one of them.

GEORGE: When I walk down the street I want people to think, 'There goes a sadder and wiser man.' Instead of which it's 'Christ. He looks a slob.' Must have a pee.

POLLY: Well, don't wake the children. George's trouble is . . . are you eating . . .

(BRIAN *shakes his head*.)

. . . he's a socialist but he doesn't like people.

BRIAN: Nor do I, much.

POLLY: You're a conservative. You don't have to.

BRIAN: No.

POLLY: There'll doubtless be a bit of something tasty in the oven, cooked by the faithful Mrs Minter. Oh, Brian, it's a nice life, yours.

BRIAN: I have an ordered life, if that's nice. All is order. Would you like some cake?

POLLY: I . . . would I like some cake? No. Why?

BRIAN: In the car there's a seed cake, a madeira cake, two dozen jam tarts, and various bunches of assorted flowers, stuff I've brought back from my constituency.

POLLY: Were you opening a fête?

BRIAN: Not especially. My constituency's run by a handful of big middle-class ladies. And I am their darling. Miss Cornfield, Miss Venables, Mrs Strickland. They love me.

POLLY: I wish ours was. You never see any of the women, ever. And it's all beer and butties. All I ever get is black pudding and black looks.

BRIAN: I just wish I had the energy of middle-class women in middle age. They'd organized this sale of work. There they were. Sturdy-legged, freckled-forearmed, horny-elbowed ladies. And the sort of arms that fill with fat, flesh-coloured flesh their flowered frocks.

POLLY: And lots of straying shoulder straps.

BRIAN: Blood donors, cake makers, good mixers, stout old-fashioned cart-horses, ploughing through day after day.

Flustered only by sex, and sometimes not even by that. I could do with even a tenth of the energy they devote to flower arrangement.

/ (GEORGE *can come back anywhere here.*)

POLLY: They're a vanishing breed.

BRIAN: No. You're a bit like that.

GEORGE: See!

BRIAN: But why, I kept wondering today. What drives the pistons? What is it that puts one firm-fleshed sensible-shoed leg in front of the other day after day after day? What thoughts do you think flood in as they ease lisle stockings down those massive legs? And in the decency of the bathroom slip into one of Arthur's old pyjama jackets?

POLLY: It's like me. Escaping boredom.

BRIAN: Boredom, they don't know the meaning of the word. And those firm capable hands. Fingers that can with equal facility bottle gooseberries, address envelopes, arrange peonies, bind wounds, decontaminate (in the event of a nuclear attack) an entire village, pray, pry and at life's end lie freckled and calm upon the sheets with no sense of life wasted or purpose lost. O fierce, foolish Tory ladies, I love you. Except that I, your Member of Parliament, your elected representative at the Palace of Westminster am an outrageous pouff.

GEORGE: Get on! Not outrageous at all. About as outrageous as St Augustine.

POLLY: He wasn't, was he? The sly devil. I'm surprised they never twig.

BRIAN: No. I'm just an agreeable young man who knows how to behave. No, they don't twig. Mind you, I've caught one or two of the 1922 Committee eyeing me uneasily, lest I should suddenly launch myself on their vast pin-striped bottoms. 'Can't have pouffs in the Conservative Party. No seat would be safe.'

POLLY: I don't think they're human at all, half of them.

BRIAN: Who?

POLLY: The 1922 Committee.

GEORGE: No. A good test is whether you can imagine them on
the lavatory. I reckon they just go in there, stand behind
the door for five minutes then come out again . . . just to
convince you they're like everybody else.

BRIAN: It's a good job I got my seat without having to go
through the cattle market. Normally you're not considered
worthy of the trust of the electorate unless you've gone
under the yoke with one of those upper-class land girls from
the front page of *Country Life*. Your credentials are a brace
of spoiled and flaxen-haired children, evidence that you
have on at least two occasions hoisted yourself on to her
massive thighs. Though quite how this makes one of more
use to the Conservative Party I am at a loss to imagine. No.
Give me a nice, clean, sad boy of nineteen any day.

GEORGE: Candidates will attend in company with their wives
and/or boyfriends. That will be liberalism.

BRIAN: That's enough anyway. I can't stand talking about it.
Some of them talk about nothing else. It's like making a
career of being five foot eleven.

GEORGE: Brian, you see, is like me. What we both crave in life
is order.

POLLY: Marriage and home is order.

BRIAN: Come on. Undies marinating in the basin, no nice cool
places in the bed. And kids. There can't be order where
there are children . . . children are anarchists,
booby-trapping the stairs . . .

GEORGE: Oh, if it were only the stairs. One's whole life mined
with affection and grief and remorse and ingratitude.
Perhaps *that's* what's wrong with me . . . perhaps in the
ninth year of my second marriage . . .

POLLY: Tenth year.

GEORGE: Perhaps in the tenth year of my second marriage I
realize too late that I am homosexual by nature. Except that
I don't like men.

POLLY: You don't like anybody.

GEORGE: Look at Brian. He is still a free man. Look at me . . .
tethered like Gulliver by a thousand tiny ropes to every

object in this house. Festooned with the fruit of a hundred
visits to the Portobello Road, weighted down with jelly
moulds, bread crocks, brass, old photographs. Yes, and
children. You're right, they're part of it. Objects like the
rest, except that they've been manufactured on the
premises, in this century, in our lifetime and we haven't
quite found a place for them yet. But they're possessions
and ornaments. And they've got to be polished in order to
do us credit.

POLLY: Here we go again.

GEORGE: Anyway, I can go back to Oxford any time I want.

ENID'S VOICE: Hello?

POLLY: Oh, God, it's Enid. What's she doing here?

(*She runs for the stairs door.*)

BRIAN: Who is it? Don't abandon me.

(GEORGE *also hides.* ENID, POLLY's *mother, enters with a
large canvas bag. She is a jolly, slightly raffish lady of about
sixty, made up in rather a slapdash way, somewhat Bohemian.*)

ENID: Hello, anybody in? It's me. Oh!

BRIAN: My name's Lowther, a friend of George's. I'm his pair.
We've just been . . .

ENID: Come again.

BRIAN: In the House. Voting.

ENID: Oh! I'm Enid, her mother. Never a popular person
with my daughter, I'm afraid. She's doubtless just run
upstairs?

BRIAN: No. She . . .

ENID: She generally does. Took the wrong turning somewhere
in childhood. Devoted to her father. Hates me. Of course
she was denied the breast. It always tells.

(*She has eventually put all her belongings down and holds out
her hand.*)

How do you do. Sorry about the paint stains. I've just been
to my sex class . . . well, actually it's my life class but this
term we're on the nude. We've got rather a nice young man
posing at the moment. He's rather a dish. But, I suspect, a
nancy. Like everybody else these days. Not that there's

anything wrong in that. More power to his elbow, that's
what I say.

(GEORGE *has come out of hiding and crept up behind her.*)

I say! There's a strange hand on my breast. I think I must
be being interfered with.

(POLLY *comes back.*)

GEORGE: Hello, you lovely old Communist.

POLLY: George. Mother. For goodness' sake. That really is
unnatural. George is the only person I know actually to be
besotted with his mother-in-law. If everybody was like you,
music-hall comedians would go out of business.

GEORGE: They have. We don't mind, do we, Enid?

ENID: No. We have a disgusting relationship. (*Kisses him.*) The
nicest thing about being old, dear, is that you can do
anything you like with a man and nobody thinks you're
flirting.

GEORGE: This has cheered me up. But you never come on a
Thursday.

ENID: I've got to go to the doctor's tomorrow so I thought I'd
come today *en route* from the Polytechnic. What're you
depressed about?

POLLY: He's got nothing to be depressed about at all.

ENID: My daughter. A very understanding person. (*To* BRIAN.)
Have you any children?

POLLY: He's not married.

ENID: He's quite capable of telling me that himself. He *is* a
Member of Parliament. So domineering. Oh, Polly, look at
your verbena toxicana. It's absolutely parched. And its
requirements are minimal. That's why I chose it.

POLLY: I don't like cacti. They're the only plants I don't like.

ENID: It's not a cacti. It's a succulent. Give you a plant and it's
like sending it to the salt mines. Come along now let's give
you a drinkie. That's better. All gone. All gone.

POLLY: I've never been any good with cacti. They need
expertise.

ENID: Expertise. One thimbleful of water every blue moon does
not constitute expertise. Otherwise we should all be fellows

of the Royal Horticultural Society, eh, Mr Lowther?

GEORGE: Let's have a look at your masterpiece.

ENID: I'm not entirely happy with it. The shoulders are good, you see, but I've never quite got the hang of arms. Whereas Zoë, at the next easel, she's just the reverse. But rather fetching, don't you think?

GEORGE: I'll take it on trust.

ENID: And he will insist on not wearing a stitch. Zoë gets quite agitated. Normally, you see, they wear what I believe is called a posing pouch.

POLLY: Oh, Mother.

ENID: Don't you oh, Mother, me. I know we're not supposed to be interested at our age. Children always assume the sexual lives of their parents come to a grinding halt at their conception.

POLLY: But you're so *New Statesman* and old-fashioned about it. It proclaims your thirties upbringing.

ENID: If that's the only thing that proclaims my thirties upbringing I think I'm doing very nicely.

POLLY: We're all emancipated now.

ENID: Not in Stanmore we're not. Things are very different there. And it's all very well to sneer at the *New Statesman*, but in the thirties it was the only thing kept one sane. You're quite shy, aren't you?

BRIAN: Me? No.

ENID: I think you are. I know one thing. If I had my time over again I wouldn't have daughters. I'd have geraniums. At least geraniums are grateful. Where've I seen you before? Television. I can't remember what it was you were talking about. You never can on television, can you! More freedom was it, or more control? Something, anyway. I quite agree, though. Mind you, all we ever watch is the wrestling. I saw a lovely programme the other night. With badgers. No, dolphins. And the D. of Edinburgh. He says dolphins are quite intelligent. And very friendly. But then he's the D. of Edinburgh so I suppose they would be.

BRIAN: I wish I'd kept my mouth shut.

ENID: Why? It seemed very sensible to me.

BRIAN: Anybody who stands up and says total freedom may not
be a good thing is immediately swamped with appreciative
letters from old ladies whose twin hobbies are prize
cucumbers and the castration of sex offenders.

GEORGE: Exactly. You look round and find you've become right
marker for the Awkward Squad . . . evangelists in belted
raincoats, defeated prep schoolmasters, hard-mouthed
ladies in gay hats. . . .

BRIAN: Regimental Sergeant-Majors in the WVS.

GEORGE: It's the S.S., Save Society by Stopping Sex, Stupid
Sods.

BRIAN: Opinions come in sets nowadays. You're either one of us
or one of them. Like this.

(*He takes out a postcard.*)

POLLY: Nice postcard. Victoria Park, Oswestry. There's no
message.

BRIAN: No.

POLLY: Who sent it?

BRIAN: I don't know. Some lunatic.

POLLY: Can I have it?

(BRIAN *shrugs and* POLLY *puts it on the mantelpiece or sticks it
in the corner of the mirror.*)

GEORGE: What is it you're off to the doctor's for? If it's
infectious don't tell me or I shall certainly get it.

ENID: I very much doubt it. Hot flushes, ladies' diseases,
nothing I could possibly come out with in company.

GEORGE: Probably psychosomatic.

ENID: I don't think Dr Proctor has heard of psychosomatic.
He's about twice as old as I am, and for the last fifteen years
he's been putting everything down to the change of life.
And I always have to take my clothes off. M.D. in his case
stands for Mucky Devil. However, one shouldn't complain,
should one, Mr Lowther? One's lucky to reach sixty
without some darns and patches in the human fabric.

GEORGE: Are you sixty?

ENID: Sixty-two, dear. Yes, sixty-two. I'm into the home stretch now. The coda. The run up to the springboard. Time's up, come in No. 17. No, no, you want to say. Not me. *Her*. I haven't had a long enough turn. She started off ages before me. But that's where the management exercises its absolute discretion.

GEORGE: Enid, you are all right, aren't you?

ENID: 'Course I am, dear. It's just an old woman rambling on. I haven't done too badly for all that. Though occasionally the system needs a little prompting. I've made it a rule never to go far without a packet of prunes. Don't pull a face, dear. Sex and bowels, I know. Shut up, Enid. I shall end up in a Home for Insufferables in Rickmansworth.

GEORGE: Not while I'm here, you won't.

ENID: Oh, Georgie. (*Kisses him.*)

GEORGE: Another drink?

ENID: No. No. Or I shall be better company than a lady should. Better be making tracks. Home again, home again, jiggety jig.

BRIAN: I can lift you as far as Baker Street.

ENID: In a motor? How marvellous.

GEORGE: Are you sure you're all right going home at this time of night?

POLLY: It's only a quarter to eleven.

GEORGE: I thought you might be nervous.

ENID: Nervous? Of what? Rape. In Stanmore. No such luck. Anyway all sex is rape in Stanmore, they're such an unforthcoming lot. Where's my bag?

GEORGE: Good God, Enid. It weighs a ton.

ENID: I know. It's one of the things about getting older, there are more and more things one can't do without. In the old days when I was a student at the Slade I used to set off in the morning, slip a sandwich and a packet of ciggies into my skirt pocket and I was set up for the day. Nowadays if I don't have everything . . . books, Kleenex, pad, envelopes, scarf, cardigan . . . I'm miserable. And most times I never open the book, write a letter, wipe my nose or put on my cardigan. But I wouldn't be settled without it.

POLLY: Come on, Enid. Brian's waiting.

BRIAN: It's all right.

ENID: Coming, just – (*Powdering her face*) – just papering over the cracks. Do you mind if I just pop upstairs to the lavvy?

POLLY: Oh, God, that's another half-hour. Don't wake the children.

ENID: I don't really want to go but one never knows whether one's going to see another, does one.
(*Exits by stairs door.*)

BRIAN: How's Andy?

POLLY: He's doing his mock A-levels next week. He's fine.

GEORGE: You see, *that's* news to me. I never even see him. The only one of the family who appears to have inherited my intellectual abilities and I never see him from one weekend to the next. This is simply his campaign headquarters, he's here just long enough to get some more lead put in his pencil, then off.

POLLY: All imagination. He's not even my flesh and blood and I know him better than you do.

GEORGE: You see him occasionally, that's why.
(ENID *enters from stairs door with* GEOFF.)

ENID: I've found an unauthorized man on the landing.

POLLY: Geoff, I'd forgotten you were in the house.

GEOFF: I've measured it all up.

POLLY: Geoff's making us an airing cupboard.

GEORGE: I hope it's all right tomorrow.

ENID: Oh, yes, silly. Now, young man, let us hie hence in yon Aston Martin.

BRIAN: It's an MG actually.

POLLY: Geoff lives Notting Hill way. Do you want lifting? Brian, you don't know Geoff, do you?

BRIAN: How do you do. It'll be a bit of a squeeze.

ENID: Good.
(GEORGE *goes out with them carrying* ENID'*s bag.*)

ENID: George, did I ever tell you: Sickert once pinched my bottom. You could see the mark for weeks.
(POLLY *and* GEOFF *are left.* POLLY *is flustered and tired.*)

POLLY: Good night, Geoff. I still haven't got your number.

GEOFF: Haven't you? I'm not on the phone.

POLLY: I never looked out that shrapnel.

GEOFF: What?

POLLY: That shrapnel. Last week, I . . .

GEOFF: Yes, if it's not any trouble.

POLLY: No, it's not any trouble. I've been keeping my eyes open for the other, but I haven't . . .

GEOFF: I fancy you.

POLLY: Yes, I do. I mean . . . yes.

GEOFF: See you.

(POLLY *and* GEORGE *now prepare for bed.* POLLY *clearing up the house.* GEORGE *is also tidying up.* POLLY *has a transistor with her which is playing chamber music.*

A recurrent theme in the play should be GEORGE *switching off this transistor whenever he can and* POLLY *switching it back on again when she notices. She should come back in her nightdress, with transistor and do some incongruous job that suddenly strikes her, like polishing some brass ornament or touching up a picture frame with paint. She goes out eventually turning the lights off, but* GEORGE *comes back, turns one of them on, now in his pyjamas. He looks at himself in the mirror.*)

GEORGE: When does it happen? When did I turn into this? This sagging cistern, lagged with an overcoat of flesh that gets thicker and thicker every year. The skin sags, the veins break down, more and more galleries are sealed off. And you never notice. There is no pain. No warning shots. No bells ring back at base to indicate that another section of the front line has collapsed. This is the body I live with and hoist into bed each night. I heave it desperately from place to place, dump it with less and less enthusiasm on someone else's body, then lug it off again and go about my business as a representative of the people. Save me, O God, from the car wash and the lawn-mower on Sundays, the steak house and the Whisky a Go Go. Deliver me from leisure and salmon pink trousers. Give me the Roman virtues, O God. Dignity, sobriety. And at the last, let my heart not be whisked across London preceded by fourteen police cars, sounding their klaxons, the transfer of my liver not be discussed by trendy surgeons (who consent willingly to make up) on late night television programmes. May I die, as I have lived, just about in one piece and my carcass not be scavenged as soon as the breath can more or less safely be said to have left my body. Shovel me into the dustbin, O Lord, without reducing me to offal in some sterile and gleaming knackers yard. And make me a decent man, O God.

(*He turns off the light, and for a second or two the stage is dark. During the last speech the sound of chamber music from* POLLY's *transistor can be heard.*

This now ceases, as the outside door is unlocked, by ANDY, GEORGE's *son. He is a boy of seventeen, seen only by the light of the fridge which he opens and takes out a bottle of milk. He takes it to the mirror and drinks it, staring at himself. Goes close and looks at it for a second. Puts the milk back in the fridge, and goes out by the stairs door.*

Lights dim.

The same. A few months later. Sunday.

GEORGE *and* ENID *are packing up some rubbish, chiefly consisting of books;* GEORGE *is clearing out his bookshelves, running his finger down the shelves and selecting volumes he doesn't want.*)

GEORGE: What time is it? I'm supposed to put the chicken in.

ENID: Shall I do it?

GEORGE: No. It's all ready. I just have to pop it in.

ENID: I hope it's free range?

GEORGE: Fat lot you care. No. It's from one of those battery farms down near the cottage. They crack on their free range establishments and a few of the hens who've earned privileges for good behaviour are allowed out in front of the sheds. Meanwhile the rest are bound and gagged inside. Battery farms. Silence, low sheds and the chimney. The blueprint for the concentration camp. Odd depressions in the ground mock the trippers herding to the coast, stir

memories of woods in Silesia, huts in a clearing and a
sergeant being sick by a wall. Here we are, bird. Shorn of
claws and beak, slung fluttering on some overhead shuttle,
to be scalded, plucked and blinded and arrive at last upon
our kitchen table, plump and white and comfortable with a
lemon and one or two onions to give you the savour in
death you never had in life. In you go at Mark 6.

ENID: Where's Polly?

GEORGE: On safari in the East End with her faithful bearer.
Apparently there is this back street in Bermondsey where
Chippendale chairs are being given away for a song by
people who haven't the sense they were born with. Or so
they've heard.

ENID: Is there time for a cup of tea?

GEORGE: I loathe Sunday. Thank God the kids are at the zoo.

ENID: Where's the tea? It used to be in this thing.

GEORGE: Ah no, there's been a radical re-thinking of the
kitchen. It's now in the tin with the picture of the royal
wedding.

ENID: H'm. I remember buying one of those at the time. I don't
know. Everything's catching up. These days you can hardly
keep ahead of the past. This shelf is new, too. And this
cupboard.

GEORGE: Yes, both erected by Geoff, the Nazarene carpenter. I
wonder whether Jesus did odd carpentry jobs around
people's houses? 'I'm sorry, Mrs Cohen, I shan't be in for
the next forty days. No. Not really a holiday. Just coming
to terms with myself really!' Now, Enid, do I want *I've
Seen 'Em All*, Memoirs of the Head Commissionnaire at
Claridge's?

ENID: No.

GEORGE: Or *The City of Nottingham Civic Handbook 1953?*
'New Factories in the Green Belt make an Imposing
Prospect'.
Don't want that.

ENID: Doesn't it bother you, them going off together?

GEORGE: The amanuensis? No. I mean, she wants company.

But I reckon he'd as soon stuff a Chesterfield. Anyway, it doesn't mean as much to them. They aren't always sniffing round for it the way we are. He said.

ENID: Here we go, dear. We always end up talking about sex. It only happens with you.

GEORGE: Anyway, I'm the one who has to mind his p's and q's. I've had one turn already. She's only on her first leg. You would have liked Liz, the first Mrs Oliver. A much maligned woman.

ENID: By whom?

GEORGE: Me chiefly. No homemaker she. She was a slattern, a soft, amiable, lovable slut. We fixed up the wedding three times and she just couldn't be bothered to get up. Politically, I need hardly say, she was of the left.

(GEORGE *possibly gets a photograph of him, Liz and Andy as a child.*)

A placid and utterly unmilitant presence at every sit-in. And the house . . . or flat, as it was then, always upside down. You'd keep on finding young men from the provinces sleeping on the floor. Fabled names in the annals of the New Left. All with monosyllabic names . . . Stan, Mike, Les, Norm. As if to have two syllables in one's name were an indication of social pretension and to prove themselves of the true faith their names had to be circumcized and trimmed of surplus syllables. What was I talking about?

ENID: (*Still looking at books*) Forgotten, dear. Wasn't listening.

GEORGE: Liz. She was Mrs Jellaby, I suppose, which is partly why I swopped her for one of the crab-apple jelly brigade. No offence.

ENID: I don't mind, dear. Polly's always taken more after Leonard than she does after me.

GEORGE: I don't know that it matters. Andy was brought up on baked beans and Rice Krispies. It doesn't seem to have done him any harm. He was a real battery boy.

ENID: How is he?

(GEORGE *shrugs.*)

He has grown.

GEORGE: Yes. Seventeen. He's found his feet . . . and other parts of his anatomy.

ENID: You used to be such pals.

GEORGE: We did, didn't we. Much more than I ever was with my dad. But of course our ages were much further apart.

ENID: I don't know where she gets all this baking her own bread from. Hard to find a more fervent disciple of bought cakes than me.

GEORGE: She's simply conducting a private rearguard action against the present day. No, they weren't. Good God. My father was actually younger. He was closer to me in age than I am to Andy. He seemed ancient, always. It's ludicrous. To look at us, you'd think we had a marvellous going on. We have two establishments, one here and the cottage. They're run in nice conjunction. Not a plum ripens before it is forthwith translated into jam. Not an egg is laid before it is summarily drowned in waterglass. Even the hedgerows are scoured and their wild, heedless fruit thrust beneath a polite crust. Oh, no. There's nothing wasted in this house, least of all opportunity. Scarcely does a plant poke its head above the soil before it's rudely dragged forth to jostle tulips in a vase. Sewing, reaping, stewing, steeping, the larder's stocked as if any day General Paulus might invest the doorstep for a siege of indeterminate duration. The larder is lined with jams in flavours of incestuous proximity . . . melon and marrow, lemon and ginger. Nothing, nothing is wasted. Nothing is allowed to break out of the endless cycle of retrenchment and regeneration. That cigarette end you have discarded, Vicar, it will find its way on to the compost heap. Part once more of the continuing process. Did you leave an old razor blade in the bathroom, madam? No. Don't apologize. It will go towards a bus destined for Addis Ababa.

ENID: There is something wrong, I suppose if we have to be dragged into the future. We ought to go forward with firm jaw and clear brow, all in profile like a Soviet poster.

Instead of looking back, dragged behind those awful hard-faced men in the Business Supplement.

GEORGE: I wish sometimes we could just go out and buy something when we need it, without all this performance of consumer's guide and best buy. I tell you. We bought that gas oven last year. There was that much consultation and consideration we might have been getting a divorce. Your house, you see, Enid, isn't like this. This isn't a house. It's a setting we've devised for ourselves. We're trying to get something over, though God knows what it is. Think of your house . . . your kitchen . . . that foxed and fly-spotted fridge on legs, your old Belling gas oven. Wood tops, stripped white and ridged by scrubbing and use rather than two days in a bath of caustic at the back of the Fulham Road. Use, not looks. Old sossed-down chairs, a house that's grown out of the life lived there, not a setting in which that life is lived.

ENID: You are an old snob, George. More right wing every day. What you want is an old-fashioned middle-class household.

GEORGE: That's not right wing. But I do. The middle-class family . . . the most exclusive interior decorator in the world. An old brown carpet slipper of a house, comfortable, roomy and lived in. This . . . this is scenery. It's been dropped in from the flies.

ENID: It'll age. It'll mellow.

GEORGE: The nicest part of your house, the thing that stamps it straightaway, so that you know exactly where you are, what level of society you're moving at, is the vestibule. That bit between the front and the inside door. Plants, a pot containing various of Leonard's broken walking-sticks. A croquet mallet and an old lacrosse stick, and a disgusting raincoat. I know that that particular sort of shabby gentility will always elude us. Our house will never look like that if we live till we're ninety-five. Better the past a void than survive like this. We're accomplices, Polly and me, with snake-hipped young men totting up back lanes in Grimthorpe and Featherstone, knocking on doors in Bishop

Auckland, peering in through barricades of plants and
ornaments for miners' widows gone a bit silly and willing to
trade the polished artefacts of a life's history for a few quid.
Reft of their associations, stripped like the eternal pine of
the polish of memory and affection and association and
brought back from northern counties to this sly southern air
across the saddle bow of some chiffon-scarved Genghis
Khan with a shop down Camden Passage and an eye for the
coming thing. You're quiet.

ENID: (*Laughs*) Good job one of us is. I'm all right.

GEORGE: Have you been feeling any better?

ENID: Oh, yes. Yes. Heaps.

GEORGE: Don't want you. Nor you. (*Chucking books in the box.
He stands back and looks at the bookshelf.*)
It's still no different. All those greens and yellows and
blues. It looks like a caravan site in book form.

ENID: Oh, no, love. They're very cheerful. I like a bright
bookcase.

GEORGE: There again. Why don't my bookshelves look like my
tutor's did . . . faded crumbling browns, sun-bleached
dustwrappers.

ENID: It's what's in them that counts.

GEORGE: They've got no dignity. They're on the game. Tarts
for some smart publishing ponce. 'Hello, dearie, don't you
recognize me in my new yellow plastic? It's Jane Austen,
dear, in my new uniform edition. Do you like it? We've had
some times together, haven't we? You've taken me to bed
more times than I care to remember.' Look out. They're
here.

(GEORGE *and* ENID *now sit silent as* POLLY *and* GEOFF
slowly edge into the room.)

POLLY: Just wait till you see this!

GEOFF: It's the most incredible thing, George, it really is. Look
at that!

GEORGE: But it's a tombstone.

POLLY: Well, it was. It isn't now.

ENID: It's going to take some cleaning.

GEOFF: I'll give it a wash.

ENID: Where did it come from?

GEOFF: Fell off the back of a churchyard.

GEORGE: 'Sacred to the memory of Joseph Banks, who departed this life August 16, 1842. Aged 28 years.'

POLLY: How's the chicken?

GEORGE: It won't be done yet.

POLLY: I'd better get my skates on.

GEORGE: Did Brian say he was coming?

POLLY: He wasn't sure. Give him a ring. Leonard and the children are staying at the zoo, aren't they? Enid, come and help me lay the table.

(GEORGE dials.)

ENID: Oh, yes, sorry, dear.

GEORGE: Lines to Manchester are engaged. Please try again later. I'm not ringing Manchester.

ENID: I shouldn't fancy it. What are you going to do with it?

POLLY: No need to do anything with it. It's something in its own right.

GEOFF: I'm going to make it into a coffee table.

GEORGE: And what about him?

POLLY: Who?

GEORGE: Joseph Banks, now lying in some nameless grave, patiently awaiting the Resurrection. Well, this is it, Joseph. Everlasting life as a coffee table in Highgate. Enid, do you fancy a walk on to the end to get some beer?

ENID: Lovely. Hold on while I just gild the lily. Then we'll pop along to the local.

GEORGE: No. Not the local. It's just the nearest pub. It's only the local if you subscribe to some nice consoling myth of community life.

POLLY: And don't stop there boozing. This won't be long. And where are you taking all those?

(GEORGE is carrying out the carton of books.)

GEORGE: These, my dear, are going to their long home.

POLLY: Oh, George, they might come in handy for . . .

GEORGE: No. They would not come in handy for anything.

They are not going to Oxfam; they are not going to the Thrift Shop. They are going into the dustbin where they belong.

POLLY: Perhaps Geoff could use them.

GEORGE: No. Nobody can use them. Nobody is going to use them. They are rubbish, waste, junk. (*He is triumphant.*) Dustbin Ho!

(GEORGE *and* ENID *depart and we hear the clank of a dustbin lid.* POLLY *comes over to* GEOFF. *They hold each other,* GEOFF *with his back to the audience staring over her shoulder at the bookcase.*)

GEOFF: Has he read all these?

(*He picks out a book, without disengaging* POLLY.)

POLLY: Doubt it. That's mine. Empson. *Seven Types of Ambiguity.* I actually made notes on it.

GEOFF: Would I like that?

POLLY: (*Almost laughing*) No. (*Then seeing the offence.*) No.

GEOFF: I might.

POLLY: You wouldn't.

GEOFF: You mean, I wouldn't understand it.

POLLY: No. I mean, yes. But I shouldn't bother. Most of these are a waste of time.

GEOFF: Is it non-fiction?

POLLY: Yes. (*Again laughing and upsetting him.*)

GEOFF: Is it I'm not fit to read them or they're too hard for me to read?

POLLY: They wouldn't interest you. Geoff. Read what you like. Don't go into a huff. What does it matter, anyway? It's all going to be cassettes now, isn't it?

(*Sound of someone coming in and they break up.* BRIAN *enters with a couple of bottles of wine.* GEOFF *kneels at the gravestone, cleaning it.*)

BRIAN: Here I am with my little lot. Am I welcome or am I not?

(*He raises his hand in greeting to* GEOFF, *sees the stone and begins to advance on it.*)

POLLY: (*Quickly*) Come and give me a hand with the lunch.

BRIAN: Yes. Yes. Yes. Yes.

(BRIAN *winks at* GEOFF.)

You making yourself useful?

GEOFF: You bet.

BRIAN: Friend of yours? What's the matter?

(BRIAN *walks round it, without saying anything, then steps over it.*)

Somebody walked over your grave? Ho ho.

(*He touches* GEOFF *with his shoe.*)

GEOFF: (*In an undertone*) Knock it off, will you?

POLLY: George is a bore. He's just thrown away a whole jorum of stuff. They'd have made such a lovely parcel for Oxfam. Geoff, nip out and see whether he's chucked out anything worth keeping. I can't bear it. You can have whatever you want.

BRIAN: Do you think Oxfam ever return anything? Oxfam graciously acknowledges the receipt of your gift but feel they must return this pair of old knickers as they would only aggravate the situation. How many are we? (*As he lays the table.*)

POLLY: Five. I don't think Andy's in. Give him a shout.

(BRIAN *shouts upstairs.*)

BRIAN: Andy! No.

(POLLY *scatters potato peelings on the floor.*)

POLLY: Oh, Dame Agnes, if you could see me now.

(*She still has hold of the book* GEOFF *picked out and is looking at her notes.*)

BRIAN: Dame Agnes who?

POLLY: Dame Agnes Bemrose, Mistress of Girton, the apple of whose eye I for a short time was.

BRIAN: Are we having a pudding?

POLLY: No-o. She thought I had a great future.

BRIAN: As what?

POLLY: It was never specified. I once fancied I'd like to be Mistress of Girton, then I decided I'd settle for being a lady novelist, rather along the lines of Virginia Woolf, and then that, too, dwindled into getting into the BBC. And now here I am, ankle deep in blighted hopes and potato peelings. 'Remember, Miss Baker, there is no Nobel Prize for Knitting.'

BRIAN: I never thought of you as at all academic. You're not that sort at all. Like me.

POLLY: Did you never want to go to university?

BRIAN: Didn't mind. Could have done. Went straight into the works instead. I wanted to get started.

POLLY: I was a bright girl. I had some interesting ideas on Coleridge's inner landscape. Then George came down to speak to the Labour Club one night in the Spring Term and that was it. You'd have done very well.

BRIAN: Not then. Now perhaps. I liked provincial life. The works all week, rugger with the boys on Saturdays and a piss-up in Knutsford afterwards. I reckon it was the army changed me. But for a certain medical corporal I was all headed for a smart wedding at the cathedral and two pages of photographs in *Cheshire Life*, winter holidays in the Bahamas and two piggy children at Oundle.

POLLY: Education didn't alter me one bit. Falling in love, sex, the children, they've altered me. I had a good education but it never went to my head, somehow. It should be a journey ending up with you at a different place. It didn't take with me. My degree was a kind of inoculation. I got just enough education to make me immune to it for the rest of my life. Now I couldn't tell you the first thing about Coleridge's inner landscape. All wasted.

BRIAN: I don't want to know about Coleridge, thank you. I just want my lunch. Or dinner as my father the mill-owner would say.

POLLY: Anyway, it's a good thing I didn't get a better degree or George would never have married me.

BRIAN: Come on.

POLLY: True. That's why he got rid of the first Mrs Oliver. She was too clever by half. But I haven't changed. Coleridge's imagery. Odd bits of junk. Picking up bits of stuff other people haven't spotted. What medical corporal?

BRIAN: Never mind.

POLLY: Now Andy's talking about leaving school, doing something useful. I haven't dared tell George. What does it matter? It doesn't get you any further, education.

BRIAN: It's not designed to. Or rather it is designed to, and that's what's wrong with it. Or so George would say. We in the Conservative Party think exactly the opposite.

POLLY: I don't know what you think at all. You don't care much, do you?

BRIAN: Not much, no.

POLLY: And Parliament. That either?

BRIAN: Passes the time. Fills in that awkward gap between the cradle and the grave.

(BRIAN *sees the postcard he gave* POLLY *stuck in the mirror. He viciously takes it out, and tears it up.*)

POLLY: Brian, I liked that.

BRIAN: Here's another one instead.

(*Takes out another postcard.*)

POLLY: Is it the same one?

BRIAN: I expect so.

POLLY: No message. Do you get lots of them?

BRIAN: Not lots. Every three months maybe.

POLLY: But why? It must be somebody who's mad.

BRIAN: Not entirely. I always get one if I've been in the news, or on television. If I raise my voice anywhere.

POLLY: What for, if there's no message? It's not even like an anonymous letter.

BRIAN: Oh, but there is a message, you see. He knows what it means and I know what it means.

POLLY: What?

BRIAN: A long time ago, at least, not so long really, when I'd just come out of the army and was still full time at the works. Before I was an MP. Quite a long time before, in fact, he must have been very smart to pick it out I was the same person.

POLLY: What same person?

BRIAN: I was had up for you know what with some youth in Victoria Park, Oswestry.

POLLY: I never knew that.

BRIAN: I should hope not. Mind you, it was so dull. It was scarcely in the papers. But *he* knows, whoever he is.

POLLY: How foul. Why don't you go to the police?

BRIAN: What for? It's not blackmail. It's just a picture of Victoria Park, Oswestry. It's actually a new one, that one. I haven't had that one before. The other one used to be rather a nice sepia photograph. They've obviously run out of stock.

POLLY: Well, I'm not having it up there. (*She tears it up.*) Why did you never say?

BRIAN: It's funny the place, really, isn't it? Lavatories, public parks, cinemas in the afternoon, the places where it happens. It can't ever be tragic, sad even, the setting's so banal. Nothing to say, why should I? Every now and again somebody pops down the road to the post. I've got now so that I can almost feel them coming.

POLLY: People are foul.

BRIAN: Yours, A Well-wisher.

(GEOFF *comes back, and* POLLY *starts to bustle round again.*)

GEOFF: What a load of old rubbish!

BRIAN: So why all this fuss about James. If it didn't take with you, why bother?

POLLY: He's a boy. He's got to get on in the world. He can't rely on being seduced at the Labour Club dance.

BRIAN: He could always try the Conservative Club.

POLLY: Watch it, you'll corrupt the youth.

(GEOFF *is still cleaning the gravestone.*)

BRIAN: Youth? Servants. (*He taps* GEOFF *with his foot.*)

POLLY: Geoff isn't servants, are you, love?

GEOFF: Aren't I?

POLLY: No, course you're not.

GEOFF: No, say it. Servants. Yes. We're servants for the people who aren't used to having servants, servants who don't make you feel guilty about it. That's probably because you're not sure our lives aren't better than yours.

POLLY: Look, Geoff, I said I was sorry.

GEOFF: Skip it.

(*GEORGE enters breathless.*)

GEORGE: Where's the bucket?

POLLY: What bucket?

GEORGE: The bucket. Quick, quick, for God's sake, where's the bucket?

POLLY: What bucket?

GEORGE: The *bucket*. The bowl, anything. Come *on*. It's the dog. It's there.

POLLY: What? Oh, no, George, you can't.

GEORGE: Yes, I bloody well can.

(*He rushes out with the dripping pail. Shouts outside as he throws the water. He returns, satisfied.*)

Got it. Purple in the face as it was passing some particularly recalcitrant stool. It leaped out of its skin. Sodden.

POLLY: It's not the dog's fault.

GEORGE: Maybe. Sometimes I think St Francis of Assisi was barking up the wrong tree. Of course it's the dog's fault. If it will choose our step.

(*He is about to throw another one, when there is a knocking at the door.* GEORGE *opens it, bucket in hand, sees who it is, turns round smartly and comes away from the door, followed in by* MRS BRODRIBB.)

MRS BRODRIBB: One moment, young man. Some person on these premises has just thrown a bucket of water over my dog. I have just met him running down the street soaked to the skin.

GEORGE: Your dog, Mrs Brodribb?

MRS BRODRIBB: My dog, Mr Oliver.

POLLY: What makes you think it was here?

GEORGE: Polly. If by dog, Mrs Brodribb, you mean that polka-dotted sewage machine on legs, yes. It was me.

MRS BRODRIBB: So, you admit it . . . he admits it. You ought to be ashamed of yourself, a man in your position, an unprovoked assault.

GEORGE: Unprovoked? Unprovoked? Mrs Brodribb, I have lost count of the number of times that creature has fouled our doorstep. It's every time he shoves his arse outside your door.

MRS BRODRIBB: Arse! Oh!

POLLY: It does happen rather often, Mrs Brodribb. I'm sure my husband didn't mean to harm him, only to teach him a lesson.

MRS BRODRIBB: If you wanted to attack a defenceless dog why didn't you choose one your own size? They have to go somewhere.

GEORGE: Then why not on your own doorstep then?

MRS BRODRIBB: Because he needs the walk. Besides, you should be flattered.

POLLY: Flattered!

MRS BRODRIBB: When Max . . .

GEOFF: Max!

MRS BRODRIBB: (*Silencing him with a look*) . . . pauses by your doorstep he is not simply relieving himself. He is leaving a message, a sign, a note.

GEORGE: A message, is it? Then I wish he wasn't quite such a frequent correspondent. Your dog, Mrs Brodribb, is a proper little Mme de Sévigné. Besides, who is it leaving a message for, for God's sake? Not for anybody at this address. We haven't any dogs. We have a goldfish and a hamster. Surely he's not contemplating starting up a deviant relationship with them?

MRS BRODRIBB: Don't you be sarcastic with me. I don't want any of your House of Commons manners here. I know one thing. I shan't ever vote Socialist after this. Not that I ever did.

GEORGE: And another thing, Mrs Brodribb. This leaving notes business. Presumably it's to do with . . . I'm sorry to have to mention this word . . . but it has to do with sex, hasn't it?

MRS BRODRIBB: (*Who has been circling round the company, stares long and deep into* BRIAN'*s face*) I've seen you on television, too. You're all the same.

GEORGE: Sex, Mrs Brodribb. But Max can go on leaving little notes for other dogs on our step until he's blue in the face, but I bet you never let him out to back them up, do you?

Except once a year with some other equally spotted bitch under medical supervision at forty guineas a time in some foul kennels in Hounslow. So what's all this message leaving, Mrs Brodribb? What are all these notes? I'll tell you what Max is, Mrs Brodribb. He's all talk and no trousers. But for future reference I am not going to have my doorstep used as a poste restante by frustrated dalmatians who never come. And I mean come, Mrs Brodribb.

POLLY: We have got a bit fed up of it.

MRS BRODRIBB: It? It? What you call it, Mrs Oliver, is an extremely sensitive creature, twice champion in his class at Crufts and a thoroughbred dalmatian. That dog, as you call it, has ten times more breeding than you have.

GEORGE: Mrs Brodribb. Shit has no pedigree.

MRS BRODRIBB: Did you hear that? Did you hear that? Such . . . language, and from one of our elected representatives. But I give you fair warning, if there is any repetition of this incident, if you ever interfere with Max again, I shall be forced to fetch my husband, diabetic though he be. And that's my last word.

GEOFF: Aw, piss off, you old cow.

(ENID *comes in with a jug just as* MRS BRODRIBB *is going out*.)

MRS BRODRIBB: If we had a real Conservative government I should have you horsewhipped.

(ENID *is mystified*, GEOFF *bursts out laughing, and there is a general hubbub.*

ENID *goes upstage into the kitchen with* GEORGE *and* BRIAN *and is told about* MRS BRODRIBB *in half-heard dialogue which goes on under the action, from various people.*)

ALL: She's a silly woman from the other end of the road. George just threw a bucket of water over her dog. The dalmatian. Ought to have thrown it over her. Quite. Who wants beer? How many are we? I hope the chicken'll be big enough. Where's salt and pepper, etc. etc?

(POLLY *comes downstage where* GEOFF *is still fiddling with the tombstone.*)

POLLY: Come on, Geoff.

GEOFF: In a sec.

(ANDY *comes in by the outside door*.)

GEORGE: Now. I never forget a face. That, unless I'm very much mistaken, is my son.

ANDY: There you go, George. Go to the top of the class.

POLLY: Andy!

ENID: Come, give me a kiss, dear. Mmm. Isn't his hair lovely. Lovely. Mmm.

POLLY: Wash your hands, love, we're all ready.

ENID: How lovely. Where've you been, dear?

ANDY: Been over the park.

BRIAN: Does it matter where we all sit?

(POLLY *indicating places*.)

POLLY: George, Enid, Andy, me, Brian.

ENID: How lovely, we're all together.

POLLY: And Geoff.

(GEOFF *comes slowly to the table as the curtain comes down*.)

END OF ACT ONE

ACT TWO

GEORGE *and* POLLY *are getting ready to go out.* GEOFF *is busy putting yet more shelves up in the kitchen.* POLLY *is ironing her skirt for the function, or sewing something on to her dress.* GEORGE *is in a dress shirt. It is evening and the children, as ever, are in bed.*

GEORGE: Put my cuff-links in, will you?
POLLY: Geoff'll do it. I've still got to get washed.
    (GEORGE *goes over to* GEOFF.)
GEORGE: (*To* POLLY) You're going to have to get a move on. (*To* GEOFF.) Are you baby-sitting?
GEOFF: Me? No. You're dropping me off, aren't you? (*To* POLLY.)
POLLY: Andy's sitting. I asked him this morning.
GEORGE: (*Edging over to the table where his watch is, so that* GEOFF *has to follow him still trying to put in his links*) Does he know what time we've got to be there?
POLLY: Don't get all agitato.
GEORGE: What time have we got to be there? Thank you.
GEOFF: (*Looking at card in mirror*) Eight.
POLLY: Eight for anything or just eight?
GEOFF: Eight.
POLLY: That means eight-fifteen.
GEORGE: It means eight. It isn't as if we were just going out to Enid or somebody.
POLLY: Better start ringing a taxi.
GEORGE: The car should have been back today.
POLLY: I don't know why we bother with the garage. Geoff is marvellous with engines.
GEORGE: (*Telephoning*) There ought to be somewhere to go to get not only service for the car but also absolution for the sin of owning it.
POLLY: Sin. I don't know what we'd do without it.
GEORGE: What I would like is the bare essentials, a car like a

145

monastic cell swept clean of dangling dolls, jokey notices, scatter cushions and . . . Hello. I want a taxi, please, to . . . Ah you're not 3232. I did dial it. Sorry you've been troubled. Goodbye, madam. A car shot of all the paraphernalia of dedicated motoring. What I want is an Austin Ascetic, a Morris Monk or a Triumph Trappist. Good evening. Could we have a taxi, please, in about . . . how long?

POLLY: Three-quarters of an hour.

GEORGE: Half an hour; 17 Passfield Gardens, Highgate. The name is Oliver.

POLLY: Say MP. It always helps.

GEORGE: MP. I wasn't giving you my initials. Never mind. The number is Dickens 0310. Dickens of *Oliver Twist* fame. DIC is the *same* as the code. I know the Post Office is asking us to use all figure numbers. But I am ringing up for a taxi not for the latest developments in telecommunications.

POLLY: We'll never get one if you're rude to them. For God's sake, be NICE.

GEORGE: The Dickens number is 432 . . . I mean 342 . . . 0310. Yes, I will hold on. Geoff, hold on for me, will you?

POLLY: I wish it wasn't tonight. We shall miss you on the telly.

GEORGE: It's old stock most of it. (*Picking up some ornament.*) Where's this thing from?

POLLY: It's a present.

GEORGE: Who the hell from?

POLLY: . . . from Geoff.

GEORGE: Oh, sorry.

(POLLY *winks at* GEOFF *behind* GEORGE's *back.* GEORGE *does his shirt up in front of the mirror and puts on his tie – he has cut himself shaving.*)

POLLY: Watch the iron for me, love, will you.

(GEOFF, *with the receiver to his ear, is now watching the iron also.*)

GEORGE: I think I've broken off my tooth again. (*He examines his mouth in the mirror.*) My mouth is beginning to look like the ruins of Hamburg.

POLLY: I can't understand you having such bad teeth. Mine are perfect.

GEOFF: It's through not having oranges in the war.

POLLY: Why is it only teeth that decay?

GEORGE: It isn't.

POLLY: You don't always have to go to the doctors to have holes in your arms stopped up, do you? Or your legs filled. It's a flaw in the design.

GEORGE: That's one thing I envy . . . no resent . . . in Andy. For all the fact he was brought up on an exclusive diet of baked beans and liquorice allsorts he has perfectly even teeth. Whereas mine are as yellow and pitted as a pub lavatory. I open my mouth and there's so much gold it's like a glimpse of the vaults at Fort Knox.

GEOFF: Hold on. (*Hands receiver to* GEORGE.)

GEORGE: Yes. Yes. What? Nearer the time. (*To* POLLY.) They want us to ring nearer the time.

POLLY: But it is nearer the time.

GEORGE: (*To receiver*) But it is nearer the time. Nearer still. You're sure there'll be one? Yes, yes. Goodbye.
(*The children start making a din upstairs.* GEORGE *goes to the stairs door and half-way up the stairs.*)

GEORGE: James. You shouldn't be out of bed. Go back to bed. What? What does she say, James? No, she can't have her pram in bed. She's brushed her teeth.

POLLY: Oh, yes, she can.

GEORGE: James. You can tell Elizabeth that decision has now been countermanded on higher authority. She can have her pram in bed. Oh God. Trouble with children . . . they're so childish. If only they were older.

POLLY: They'll get older . . . in time.
(POLLY *takes off her blouse and puts on the one she's been ironing.*)
Be a love, Geoff, and tell them a story.
(GEOFF *goes upstairs.*)

GEORGE: You ought to be a bit more careful, undressing in

front of Geoff. You embarrass him.

POLLY: He doesn't mind.

GEORGE: He'll think you're doing it on purpose.

POLLY: You said it embarrasses him. You mean it embarrasses
you. You forget I was brought up a member of the middle
classes. We are not embarrassed by our bodies.

GEORGE: You are thirty-two. You are rapidly approaching the
age when your body, whether it embarrasses you or not,
begins to embarrass other people.

POLLY: Speak for yourself.

GEORGE: I do not fart about the house in my underpants.

POLLY: I've seen you in your underpants.

GEORGE: Of course you've seen me in my underpants. You are
my wife. Seeing me in my underpants is part of the duties,
responsibilities and possibly even the pleasures of marriage.
All I am saying is that I do not fart about in the house in
them. You have never seen me in this room, for instance, in
my underpants.

(POLLY *thinks very hard*.)

POLLY: (*Triumphantly*) Yes, I have.

GEORGE: When?

(POLLY *crestfallen. She can't remember.*)

We ought to be making tracks.

POLLY: No. I know I have.

GEORGE: I'm sorry we're late, Prime Minister, but my wife and
I were detained in argument, as to when was the last
occasion she saw me in the living-room in my underpants.

POLLY: And saying that about his present.

GEORGE: I didn't know it was his. Be honest, you don't like
it . . .

POLLY: No, but, I'm trying to encourage him. Educate him a
bit.

GEORGE: What in? The liberal art of accumulating unwanted
scrap. I suppose you think by teaching him to line his nice
little Notting Hill nest with articles like that is education.

POLLY: It's a kind of education. It's better than nothing.

GEORGE: It's corruption. He'd be better off with the usual

fifteen Penguins and a blow-up of Buster Keaton.
(GEORGE *is by now more or less kitted out. He puts on his jacket and regards himself in the mirror.*)
I wish I was a bit more left wing. Then I needn't wear this thing on grounds of conscience.

POLLY: You look very good. Really slim.
(*Pause.*)
You aren't going in those socks?

GEORGE: What socks? I haven't got any others.

POLLY: You can't go to Downing Street in grey socks. What if somebody looks up your legs?

GEORGE: As I'm swinging from the chandelier, you mean? If one remembers that the Lord Chancellor wears button boots and football socks, I reckon these are pretty discreet.

POLLY: I wonder what colour Geoff's socks are?
(*She makes for the stairs door.*)

GEORGE: I am not wearing Geoff's socks.

POLLY: Here. I know.
(*She goes to a drawer and takes out a pair of worn black tights.*)
I knew these would come in.
(*She starts cutting off the legs about half-way up.*)

GEORGE: I can't wear those. They're yours. They won't fit me.

POLLY: They stretch, stupid.

GEORGE: Anyway, they're very hot to the feet. I shall sweat.

POLLY: You're a Socialist. They expect you to sweat.

GEORGE: 'I wonder whether you'd be interested to know, Prime Minister, that beneath this suave Geraldo-like exterior, I am wearing a pair of ladies' black tights.' 'Really? This is something that transcends politics. Tell me more.' I'll feel easier when Andy turns up.

POLLY: He's generally very reliable.

GEORGE: Probably servicing some sixteen-year-old classmate with more abortions than O-levels.
(GEORGE *picks up the telephone to ring a taxi again.*)
He's on the phone. Andy, where are you? We're stuck here waiting to go out. You're supposed to be at home

149

baby-sitting. What? . . . (*To* POLLY.) He is at home. He's upstairs. Sorry. No, no. Carry on. Be my guest. I'm only the subscriber.

(*He puts the receiver down, then picks it up again, and listens.*)

POLLY: George!

GEORGE: Ssh! (*After a while putting it down.*) They weren't even talking about me.

POLLY: Why should they be?

GEORGE: I am just curious to know what he is like when I'm not there, that's all. Anyway, I am ready. (*He settles down on the sofa.*) Time for a few apoplectic moments with the *Daily Express.*

POLLY: Try that taxi again.

GEORGE: Give it five minutes. Here we are. 'Pru Venables, niece of Rear-Admiral Sir Murdo Venables. Pru . . . here seen showing a larger expanse of upper thigh than her work with mentally handicapped children would seem to warrant, though, you will note, with her parts discreetly veiled in shadow, thinks Mr Heath is super.'

(*He gets the scissors and cuts it out and sticks it with the other cuttings on the wall.*)

POLLY: How's Brian? Did you have lunch yesterday?

GEORGE: I had lunch with him yesterday. Aren't you getting ready?

POLLY: What about?

GEORGE: Just lunch.

POLLY: No more postcards?

GEORGE: Postcards? He didn't say. Forget about it. It's not so extraordinary really. Somebody who's mad. If you ever raise your voice in public you know damn well before you've got two words out there'll be some clown stampeding for the Basildon Bond. 'Any Answers', that's the real voice of the English people. Envious, cruel, angry and complacent. And the *Express*. It's nice to know the enemy's still there.

(ANDY *appears.*)

What-ho. By salad cream out of fish fingers, my

Birds Eye boy.

ANDY: Light my fire. Is there any food?

(ANDY *kisses* POLLY. *And dashes dandruff off* GEORGE's *shoulders*.)

GEORGE: Sorry. It must have come off the comb.

ANDY: There you go, George. Smart.

GEORGE: I don't often wear it, it's . . .

ANDY: No. No. It suits you.

POLLY: Doesn't it?

ANDY: It's you, Dad. Very fetching. Quite the Young Conservative.

GEORGE: What's happening about school, said he, shifting smartly to the offensive.

POLLY: Not now, George, there isn't time.

GEORGE: You're the one who hasn't got any time. Jillo. Come on. Put your skates on. Have you thought what you want to do yet? I mean, eventually.

ANDY: No.

GEORGE: No.

(*Pause*.)

Nothing at all?

ANDY: I'd sort of hoped, you know, I was going to want to become an architect.

GEORGE: Yes.

ANDY: But it doesn't seem to be coming, the urge, so now I think I ought to drift for a bit.

(GEORGE *is silent*.)

I'm easy . . . I . . . you know . . . I . . . don't care.

GEORGE: I know you don't care . . . What I don't see is why you have to care.

ANDY: But look, then say I don't care. Which I don't . . .

GEORGE: Andy, care about what?

ANDY: About the work, you know, what I'm doing, I, you know, well, I go along with it, right. I get my A-levels, say. I don't care. I get a degree, maybe say . . . I don't care. I get a job. I don't care. I mean, George. When does it happen? When do I start to come into it? Me. Not until I've got this sodding great jingling ring of qualifications to unlock the doors I'm not particular to go into. So why not stuff it right now? I was trying to see the point of it. And that if I went to university it would be a waste of time. It's three years of my life.

(*Here or elsewhere* POLLY *should interrupt the scene, without speaking, by rushing in looking for things, e.g. toilet roll, or searching in cupboards, finding what she wants and going out again.*)

GEORGE: Three years! Look, how old are you? Eighteen.

ANDY: Seventeen.

GEORGE: Seventeen. I didn't even get to university till I was twenty-two. I was stuck on some deserted aerodrome in the twilight of Empire for two years first. You'll be finished when you're twenty-two. And you talk about time. Time is the one thing you have got. If there's one thing I envy you for, it's not your cool and your easy birds and an arse like a split grapefruit, it's time. You've got all the time in the world. You've still got the option. And this time, the drifting, what will you do with it, now that you've got it?

ANDY: Travel, social work. I hadn't thought.

GEORGE: No, I seem to be the only one doing any thinking. What sort of social work?

ANDY: Stop trying to pin me down.

GEORGE: All work is social work if you do it right.

ANDY: He said.

GEORGE: And if society's organized right.

ANDY: But it isn't, is it? You can't see it, because you're involved in the system.

GEORGE: System. The phrases are so worn I wonder you've the face to use them. System. What system? The system that makes me thirty years older than you are. The system of me not being willing, or indeed able to pour myself into a pair of turquoise matador pants and grow ringlets down to my shoulders. The system of clinging to plain hard logical thought instead of being at the whim of vague gusts of feeling and fellowship. Yes, I am part of that system.

ANDY: No. It's, like, sharing. You know. Being kind to one another. The system feeds you palliatives. The whole meaning of life is lost.

GEORGE: So. What does it mean? You say we're losing it – you must know what it is.

ANDY: It's not saying that's mine, that's yours. Not caring about colour, race . . .

GEORGE: Do I care about colour?

ANDY: I didn't say you did.

GEORGE: Well then . . .

(POLLY *comes in and out quickly.*)

POLLY: Have you got that taxi?

(GEORGE *goes on with his conversation with* ANDY *as he telephones.*)

ANDY: You see, George, you've only got to read Marx to see . . .

GEORGE: I have only to . . . No. *You* have only got to read Marx. I already have. What do you think I was doing stuck on my bed in the RAF for two years? Anyway, where've you been doing Marx?

ANDY: We do it in Religious Instruction.

GEORGE: Ah.

ANDY: Dave says . . .

GEORGE: *Who* says?

ANDY: Dave. He's taking us for teaching practice.

GEORGE: Dave. Dave.

ANDY: He says . . .

GEORGE: There's no need to tell me what Dave says. I know what the Daves of this world say.

ANDY: But you don't, George. You never listen. It's just your disillusion. You lump people together, goodies and baddies. You don't differentiate between . . .

(GEORGE *holds up his hand to stop him.*)

GEORGE: Hallo. I want a taxi to 17 Passfield Gardens, Highgate. Yes . . . yes, I did ring before if you remem . . . My number is Dick . . . sorry 342 0310. Yes . . . yes . . . I'll hold on. . . . Love is all you need. That's your philosophy, isn't it? Come to me at forty trailing your wife and kids and your whole communal family when any number of joints won't disguise the fact you're fat and cross and tired and tell me then that love is all you need. Try getting that together. Yes . . . yes . . . Passfield Gardens.

ANDY: George. I have said, you know, nothing.

GEORGE: That's 'you know' right. You have said 'you know' bugger all. Love is not all you need.

ANDY: I never said it was.

GEORGE: No. That's how subtle you are. But you bloody well think it.

ANDY: I've said nothing. I've made no charges. What I think you don't know. You've not the faintest idea. You're not even interested. It's shadow boxing.

GEORGE: Knowledge and subtlety and understanding and law. . . . I am holding on, madam, like grim death . . . law, that's what you need. Grubbing away on committees and nagging at officials and teasing away at the law; taking it in and letting it out until it fits even approximately the people who have to wear it.

ANDY: And talk, George. You forget talk. Lots and lots of talk. Witty talk. Clever talk. Dirty talk. Parliamentary talk. You're a killer, Dad, you really are.

GEORGE: Listen. Shocking though it may seem to your mawkish Maoist mentality, ninety per cent of the people in this world are thick. Stupid.

ANDY: Who, Dad? You, me? Not you, me. The others.

GEORGE: That's right. The others. People who with pushing and planning, welfare and incentives can just about be brought to see their own nose end . . . And by that nose end they are led. By me. And in due course by you.

ANDY: You're wrong, George. You are wrong. Look, each person is special . . .

GEORGE: Special. On the Kingston by-pass on a Sunday afternoon show me how special.

ANDY: Not if you like them . . . if you try and . . .

GEORGE: Liking them doesn't feed them, and liking doesn't

house them. Liking them doesn't stop them turning the
place into a midden or turning out in their stinking, fuming
tin boxes, Sunday by Sunday, perambulating their
boredom, about the countryside.

(*Pause.*)

So what are you going to do?

ANDY: I've told you. I don't know.

GEORGE: Of course you could go into Oxfam, or War on Want.
The amount of stuff we contribute they're practically family
firms. I don't know, Andy. The only thing that matters in
life is work. W-O-R-K.

ANDY: Come on.

GEORGE: No.

ANDY: Look, I *believe* you . . .

GEORGE: No, really. I tell you there are times when family and
kids are . . . yes, I am holding . . . all the things that are
supposed to make life worth living are marginal and
nothing compared with work.

ANDY: But . . .

GEORGE: No, wait.

ANDY: Work. You talk about work. Parliament? You? You
never stop sounding off about it . . . threatening to go back
to Oxford . . .

GEORGE: I know, I know . . .

ANDY: The worst thing you ever did, you said, what dregs there
are in it. Come on. I reckon it's pretty irrelevant nowadays.
Esso, ICI, Shell. That's where the power is. The
Conglomerates.

GEORGE: The what?

ANDY: The Conglomerates . . . Esso, ICI . . . Shell . . .

GEORGE: The Conglomerates. I bet that's Dave!

ANDY: Well, what did Parliament ever do? It never did much
for me, anyway.

GEORGE: It never did much for you . . . it brought you into the
bloody world. You were born in 1953 in Charing Cross
Hospital under the auspices of the National Health Service.
The National Health Service, a phrase still capable of

bringing a sly smile to people's faces. You shrug it off, the Welfare State, another sneering phrase. It's nothing to you. You've grown up with it, you were born under it. You take it for granted now. You don't remember the years when it was put together, at the desks of little men with bad teeth and terrible haircuts, runtish little civil servants born during the Depression, smoking too much in their cold government green offices in Nissen huts on bomb sites shivering through that winter of 1947 that went on until June. Hammering it out clause by clause, section by irrelevant section. Food rationed, clothes rationed, coal rationed, working by candlelight in power cuts, left standing in the tube by the hour together. Battering it out and forcing it through in the teeth of the Conservative Party, in the teeth of the medical profession, in the rotten nicotine-stained teeth of half the nation, they got it through and laid the corner-stone of a civilized life. And I glory in that. Snobbish, sceptical sneering socialist that I am, I glory in it.

ANDY: Great days, Dad. Those were the days, Dad.

GEORGE: Socialist that I am I glory in it. And it was done, please note, not by kindness and benevolence, not by moist good fellowship and rattling beads and tuning into the universe. But by grit and thought and work. Back-breaking, life-destroying, ill-tempered work. . . . Work that comes out of guilt and fear and want and all those phantoms your generation is very happy to be without. And you sit there with that stupid transcendental grin on your face and say it's irrelevant.

ANDY: Save it, Dad. Save it for some other stupid sod. One of the ninety-nine per cent. No point in wasting it on me. I'm one of the chosen. That's right, isn't it? Anyway, it's all relative.

GEORGE: What?

ANDY: It's all relative.

GEORGE: Which particular revolutionary handbook did you pick that one up from? Or is that Dave? It isn't all relative. Some things are absolute. Humbug is absolute. Rubbish is absolute. Sloppy, sentimental and worthless. And waste.

And it is a bloody waste. You'll end up like our friend, upstairs stripping wardrobes for a living. (*To receiver*.) What? Yes. But I've been holding on for the last ten minutes. I *did* ring earlier. Half an hour ago. What? How do you mean too late? When I rang before you said it was too early. Now you say it's too late. How do . . . well, whose fault is it? Of course it's your fault. Oh . . . get stuffed.

(GEORGE's *indignation is spread between the operator and* ANDY.)

Words fail me. They always do in the end. Worst method of communicating with anybody. Sorry.

ANDY: Come on, Dad, we have a laugh, don't we?

GEORGE: (*Shouting upstairs*) There's no taxi. I'll go and try and catch one down the road. Be ready.

(POLLY *comes down almost at the same moment as* GEORGE *is putting on his coat*.)

(*To* ANDY.) Sorry.

POLLY: What was that?

ANDY: The *Oxford English Dictionary* triumphs again.

(GEOFF *comes downstairs*. ANDY *goes upstairs*. POLLY *is all dressed up, ready*.)

POLLY: Nice?

GEOFF: Very nice.

POLLY: Can you do this?

(GEOFF *begins to fasten her ear-rings on*.
ANDY *returns for some milk*.)

ANDY: (*He goes upstairs again*.) Excuse me. Sorry to interrupt.

POLLY: He's only doing my ear-rings, love.

GEOFF: He knows?

POLLY: No. Anyway. No. He's been having a set-to with George. Where are you off to tonight?

GEOFF: Nowhere.

POLLY: Nowhere?

GEOFF: No.

POLLY: You could stop here and watch George on the telly if you wanted.

GEOFF: No. Is Brian going to this thing tonight?

POLLY: Who?

GEOFF: Brian.

POLLY: I suppose so. It's a duty do. MPs and their ladies. You call him Brian?

(POLLY *should embark on some job at this point entirely out of keeping with her get-up. Dusting or cleaning up or polishing.*)

GEOFF: Why not?

POLLY: What does he call you?

GEOFF: Doesn't call me anything.

POLLY: Do you think he fancies you?

GEOFF: Have you seen the chuck? (*He is clearing up his tools.*)

POLLY: The what?

GEOFF: For the drill.

POLLY: He probably does. What does it look like? Have you ever been in bed with a man?

GEOFF: Come on. Everybody has some time or other.

POLLY: Have they? James had it somewhere this morning. George hasn't.

GEOFF: Not bed, but at school. As a kid. Something, there must have been.

POLLY: What I said, but he says not. That's his generation for you. Things used to be different. More fraught. Is this it?

GEOFF: And now he's too old to start. Lend us that. I'll sweep up.

POLLY: But you can tell Brian fancies you, the way he never talks to you.

GEOFF: You'll get all mucky.

POLLY: Don't you think so?

GEOFF: Maybe, maybe. And if he does, then?

POLLY: Nothing. Do you know when someone fancies you?

GEOFF: You tell me.

POLLY: You told me.

GEOFF: What're you after?

POLLY: Nothing. Just interested. Has he touched you? Brian. He's very well off.

GEOFF: Do me a favour. Ask him, why don't you? If you're so keen. Get it all mapped out. I'm only part-time here, you know.

POLLY: Sorry. Well, stop fiddling about and talk to me.

(*He is about to kiss her, when the taxi hoots outside and* GEORGE *is heard coming in.*)

GEORGE: Come on. Geoff, we'll have to drop you at Oxford Circus, there's not time to go your way.

(*He opens the stairs door and shouts, only* ANDY *is either just coming down or has been behind the door all the time.*)

We're going now. I don't know what time we'll be back. Damn. I never rang Enid. She was going to the hospital today.

POLLY: There isn't time now, love. Switch the programme on, you're missing it. And make sure James does a pee. Your supper's in the oven.

(*They go.*

ANDY *switches on the set. He gets something from the fridge: cake, or a mixture of unsuitable food which he puts beside him on the sofa without a plate. The television warms up. He tries several channels before* GEORGE *appears.*)

GEORGE (TV): Somehow society ought always to be kept open. There must be a choice. Until you give people a choice there will always be people going up society by the wrong ladders . . . sex, fashion, crime.

VOICE (TV): But you say there must be options. What I don't understand is what changes you would make in the State System as it exists today.

GEORGE (TV): Look, I am a product of the State System and admirable though it may be in some respects in others it is appalling.

VOICE (TV): Appalling.

GEORGE (TV): But it isn't education simply. You see, I believe that some people are better than others, better not because they're cleverer or more cultivated or God knows . . . (*he laughs*) because they're better off. But because they're more . . . more human. I used to believe that the relation between such people and education was one of cause and effect . . .

(ANDY *who has been watching it for a long time with his hand on the switch either switches it off or switches it over. He takes a long swig from the milk bottle and switches it off altogether as the lights fade briefly, and go up again on* GEORGE, BRIAN *and* POLLY, *sitting round the kitchen table.*)

GEORGE: It's autumn. Autumn. The start of term. The real beginning of the year. I've always kept terms, ever since I was five years old. Autumn when you moved up a class, changed teachers, got a new exercise book. New satchel, school socks. I even went into the RAF in September. And Oxford in October, trunks in the lodge, leaves down Park Road. Track suits. And now Parliament again. Still in terms.

There are people whose year begins with the calendar. Begins, as Fleet Street decrees it should begin, with travel brochures and sales in Oxford Street. How many? Most people, I suppose. Wish class away there would still be this: we are two nations because our years have different bones. Terms are part of the crumbling skeleton of the Christian year. Advent, annunciation, birth, passion and pentecost.

Our year begins as theirs does. Theirs . . . whose? The masses. The people. The voters. I was in America a year on a scholarship. After Oxford. There were no terms there. It was time with the stays taken out of it, no rhythm to the calendar, no Christian holidays, no Easter or Whitsuntide. A secular state. There were sudden holidays in the middle of nowhere. Like missing a step on a stair. Lincoln's birthday. Labour Day. Odd, capricious. I like ceremony. I like pattern.

(*The lights go up as he addresses these last remarks to his wife and* BRIAN.)

Perhaps I am a Christian. Perhaps that's what's wrong with me. Or boredom.

POLLY: If you're so bored you could put the milk bottles out.

BRIAN: Boredom at least implies there's something better.

(GEORGE *does put the milk bottles out.* POLLY *is referring to a printed list, getting together some clothes. She holds up a little pink blazer.*)

POLLY: Look at his little jacket. Doesn't it look pretty?

GEORGE: How much is this Greyfriars trousseau going to cost?

POLLY: Nothing. It's coming out of Aunt Betty's money.

(GEORGE *fingers a waspish football jersey.*)

GEORGE: I particularly resent money spent on kitting him out for competitive games.

POLLY: All games are competitive.

GEORGE: How's he going to get to the flaming school, with the streets thick with sex maniacs?

POLLY: They have a rota. I've got into a group. It's Thursdays our day.

GEORGE: Thus dragging us willy-nilly into association with all the other educational queue jumpers. If there's one thing I don't fancy at nine o'clock in the morning it's chauffeuring round a cartload of Jasons and Jeremys.

POLLY: Half-past eight.

GEORGE: Cash name tapes. They were always great dividers. Like three initials. What's this?

POLLY: His hair.

GEORGE: All this?

POLLY: It says they prefer it short.

GEORGE: Short? (*He runs upstairs.*) It's not a flaming monastery.

POLLY: You all right, love?

(BRIAN *nods.*)

It's all show is this. Andy's the one. Now he's back at school what does it matter.

BRIAN: He *is* back?

POLLY: Never left. It was all talk. In this house it generally is. You have to take it all with a piece of cake.

GEORGE: He looks like a little lavatory brush. I wonder are there any other alterations to the fabric the school requires. Eyelashes clipped to regulation length? Circumcision perhaps?

POLLY: If he doesn't mind, I don't.

BRIAN: Anyway, all games are not competitive.

POLLY: All competitive games are.

GEORGE: Yes. I suppose now we've seen him safely on to the escalator you'll start worrying about Elizabeth. Already at five more eccentric than Edith Sitwell ever was. I wonder whether there's a handily situated atheist convent?

POLLY: I shouldn't worry. She'll probably slump into marriage same way as I did. I was a bright girl, you know.

GEORGE: You were not a bright girl. You talked like a man and you smoked cigars. That is not intellect.

POLLY: I was brighter than anybody else in my year.

GEORGE: And where are they now, your year? Gossip columnists on the *Evening Standard*, publishers' readers, hostesses on late-night television programmes, the commanding heights of the economy. You're well out of it.

POLLY: I ought to say at this juncture that since I didn't manage to get to Sainsbury's there is nothing for supper.

GEORGE: Eggs?

POLLY: No.

GEORGE: Can't you raid the store cupboard?

POLLY: Yes, if you fancy gooseberries on toast. Couldn't we go out?

GEORGE: No sitters. Incidentally, Geoff rang when you were out.

POLLY: Geoff? What about?

GEORGE: Nothing much. Talk. He hasn't been round for a bit, has he? I've not seen him anyway.

POLLY: If you can think of anything else for him to do. I can't.

GEORGE: I'd just got used to him. I quite like him. He said he might come round.

POLLY: Here? When?

GEORGE: Any time. Tonight, I suppose.

POLLY: What time?

GEORGE: Didn't say. Doesn't matter, we're not going out.

POLLY: I was just thinking could we not go out? To eat.

GEORGE: How can we? Why do you suddenly want to go out, anyway? There'll be enough meals out starting tomorrow.

Why do we have to eat at all? Couldn't we just give it a miss?

POLLY: I suppose you're bored with eating now?

GEORGE: Yes. In at one end of the tunnel and out the other.

POLLY: Shall we go out or shan't we?

BRIAN: Don't bother about me. I don't mind one way or the other.

POLLY: I didn't have any lunch. We haven't been out for ages. (*Pause*.)

GEORGE: No. Look. Why don't I go out to the Koh-I-Noor and fetch some? Then you won't have to do anything.

POLLY: It's not that . . . all right.

(GEORGE *goes out*.)

Oh, God. Why is it always me that gets the tap end of the bath?

(POLLY *puts the oven on*. BRIAN *says nothing*.)

Have *you* seen Geoff?

BRIAN: Have I seen him?

POLLY: You do see him, don't you?

BRIAN: Yes. Sometimes.

POLLY: Sometimes. I wondered whether that was what you were glum about.

BRIAN: No. Oh, no.

POLLY: Because he's going away. Did you know that?

BRIAN: Yes.

POLLY: Do you know where?

BRIAN: Yes.

POLLY: Where?

BRIAN: Torremolinos.

POLLY: What to do?

BRIAN: He has this friend who's opening a restaurant.

POLLY: Another friend. So. There we are.

BRIAN: What? Oh. Yes.

POLLY: Don't you want to know how I found out?

BRIAN: Found out what?

POLLY: You and Geoff.

BRIAN: It wasn't that much of a secret.

POLLY: You never told me.

BRIAN: No, I suppose not.

POLLY: He started wearing your after-shave lotion.

BRIAN: You can buy it in shops. I don't have it specially blended.

POLLY: That and . . . vibes.

BRIAN: Vibes.

POLLY: You can tell you knew each other better than you let on.

BRIAN: Not much better. He's still a bit of a mystery to me.

POLLY: So in the end I asked him point-blank. And he told me.

BRIAN: Yes. He told me he told you. He may be coming round later on to collect his stuff.

POLLY: He didn't tell me.

BRIAN: He told me about you.

POLLY: He didn't tell me about you. Why is that, I wonder?

BRIAN: He knew I wouldn't mind. In my situation one can't really afford to. I was . . . a bit shocked about you.

POLLY: Shocked. You were shocked? What had you to be shocked about?

BRIAN: Polly, you are married.

POLLY: Yes. But I loved him.
    (*Pause*.)
    No, I didn't. Did you?

BRIAN: No.

POLLY: Did he love you?

BRIAN: Oh, no. He obliges, but he's not that way, anyway.

POLLY: But it's a good job I didn't love him. Otherwise I should have been a bit, you know, cross.

BRIAN: Cross. What a funny word.

POLLY: I should have had a right to be cross.

BRIAN: It's like a French farce. I go out one door, you come in at the other.

POLLY: I suppose this is what's meant by talking it over like grown-up people, i.e. neither of us could care a damn.

BRIAN: I care. He wasn't in love with you, though?

POLLY: No. What did he talk about to you?

BRIAN: Questions mainly. Lots of questions.

POLLY: What about?

BRIAN: Anything. What did I think of President Kennedy. Had there been a plot. Would there be another war. Had I ever spoken to the Prime Minister.

POLLY: Yes, that's it. That's like it was with me.

BRIAN: And looking for a way in, somehow. As if it were all to do with being clued up. Question and answer, but not to any purpose.

POLLY: And you can't put him off, can you? He gets moody. I know I wasn't much help. I got a bit bored.

BRIAN: I wasn't bored. I felt . . . a bit sorry for him.

POLLY: I didn't.

BRIAN: You're not coming out of this very well.

POLLY: Did you smoke with him?

BRIAN: I don't smoke. Oh *smoke*. No. No. He asked me. I wouldn't.

POLLY: I did.

BRIAN: Nice?

POLLY: No. Made it less boring. I was sick once. Just like having a baby. 'Course I've seen more of him than you. Perhaps you'd have got bored. Except that was what I wanted really, a good boring man. George is so interesting all the time it gets boring. Whereas having a boring man was rather interesting.

BRIAN: I don't think you were all that well suited.

POLLY: What about . . . sex?

BRIAN: It was actually quite a bit before we got on to sex.

POLLY: Do you know, I found that. I think these days it seems to come quite low down on the list. There's a good deal of . . . I don't know . . . well just cuddles.

BRIAN: Yes.

POLLY: I find that a bit disturbing.

BRIAN: Do you? It's what they like. It's one of the differences nowadays. I've noticed it before.

POLLY: Why don't they get on with it, do you think?

BRIAN: They . . . are . . . the young . . . him, Andy . . . nicer than we were, I reckon. I think things are different.

Drifting, not pushing. Accepting.

POLLY: You?

BRIAN: Me, I suppose. Things in general. Not . . . not scoring. And it's not pot. It's them. And it's admirable. I wish it were me.

POLLY: He said I was very warm. Didn't he say that to you?

BRIAN: No. He said . . . no. He didn't say that.

POLLY: I suppose I am rather warm, really. George says I'm warm. You never know, do you?

BRIAN: What?

POLLY: *You* do, I suppose. But what you're like. Until there's been someone else, and there never was, you see – so I didn't know I was warm . . . anything . . . I thought that was just George. But now there's been someone else, I suppose, I must be. And you find you're something else besides. Someone else he, George, doesn't know, and now I've got to go back to being just what I was. And it's going to be so . . . (*she is crying*) boring.

(ANDY *is heard coming down the stairs and* POLLY *quickly switches on her transistor.*)

ANDY: What's up?

POLLY: (*Above the music, which is very loud and martial, say Sousa*) Nothing, love. (*She blows her nose.*) I'm just affected by the music.

ANDY: Is it George?

POLLY: Dad? No. Honestly. Is it, Brian?

BRIAN: No. We were just having a jolly good cry together. It's our age, you know.

ANDY: What's happened to all the food?

POLLY: George has just gone out for something. Look in the store cupboard if there's anything you fancy.

(ANDY *looks and comes out with a bottle of gooseberries, which he opens and begins spooning them out, occasionally drinking the juice from the bottle.*)

ANDY: You're sure you're all right?

POLLY: Positive. Honestly.

(*They sit in awkward silence for a bit while* ANDY *spoons in the gooseberries, and they watch him.*)

ANDY: Good these are.

POLLY: Good. They're last year's. This year they were nothing at all. (*To* BRIAN.) Nothing at all.

BRIAN: Were they?

POLLY: Nothing. Greenfly.

(*She still sniffs silently.*)

ANDY: (*To* BRIAN) Do you want any?

BRIAN: No. I . . . No.

(*Knock at the door.*)

POLLY: (*Leaping up*) That'll be Geoff.

(*She runs very quickly upstairs.* ANDY *shrugs and answers the door.*)

GEOFF: How do.

ANDY: She's upstairs. You know Brian?

(GEOFF *raises hand to* BRIAN.)

GEOFF: I called round to collect the rest of my gear.

ANDY: (*Through stairs door*) Mum. Geoff. Do you know where it all is?

GEOFF: More or less.

(ANDY *sits down again, goes on with the gooseberries. The silence is still pretty awkward.*)

ANDY: Gooseberry?

GEOFF: What?

ANDY: Home-made. (*Holding out bottle.*)

GEOFF: No, thanks. No, OK, I will. (*He tries one.*) You seen my set-square?

ANDY: In James's box, try.

(GEORGE *now appears with two carriers and several silver foil cartons of Indian food, which he dumps on the kitchen table.*)

GEORGE: Hello, stranger. We were just saying you'd not been round. You staying for supper?

GEOFF: No.

GEORGE: Indian food. There's always plenty.

ANDY: Except for the Indians.

GEOFF: I'll see to it, shall I?

GEORGE: Would you?

(GEOFF *puts food in oven, etc.*)

Drink? (*To* BRIAN.) No? No.

(GEOFF *has now got most of his gear together.*)

Are you going?

GEOFF: Yes.

BRIAN: To Spain.

GEORGE: Spain?

GEOFF: I'd borrowed one or two books. I don't know where
they go.

GEORGE: Take some more if you want.

GEOFF: I'd better not. It'll be a bit before I'm back.

GEORGE: Whereabouts?

GEOFF: Torremolinos . . . I'm going to help set up this
restaurant.

GEORGE: Torremolinos?

GEOFF: Yeah. It's goodbye to The Smoke. Anywhere.

(GEOFF *is putting the books back on the shelf.*)

GEORGE: Take some. It's not exactly Wittenberg,
Torremolinos.

GEOFF: What? I can never follow you.

ANDY: It wouldn't suit him so he can't see why it should suit
you either.

GEORGE: I just don't think Torremolinos Public Library will be
much cop.

ANDY: I envy you. I wish it were me.

GEOFF: I don't know what to choose.

ANDY: Here. I'll choose some.

GEOFF: (*To* ANDY) I had a tape measure. Have you seen it . . .

GEORGE: It's on the sink. I shouldn't worry about books, Geoff.
Books are on their way out, nowadays, didn't you know
that? Words are on their last legs. Words, print and also
thought. That's also for the high jump. The sentence, that
dignified entity with subject and predicate, is shortly to be
made illegal. It probably already is in Torremolinos.
Wherever two or three words are gathered together, you
see, there is grave danger that thought might be present.
All assemblies of words will be forbidden, in favour of

patterns of light, videotape, every man his own telecine.
Oh, and vibes. Yes, vibes. Does she know you're here?

GEOFF: A lot of the time I never understand what you're saying.

(GEORGE *goes upstairs for* POLLY.)

ANDY: You're not missing much. Mum.

GEORGE: You'll wake the kids. I'll get her.

(POLLY *comes downstairs*.)

POLLY: You're going then?

GEOFF: Yes.

POLLY: Is there anything you want?

GEOFF: No.

ANDY: Cheers.

POLLY: Where you going?

ANDY: Only out.

(*Goes out by outside door.* ANDY *should sense he is spare before going.* GEOFF *is left with* BRIAN *and* POLLY.)

GEOFF: Well, I'm off.

POLLY: Oh, are you off?

GEOFF: Yes. I'd better. Not mad, are you?

BRIAN: Me? No.

POLLY: No.

GEOFF: My fault really.

POLLY: You don't want a cup of tea?

GEOFF: No. Something I wanted to say. It . . . it wasn't sex. I
    mean, it was. I wasn't after anything, but it's the least part
    of it. Nobody ever explains to you how the system works,
    what the timetable is, sort of. There ought to have been
    somebody when I was . . . I don't know . . . somebody to
    say, 'Look, this is the last bus. If you're not on this one
    you're going to have to walk.'

(POLLY *remembers something he has left and is about to give it to him*.)

No. Have that. We're free-loaders, people like me.
Hitch-hiking. Whereas you . . . all you . . . you're on the
motorway. We're other routes. We're . . . we're lumbered.

(GEOFF *goes leaving* POLLY *and* BRIAN *rather lost.*
GEORGE *comes back.*)

GEORGE: Geoff gone?

POLLY: Mmm.

GEORGE: I wanted to say goodbye. I shall miss him, you know.
I'd got quite to like him. Wasted, you know a boy like that.
Wasted. He was quite bright. He's somebody in the
dustbin. Torremolinos.

POLLY: He'll be all right. He's beautiful. He won't be in the
dustbin for long. He's got his head screwed on right.

GEORGE: No. You don't see it, Polly. You think because he's
pretty and knows a Chesterfield when he sees it that he's
got a pretty nice life. But I tell you, it's waste. It's like
Dickens. Fortunes in the dust heap. How do we cast the
net wider or make it with the finer mesh? Or are nets what
we want? Somehow you see society's got to be kept open.
We can't afford to lose people. Somehow boys like that . . .

POLLY: Shut up.

GEORGE: What?

POLLY: One thing about Geoff . . .

GEORGE: Why?

POLLY: Just for once, let it pass. Shut up. No comment. You
always have to fetch everything down to words.

GEORGE: What else would you prefer . . . the music
programme?

POLLY: Nowhere, there's nowhere safe . . . from words with
you. No . . . no secret room, but what you have to be in
there like an auctioneer's clerk, cataloguing, describing,
relating, reducing everything to a collection of objects,
sticking labels on them. Lot numbers. And though
nothing's been changed, nothing taken away, just listed,
catalogued and explained . . . yet it's less. You make it less,
George. It's not a place any more.

GEORGE: It just happens that all I was saying was . . . Geoff is a
very good example of something . . .

POLLY: He isn't an *example*. That's it. Can't you see? Always
this is what it's like. It's as if this or as if that. No. This is
what it is. There isn't a gap. You don't have to be
describing always. Not for me, anyway. Just leave it. Don't

say it. (*She is crying*.) All your talk, and you see less than
anybody else. You can't even see what's under your nose.

GEORGE: Like what?

POLLY: Like . . . Oh, Georgie . . . I don't know . . . like what
people are . . . I don't know . . . like . . .

GEORGE: Like?

POLLY: You're the dead one, George. Irony, litotes,
zeugma . . . that's all you are. Just a figure of speech.
(BRIAN *gets up*.)

GEORGE: Don't go, please.

BRIAN: No, actually I'd better go.

GEORGE: (*To* POLLY) Look. What is all this about? What am I
supposed to have done?

POLLY: Nothing. Nothing.

GEORGE: Nothing. Right. (*As if that settles it*.) And what about
you?

BRIAN: Me?

GEORGE: You're not exactly Nancy with the Laughing Face.
Will one of you tell me what I'm supposed to have done?

BRIAN: You? You've done nothing. Look. There is something
I . . . well, I ought to explain before tomorrow. Remember
those postcards?

GEORGE: Ignore them . . . it's . . . forget about them . . .

BRIAN: No. Something else has happened since then.

ENID'S VOICE: Hello!
(BRIAN *gets up hurriedly*.)

POLLY: Oh, Christ. That's all it wanted. No, stay.

BRIAN: No, I'll nip out . . .
(ENID *puts her head round the door*.)

ENID: Coming, hiddy, or not.

GEORGE: Now then.

ENID: Cheer up, dear. I'm not stopping. I've got a taxi waiting.

POLLY: Taxi? Where to?

ENID: Stanmore, where else?

POLLY: That'll cost the earth.

ENID: No. It won't, you see, because . . .

GEORGE: What's happened about your tests?

ENID: That's what I called in to say. I've been living in fear and
trembling and eventually screwed up my courage to the
sticking point – Hello, Mr Thing, didn't see you
there – went to see dirty Doctor Proctor who, of course, has
had the results for a week and never bothered to tell me.

GEORGE: And what is it?

ENID: Nothing at all. I'm all right. I said what about the shadow
and he said well that's all it was, a shadow, no substance to
it at all. (*To* BRIAN.) Sorry to visit all this on you.
(BRIAN *should go upstairs.*)

GEORGE: Oh, Enid. (*Kisses her.*)

ENID: I really thought it was the fell sergeant this time. I made
my will, everything, and such a weep doing it.

POLLY: Enid, you are a twerp.

ENID: Twerp! I thought it was curtains.

GEORGE: I did.

ENID: Did you? I'm glad you didn't tell me. Anyway, all gone.
So I went to my class tonight the first time for three weeks.
And Zoë and I went out for a little celebration with the
male model who turns out to be a taxi-driver in his spare
time and not a nancy at all. He says it's coming from Leeds.
They all talk like that. You all right, dear?

POLLY: Yes. 'Course I'm all right.

GEORGE: And how do you feel?

ENID: At this moment, dear, a bit tiddly. Sure?

POLLY: Yes.

ENID: I suppose it ought to teach me to mend my ways. But I
can't see how. George dear, would you do something for
me. Go along to the end and get me some ciggies. It's for
Gerry. He's been ever so good.

GEORGE: I've got some here. He could have those.

ENID: No, dear, those aren't the sort he likes.

GEORGE: Well, what sort?

ENID: Oh, any sort. He's not fussy. Off you go before they
close.
(POLLY *and* ENID *are alone.*)
You been crying, dear?

POLLY: No.

ENID: What about?

POLLY: Nothing. I haven't.

ENID: Last time I saw you crying . . .

POLLY: I haven't been.

ENID: . . . was when you were fifteen. Over Michael Fitton.

POLLY: Who?

ENID: Michael Fitton, dear, don't you remember? A funny boy
    with weak ankles who played the violin and lived in the
    Drysdales.

POLLY: That's right. With ginger hair.

ENID: He's gone to New Zealand. I saw his mother in
    McCorquodales last week. You wouldn't think there'd be
    openings for violinists in New Zealand, would you? She
    said they were crying out for them.

POLLY: (*Crying*) Oh, Mum. You are lovely.

ENID: Then there was Roger Mowbray. He stood for the council
    this year.

POLLY: His . . . his feet used to smell.

ENID: Terrible. Probably still do. He didn't get in anyway. That
    was a narrow escape, too. You were quite smitten with him.

POLLY: I never was.

ENID: Yes, you were. You've forgotten, but you were. I
    remember Leonard saying.
    (*Pause.*)
    Is it that young man?

POLLY: (*Still crying*) Sort of, I suppose. Oh dear. Things
    altogether, really. Things going on. And on. This is the way
    things are going to be now.

ENID: Blow your nose, dear.

POLLY: The family's complete, we don't want any more. . . . If
    I had another baby I think George would strangle it . . .
    and then him.

ENID: Who?

POLLY: George . . . George is . . . like he is . . . And this is our
    hand. It's been dealt and now all there is to do is to play it
    for, what? Thirty years.

ENID: (*She is smoking*) Thirty years.

POLLY: You don't smoke.

ENID: Oh, I do occasionally. Special occasions.

(*Pause.*)

You wonder sometimes how you land up where you do. I look across at Leonard sometimes on a night and think of myself running up the steps of the Slade all those years ago. Only it doesn't seem all those years ago. I thought life was going to be like Brahms, do you know? Instead it's, well it's been Eric Coates. And very nice, too. But not Brahms.

POLLY: You and Dad have been very happy I've always thought.

ENID: Oh, yes, it's been very happy.

POLLY: I've got so much left. Spare. I suppose I ought to be more like you and further education.

ENID: Going to classes? Oh, no, that's not the answer, classes. Don't start on that. I've been to so many classes. Pottery classes, first aid classes, classes in bookbinding and the first principles of Economics. Keats. Yoga. Poland, Cockpit of Europe. Judaism, an Introduction to Flower Arrangement. Classes in primary schools and scout huts, vestries in the black-out, sat there with my pencil and pad, improving myself, leaving Leonard's supper ready. Making contact, taking up the slack, such an awful lot of slack left to take up somehow. Like a pie, marriage, so much pastry sliced off the dish. Oh, no, don't start on that. That's not the answer.

POLLY: Did you have any affairs?

ENID: One or two. At least I suppose that's what they were. You never know, do you? I'm supposed to offer advice, aren't I? Your silly old mother. I'm not much good as Evelyn Home.

POLLY: I'm better for the cry, it's all right.

ENID: People ask you for help and all you do is root about in your own trunk trying to come across something similar.

POLLY: It's all right.

ENID: I wouldn't tell him.

POLLY: No? I wanted to.

ENID: It's like setting him a test. No. Marriage isn't Outward
Bound, dear. Keep it to yourself, if he doesn't know.

POLLY: No. He doesn't know.

ENID: Stop talking now. Or I shall get on your nerves.

POLLY: No.

ENID: Yes. The trouble with both of us, dear, is that we've both
been hit with the doolally stick.

GEORGE: (*Coming in*) Hit with what.

ENID: The doolally stick. A bit daft, it means, the pair of us,
your wife and I.
(*Taxi hoots.*)
That's Gerry. He's taking me all the way back to Stanmore
for nothing. He's lovely. Is everything all right?

GEORGE: Champion, champion.

ENID: (*Kisses* POLLY) 'Bye, dear. I'm afraid you've got your old
mother for another few years yet.

POLLY: Enid. (*And for the first time kisses her with genuine
affection.*
BRIAN *reappears. Taxi hoots.*)
That's Gerry again. So impatient. Toodloo.

GEORGE: That's some good news, anyway.

POLLY: Is it?

BRIAN: I wondered . . . Anyway, I'll be off.

GEORGE: What is it, for Christ's sake? I can't see why you
worry about it? It is that, isn't it? The postcards.

BRIAN: No. No. That's to say, whoever it is has obviously
got a bit tired of the situation. I'm still not certain what
I'm going to do. He . . . has sent . . . they must have
saved the clipping . . . from the newspaper. And sent it to
my agent.

GEORGE: So what's happened?

BRIAN: Blessington, my agent, is an admirable man, who puts
down half a bottle of whisky a day and has two convictions
for drunken driving, but otherwise a pillar of society. With
three teenage sons. The upshot is he has made some
inquiries, and, as he put it, sounded opinion in the

constituency and . . . I am not going to be asked to stand
again.

GEORGE: But that's monstrous.

POLLY: They can't do that, can they, just chuck you out in
between elections?

BRIAN: No. Not now. Not straight away, not without there
being a fuss.

GEORGE: You can sit it out. There's three years at least before
they can shift you.

BRIAN: It all depends. I can say, you see, I want to devote more
time to business. That's an eminently respectable reason.

GEORGE: The sods. When you consider that there are many
Members of Parliament, and alas not merely in the
Conservative Party, men who have never had a moment of
self doubt in their lives. We don't expel them for greed, for
arrogance, for debating the state of the nation in voices that
would get them thrown out of a saloon bar, for spending
lunchtime in strip clubs or trundling their throbbing pink
tools round to little blondes in Victoria. What is it in this
particular sin?

POLLY: What are you going to do?

BRIAN: If I give up, you mean?

GEORGE: You mustn't give up.

BRIAN: Go back full time to the works, I can. Couldn't do that
if there were a hullabaloo, you see. And it's a bit late to
strike out.

POLLY: You could always do social work.

BRIAN: What?

POLLY: Some sort of social work.

BRIAN: Me? Can you see it? Expiate my sin stroke crime by
picking old men off bomb sites and feeding them tea and
wads in some East End church hall. Along with a lot of
other damp young men, fugitives from teachers' training
colleges, ex-altar boys, schizophrenics going straight and
High Church young men who make daring jokes about
vestments. The lame ducks. The ones who brought a note.
No, thank you.

GEORGE: You're going to fight it?

BRIAN: I may do. I may not. I haven't thought it out yet. I only got to know this morning.

GEORGE: It's blackmail.

BRIAN: That's right, it's blackmail. But don't get worked up about it.

GEORGE: Worked up, Christ!

BRIAN: Some people might reckon I'm half a man. But then so are you, George, in a different way. So are all politicians. Come close and you'll see a scar. We've all had an operation. We've been seen to, doctored, like cats. Some essential part of our humanity has been removed. It's not honesty or straightforwardness, or the usual things politicians are supposed to lack. It's a sense of the ridiculous, the bloody pointlessness of it all, that's what they've lost. They think they're important. As if it mattered.

GEORGE: Now. Has he put anything down on paper?

BRIAN: Who?

GEORGE: Your agent.

BRIAN: He wrote me a letter.

GEORGE: Saying what?

BRIAN: Saying what I told you.

GEORGE: Outright? Not just hints or . . .

BRIAN: Hints! He gave the actual date of the newspaper.

GEORGE: Then you've got him. Where is it?

BRIAN: What?

GEORGE: Because if he actually committed himself on paper.

BRIAN: I threw it away.

GEORGE: What? But you only have to show that letter . . .

BRIAN: I don't want to show that letter to anybody.

GEORGE: But there's a principle.

BRIAN: George. Fuck principle. I wasn't going to say anything because I knew we'd have to have all this to go through. Just keep out of it. Smashing, isn't it? A lively little liberal scuffle. A nice straightforward battle between right on the left and wrong on the right. Where you can go in with fists flying and hang the consequences.

GEORGE: I know it's harder for you to see it, but . . .

BRIAN: No, I see it. A clear issue. Vermin. The Tory beast. The old ogre of intolerance as it still stalks the constituencies. That's how she fits in, that dog woman, Mrs Boothroyd.

POLLY: Brodribb.

BRIAN: A target a mile wide and all stupid. Safe enough there, George.

GEORGE: That's balls. Whoever it was it's monstrous. You can't think it's just that.

BRIAN: Not just, though that's part of it. You'd like a good fight, wouldn't you, George?

GEORGE: Yes, I would. It's a scandal.

BRIAN: It's a scandal. And they're pretty hard to come by, aren't they, situations where there isn't something to be said on both sides? No balance. No assessment needed. No. That's what you're missing and you'd enjoy it too much. Something really solid to fetch the phrases out, get the life-giving adrenalin flowing. Well, I wouldn't waste them on me. Save them for the old age pensioners.

GEORGE: Brian.

BRIAN: No offence, George. I appreciate it. Night, love.
(*He kisses* POLLY.
Exits.)

GEORGE: He's worked up about it now. I'll go after him.

POLLY: No.

GEORGE: But he's wrong. He must put up a fight about it. It's years ago. My God if they can do that . . . he'll come round. I mean. What do you think? It's pathetic.

POLLY: There've probably been other times.

GEORGE: Have there? Not that anybody knows about. Anyway, what if there have. These days. It's nothing. Nothing. Bassington.

POLLY: Blessington.

GEORGE: I'd like an electric device to send a short sharp shock through the arses of men like that. And when was it, 1955, '56. Fifteen years ago. Five minutes with a soldier in the

park. Jesus Christ. What is there in that that makes him
unfit to represent the people. What next, it makes you
wonder, nose picking?

(POLLY *slips out during this speech, crying.*)

'It has come to our notice that in March 1953 in the course
of a weekend at the Hyde Park Hotel on three separate
occasions and notwithstanding there was a lavatory only a
few yards down the corridor, you nevertheless took it upon
yourself to piss in the basin. This, taken in conjunction
with the fact that you have frequently failed to change your
underwear twice daily has raised grave doubts as to your
suitability to continue to represent this constituency and the
committee has therefore decided that . . .'

(*He finds he is alone. He sits down on the sofa, silent and
jaded. He begins to get ready for bed. Unbuttons his shirt, puts
out some of the lights. Faintly, as ever, music upstairs.*

ANDY *comes in through the outside door.*)

ANDY: George.

GEORGE: Hello.

ANDY: S'Mam?

GEORGE: Bed, I think. Been out?

ANDY: Yep. Geoff go?

(GEORGE *nods.*)

Any food?

GEORGE: In the oven.

(ANDY *goes into kitchen.*)

Better turn it off. And throw away what you don't want.

ANDY: You not eating?

GEORGE: No.

ANDY: (*Poised with several cartons over the waste bin*) Sure?

GEORGE: No.

(*He drops in the cartons with a thud and a shrug. This
dumping must be quite explicit and pointed, dumping several
cartons distinctly and separately, opening waste bin with his foot
each time.*)

ANDY: S'matter?

GEORGE: Tired.

179

ANDY: Go to bed.

GEORGE: In a minute. She kick you out?

ANDY: Who?

GEORGE: You tell me.

ANDY: No. (*Pause*.) No.

GEORGE: So.

ANDY: I went down the pub.

GEORGE: What for?

(*Pause*.)

ANDY: A drink. Two drinks. Smoke.

GEORGE: Thought you didn't go in for pubs much.

ANDY: Who?

GEORGE: You. Youth. Young people. The younger generation.

ANDY: Us.

GEORGE: Us. That's the big difference. We were never us.

ANDY: I don't feel it.

GEORGE: I didn't then. We'll go down as the last generation
    before the pill. Still making sly visits to back-street
    herbalists for the tell-tale pink and purple packets. We . . .
    I . . . went by train to country stations, Shepreth,
    Melbourne, Foxton. Distance was still measured in cycle
    rides, not yet annihilated by the motor car. And with
    army appetites found out good places to eat. Good meals
    used to be an achievement then, good restaurants anyway.
    Not like now, an indulgence, an ordeal or a chore. Then
    really found reason to welcome Suez. For there we were
    scattered all over England and suddenly we linked hands
    and became a generation. By which time I was
    twenty-eight. Some youth.

ANDY: That's the new period in A-levels. Contemporary History
    from Munich to Suez.

(GEORGE *laughs*.)

GEORGE: Andy.

ANDY: Yes.

GEORGE: I don't mind, you know . . . I go on at you . . . but
    say, if you wanted to bring anyone back here, you can.

ANDY: No.

GEORGE: You never do.

ANDY: No . . . it's . . . there's never any need.

GEORGE: I don't mind. Polly might. But it's all the same to me whatever you do, really.

ANDY: Thanks.

GEORGE: I mean, to stop if you want them to . . .

ANDY: I knew what you meant. I reckon I'm off to bed.

GEORGE: I suppose that would take some of the fun out of it. Or isn't it fun any more? I suppose you're so cool you never notice. You do have a bird?

ANDY: Sometimes.

GEORGE: That isn't what I meant.

ANDY: Isn't it? You're frightened of getting old, Dad, aren't you? Oh, yes, you are, Dad. You think somehow, Dad, I'm going to supply the vitality. Well, I'm not, Dad. Do you know what your trouble is, Dad?

GEORGE: What's all this Dad business? What's the matter with George all of a sudden?

ANDY: You've stopped looking at things. You don't look and then alter. That's being old, Dad. Not changing any more. So do you want to know something? If you want precise information, I've never been to bed with anybody ever.

GEORGE: I'm sorry.

ANDY: Ever. Have you ever thought what's happened to all the shy people? What's become of them all of a sudden?

GEORGE: Right.

ANDY: Whatever happened to reserve, Dad, and self-consciousness? Was it your government that got rid of guilt? Tell me this, Dad. How is it easier, how is it easier to reach out and touch someone for the first time? Why is it easier for me now, than it was for you then, whenever that was? Because that's the irreducible fact. You envy me, sniffing out what I do, fishing out where I've been, trying to calculate exactly where I've got to in the sexual stakes. Well, listen, Dad, there's nothing to envy yet. You can sleep easy at nights, because I haven't even started.

GEORGE: OK, OK.

ANDY: But I tell you this, Dad . . .
   (POLLY *comes down in her dressing-gown with transistor.*)
   When I do start, and I care, and you say things like that to
   me, then I shan't simply tell you to mind your own bloody
   business, I shall just go. Leave.
GEORGE: Yes, you do that, *Son* . . . You do that. You're the
   New Puritans, you lot. Get through the haze of pot and
   cheap fellowship and underneath you're like everybody
   else, harsh, censorious bastards.
ANDY: And sometimes, Dad, keep your mouth shut. That's
   cool. I commend it to you.
   (ANDY *goes upstairs.*
   GEORGE *sits for a moment on the sofa.*)
POLLY: Come on, love, I'm sorry.
GEORGE: What a foul day it's been. All in all.
POLLY: Yes. About Enid. Is she all right, do you think?
GEORGE: Enid? I don't know. I wondered. It seemed funny.
POLLY: Yes, it did.
GEORGE: I can ring that doctor, if you like?
POLLY: No.
GEORGE: Her I care about, don't I?
POLLY: What? Come on, I didn't mean it.
GEORGE: Anyway, if it isn't all right, it must mean . . . there
   isn't anything to be done. Oh-o-oh. Feel old. And
   tomorrow it's the new session. A few more years in the
   cold. Then perhaps a Minister for five years, ten if we're
   lucky. Then I shall be sixty and out. My name to a statute,
   perhaps, and that's my posterity. That and Andy.
POLLY: And James and Elizabeth.
GEORGE: I was a lackey of Transport House. The sum of a small
   irrelevant career in English public life in the second half of
   the twentieth century.
POLLY: I wonder, wherever we lived, if we'd be the same?
   Outside London. East Anglia, say. How do people live
   there?
   (*Pause.*)
   Or Truro.

GEORGE: (*Who has slit open a postal packet containing the local paper sent from the constituency*) Truro?

POLLY: The provinces. Anywhere. People are nicer. Better, anyway. It's London that's wrong.
(*She should retrieve the string and brown paper, tidy to the last, and put it away in a drawer.*)

GEORGE: I was thinking if they'd ever have me back at Oxford we could live in the country all the time. The Cotswolds practically. A lot of them do.

POLLY: Except if we lived outside London, the provinces say, are there people like us? It might be like staying up at Cambridge during the long vac. Having to make do with people who were there, whether you liked them or not.

GEORGE: What?

POLLY: Nothing.

GEORGE: Or just come up here at weekends.

POLLY: London. Come on up.
(POLLY *pauses with hand on light switch as* GEORGE *gets up with the local paper. He sees an item that interests him.*)

GEORGE: That's funny. Do you remember, a long time ago I had a West Indian woman who thought next door were poisoning her cats?

POLLY: No. (*Goes off.*)

GEORGE: I thought she was mad. She wasn't. They were. She's taken them to court and they've been fined.
(GEORGE *switches light off, light streams from stairs door, and he goes upstairs as the curtain comes down.*)

HABEAS CORPUS

CHARACTERS

ARTHUR WICKSTEED, a general practitioner
MURIEL WICKSTEED, his wife
DENNIS WICKSTEED, their son
CONSTANCE WICKSTEED, the doctor's sister
MRS SWABB, a cleaning lady
CANON THROBBING, a celibate
LADY RUMPERS, a white settler
FELICITY RUMPERS, her daughter
MR SHANKS, a sales representative
SIR PERCY SHORTER, a leading light in the medical profession
MR PURDUE, a sick man

All scenes take place in and around the Wicksteeds' house in Hove.

When the play opened at the Lyric Theatre on 10 May 1973 the cast was as follows:

ARTHUR WICKSTEED	Alec Guinness
MURIEL WICKSTEED	Margaret Courtenay
DENNIS WICKSTEED	Christopher Good
CONSTANCE WICKSTEED	Phyllida Law
MRS SWABB	Patricia Hayes
CANON THROBBING	Roddy Maude-Roxby
LADY RUMPERS	Joan Sanderson
FELICITY RUMPERS	Madeline Smith
MR SHANKS	Andrew Sachs
SIR PERCY SHORTER	John Bird
MR PURDUE	Mike Carnell

Directed by Ronald Eyre
Designed by Derek Cousins
Music by Carl Davis

Presented by Michael Codron in association with Stoll Productions

AUTHOR'S NOTE

The text printed here is as first performed at the Lyric Theatre, London, in May 1973. In the rehearsal version of the play I included no stage directions in an effort to achieve as fluid a presentation as possible. In the printed version I have marked a minimum of entrances and exits to make the action more readily comprehensible to the reader.

The play was presented on an open stage furnished with three chairs. All props, telephone, parcel, etc., were handed in from the wings. Much of the dialogue was delivered straight to the audience to an extent that makes it tedious to indicate all remarks taken as asides.

I would like to thank Ronald Eyre for his invaluable assistance with the text.

WICKSTEED: Look at him. Just look at that look on his face. Do you know what that means? He wants me to tell him he's not going to die. You're not going to die. He is going to die. Not now, of course, but some time . . . ten, fifteen years, who knows? I don't. We don't want to lose you, do we? And off he goes. Sentence suspended. Another ten years. Another ten years showing the slides. ('That's Malcolm, Pauline and Baby Jason.') Another ten years going for little runs in the car. ('That's us at the Safari Park.') 'So what did the doctor say, dear?' 'Nothing, oh, nothing. It was all imagination.' But it's not all imagination. Sometimes I'm afraid, it actually happens.

MRS WICKSTEED'S VOICE: Arthur! Arthur!

MRS SWABB: It's all in the mind. Me, I've never had a day's illness in my life. No. I tell a lie. I once had my tonsils out. I went in on the Monday; I had it done on the Tuesday; I was putting wallpaper up on the Wednesday. My name is Mrs Swabb (hoover, hoover, hoover) someone who comes in; and in all that passes, I represent ye working classes. Hoover, hoover, hoover. Hoover, hoover, hoover. Now then, let's have a little more light on the proceedings and meet our contestants, the wonderful, wonderful Wicksteed family. Eyes down first for tonight's hero, Dr Arthur Wicksteed, a general practitioner in Brighton's plush, silk stocking district of Hove. Is that right, Doctor?

WICKSTEED: Hove, that's right, yes.

MRS SWABB: And you are fifty-three years of age.

WICKSTEED: Dear God, am I?

MRS SWABB: I'm afraid that's what I've got down here.

WICKSTEED: Fifty-three!

MRS SWABB: Any hobbies?

WICKSTEED: No. No. Our friends, the ladies, of course, but nothing much else.

MRS SWABB: Do you mind telling us what your ambition is?

WICKSTEED: Ambition? No, never had any. Partly the trouble, you see. When you've gone through life stopping at every lamp-post, no time.

MRS SWABB: Next we have . . .

MRS WICKSTEED: I can manage thank you. Elocution was always my strong point. Speak clearly, speak firmly, speak now. Name: Wicksteed, Muriel Jane. Age? Well, if you said fifty you'd be in the target area. Wife to the said Arthur Wicksteed and golly, don't I know it. Still potty about him though, the dirty dog. Oh, shut up, Muriel.

MRS SWABB: And now . . . this is Dennis, only son of Arthur and Muriel Wicksteed. And what do you do, Dennis?

DENNIS: Nothing very much. I think I've got lockjaw.

MRS SWABB: Really? Whereabouts?

DENNIS: All over.

MRS SWABB: Are you interested in girls at all?

DENNIS: If they're clean.

MRS SWABB: That goes without saying. You don't want a dirty girl, do you?

DENNIS: In a way, I do, yes.

MRS WICKSTEED: Dennis!

MRS SWABB: And now we have the doctor's sister, Miss Constance Wicksteed. Connie is a thirty-three-year-old spinster . . .

CONNIE: I am not a spinster. I am unmarried.

MRS SWABB: And to go with her mud-coloured cardigan Connie has chosen a fetching number in form-fitting cretonne. Have you any boyfriends, dear?

CONNIE: No.

MRS SWABB: Connie, you big story! What about Canon Throbbing, our thrusting young vicar? Why! That sounds like his Biretta now.

(THROBBING *crosses on his power-assisted bicycle.*)

Now, Connie, would you like to tell the audience what your ambition is? Go on, just whisper.

CONNIE: I'd like a big bust.

MRS SWABB: And what would you do with it when you'd got it?

CONNIE: Flaunt it.

MRS WICKSTEED: Connie!

MRS SWABB: Three strangers too are in the town. A lady and her daughter. . . .

SIR PERCY: Out of my way, we're wasting time: I am Sir Percy Shorter. Shorter, Percy, KCB, President, British Medical Association. Venuing this week at Brighton.

MRS WICKSTEED: Percy!

WICKSTEED: My wife's sometime sweetheart.

MRS WICKSTEED: The man I spurned.

SIR PERCY: Well? Aren't you going to ask me what my ambition is?

MRS SWABB: President of the British Medical Association! What more can a man want?

SIR PERCY: Revenge.

MRS SWABB: I don't like it. Two strangers now are in the town, a lady and her daughter . . .

LADY RUMPERS: England, my poor England. What have they done to you? Don't touch me. That's one thing I've noticed returning to these shores. There's a great deal more touching going on. If I want to be touched I have people who love me who can touch me. Touching is what loved ones are for, because loving takes the sting out of it. Delia, Lady Rumpers, widow of General Sir Frederick Rumpers. Tiger to his friends and to his enemies too, by God. Does the name Rumpers ring a bell?

WICKSTEED: Very, very faintly.

LADY RUMPERS: Time was when it would have rung all the bells in England. Rumpers of Rhodesia, Rumpers of Rangoon — when the history of the decline of the British Empire comes to be written, the name Rumpers will be in the index. For many years we were stationed in Addis Ababa. Tiger was right-hand man to the Lion of Judah.

MRS SWABB: Haile Selassie.

LADY RUMPERS: There followed a short spell in K.L.

MRS SWABB: Kings Langley.

LADY RUMPERS: Kuala Lumpur.

MRS WICKSTEED: Of course.

LADY RUMPERS: Then we fetched up in Rhodesia. In a green meadow on the outskirts of Salisbury, roses bloom and the trees are alive with the songs of multi-coloured birds. There we laid him.

(DENNIS *sniffs*.)

I am upsetting you?

CONNIE: He has hay fever.

LADY RUMPERS: From end to end I've searched the land looking for a place where England is still England.

WICKSTEED: And now she's hit on Hove.

LADY RUMPERS: My daughter. . . .

(*Everyone looks but no one enters*.)

Felicity, at present changing her Hammond Innes. We had a terrible experience coming down. We had to move our compartment three times to avoid a clergyman who was looking up her legs under cover of the *Daily Telegraph*.

MRS WICKSTEED: And such a respectable newspaper.

LADY RUMPERS: I lie awake at night in a cold sweat wondering what would happen if Felicity's body fell into the wrong hands.

MRS SWABB: But this is a doctor's. Doctors can touch anybody, because they don't have the feelings to go with it. That's what they go to medical school for.

LADY RUMPERS: Rubbish. Doctors are as bad as anyone else. I could tell you of a doctor who once touched me and I will never forget it.

MRS SWABB: There's no need to tell me, I know.

MRS WICKSTEED: You know? How do you know?

MRS SWABB: Because I am Fate. I cut the string.
    I know all goings out and comings in.
    Naught escapes me in a month of Sundays:
    I know if they change their undies.
    Hoover, hoover, hoover.
    Hoover, hoover, hoover.
Now a scene setting scene to set the scene and see the set,

set the scene up and see the set up.

WICKSTEED: A thorough examination? Are you ill?

THROBBING: Never felt better. Your sister, Connie, and I are about to get married.

WICKSTEED: She hasn't told me.

THROBBING: Probably because I haven't told her. But this is her last chance. Ten years of courtship is carrying celibacy to extremes.

WICKSTEED: Poor girl.

THROBBING: And I thought before I embarked on the choppy waters of the *vita coniugalis* I'd better have the vessel overhauled. If I can stretch my metaphor.

WICKSTEED: Ah well, drop your trousers.

THROBBING: What for?

WICKSTEED: The longer I practise medicine the more convinced I am there are only two types of cases: those that involve taking the trousers off and those that don't. I'm waiting.

THROBBING: I'm a bit shy.

WICKSTEED: Why? No one will come in.

(MRS SWABB *instantly does so, as the* CANON *drops his trousers. And pulls them up again.*)

MRS SWABB: Hoover, hoover, hoover.

WICKSTEED: Get out.

MRS SWABB: Hoover, hoover, hoover.

THROBBING: Couldn't I go behind a screen?

WICKSTEED: In the course of thirty-odd years in pursuit of the profession of medicine, Canon Throbbing, a profession to which I unwittingly yoked myself in my callow youth, people have been taking their trousers off in front of me at the average rate of five times a day, five days a week, fifty-two weeks in the year. This means that at a conservative estimate and allowing for some duplication I have seen twenty-five thousand sets of private parts. The most conscientious whore could not have seen more. In the light of such statistics you are displaying not so much modesty as arrogance. TAKE THEM OFF.

(THROBBING *goes off*.)

WICKSTEED: We were taught many things at medical school, padre, but seeing through several thick layers of winceyette was not one of them.
Off?
Yes.
Turn round.
Bend over.
Get any feelings of nausea at all?

THROBBING: No.

WICKSTEED: Well God knows I do. It's all guesswork you know. I delve in their ears, I peer up their noses. I am glued to every orifice of the body like a parlour-maid at a keyhole.

THROBBING: May I get up now?

WICKSTEED: Shut up. And so it goes on. Day after day. Week after week. They troop in with their sore throats and their varicose veins. They parade before me bodies the colour of tripe and the texture of junket. Is this the image of God, this sagging parcel of vanilla blancmange hoisted day after day on to the consulting-room table? Is this the precious envelope of the soul? Is this. . . .

THROBBING: Is this on the National Health?

WICKSTEED: No. Why do you want to get married, anyway?

THROBBING: Because . . . because I look up girls' legs.

WICKSTEED: Marriage won't stop that.

THROBBING: Won't it?

WICKSTEED: I'm afraid not.

THROBBING: You mean, you still do?

WICKSTEED: Me? No. I'm a doctor.

THROBBING: Well, I do, and I'm a clergyman.

WICKSTEED: My poor sister. Because she's flat-chested he thinks she's religious.

(THROBBING *climbs on his bicycle and exits.*)

CONNIE: I don't love him.

MRS WICKSTEED: Love? You look on the shelf and you'll find it cluttered with dozens of spinsters gathering dust and all of them labelled 'I was waiting for love'. I married Arthur for

love and what did I get? The mucky end of the stick. I
could kick myself.

WICKSTEED: Do you know who I could have married?

MRS WICKSTEED: Do you know who I could have married?

WICKSTEED: Sir Percy Shorter.

MRS WICKSTEED: Sir Percy Shorter.

WICKSTEED: Twice the man Arthur ever was.

MRS WICKSTEED: Twice the man Arthur ever was.

WICKSTEED: Or will be.

MRS WICKSTEED: Or will be. I get to look more and more like
the Queen Mother every day.

DENNIS: Mother.

MRS WICKSTEED: Yes?

DENNIS: I've got some bad news.

MRS WICKSTEED: Yes?

DENNIS: I've only got three months to live.

MRS WICKSTEED: Three months? Two months ago you only
had ten days.

DENNIS: I made a mistake.

MRS WICKSTEED: And what's happened to the galloping
consumption you had last Thursday? Slowed down to a trot
I suppose. What is it this time?

DENNIS: I've got a very rare disease.

MRS WICKSTEED: You've got an extremely common disease.
You've got a dose of the can't help its. You'd better ask
your father.

DENNIS: He doesn't care.

WICKSTEED: That's true enough.

DENNIS: It's called Brett's Palsy.

(*He shows her a medical book.*)

MRS WICKSTEED: Tiredness, irritability, spots, yes. And
generally confined to the Caucasus. If this germ is confined
to the Caucasus what's it doing in Hove?

WICKSTEED: Over here for the hols, I suppose.

MRS WICKSTEED: Tragic. And he came through puberty with
such flying colours.

CONNIE: Every day and in every way they're getting bigger and bigger and bigger.

DENNIS: I'm going to die, Connie.

CONNIE: Every day and in every way they're getting bigger and bigger and bigger.

DENNIS: I'm dying and no one will believe me.

MRS SWABB: Listen to this. 'Lucille is from Sydenham. Her hobbies are water-skiing and world peace.'

DENNIS: That's my magazine.

MRS SWABB: Someone hid it on top of the wardrobe.

CONNIE: If I had those I wouldn't need hobbies.

MRS SWABB: No dear. Look. 'Send off this postcard and a beautiful bust can be yours this summer for only £5.'

DENNIS: Two fifty each.

CONNIE: False ones. Do you think so?

DENNIS: I would, Connie, if it were me.

MRS WICKSTEED: Connie? Connie? Who's Connie? I've told you before, Dennis. Connie has a title. She's your Aunt Connie.

CONNIE: Aunt isn't a title.

MRS WICKSTEED: It's the nearest you'll ever get to one. Calling your aunt by her Christian name. I knew a girl once who called her parents by their Christian names. She had a baby before she was seventeen. And what was the father called? She hadn't even bothered to ask. So much for names. (*Exits.*

MRS SWABB *fills in the postcard.*)

CONNIE: It's no use. Look at my legs.

MRS SWABB: Very nice legs, if you ask me. There are people running about with no legs at all, who'd be more than happy to have yours.

CONNIE: By rights with me it ought to be all lemon tea and neutered cats. But it isn't. I look like this on the outside but inside I feel like Jan Masefield.

MRS SWABB: No, dear, Jayne Mansfield.

CONNIE: No. Jan Masefield. She was a girl in the front row at my school. Actually it was the second row but it looked like the front row.

MRS SWABB: I'll post this postcard personally
    I'm sure it's for the best
    You wait she'll be a different girl
    With the Cairngorms on her chest.

DENNIS: Is that a lump there?

CONNIE: Yes.

DENNIS: Oh God.

CONNIE: Your fountain-pen. You want to say: look, this body doesn't really suit me. Could I move into something different? But you can't. The body's a tied cottage. At birth you're kitted out with mousey hair, bad legs, and no tits . . .

MRS SWABB: That's right dear. You get it off your chest. Look out, it's the priest with five fingers.

THROBBING: Precious. Dr Wicksteed's given me a clean bill of health. Isn't it wonderful?

DENNIS: I've got Brett's Palsy.

THROBBING: How interesting.

DENNIS: Three months to live.

THROBBING: As long as that? It's the green light, Connie.

DENNIS: She hasn't said yes yet.

THROBBING: With you sitting there she hasn't had much chance. Haven't you anything to do?

DENNIS: No.

THROBBING: If I had only three months to live I'd have a hundred and one things to do.

DENNIS: Like what?

THROBBING: Take my library books back, stop the papers, warn the milkman—

DENNIS: Death isn't like going away on holiday, you know.

THROBBING: Oh yes it is. It's going away for a long, long holiday to a place by all accounts every bit as nice as Matlock. For some of us anyway.

CONNIE: Dennis doesn't believe in heaven, do you Dennis?

DENNIS: No. I don't know what it means.

THROBBING: Nor did I till I met you, dearest. You'd better not sit near me. I've just been visiting the sick.

CONNIE: Dennis!

(*Exit* DENNIS *hurriedly*.)

THROBBING: Alone at last.

CONNIE: Yes.

THROBBING: Just you and me.

CONNIE: Yes.

THROBBING: The two of us.

CONNIE: Yes.

THROBBING: How old are you, Connie?

CONNIE: Thirty-three.

THROBBING: What a coincidence.

CONNIE: You're not thirty-three.

THROBBING: No, but my inside leg is! Oh, Connie.

CONNIE: Canon, please.

THROBBING: Forgive me: I was carried away. Connie. Will you
marry me? Will you marry me?

MRS SWABB: Right now it's make up your mind time for thirty-
three-year-old 'I keep myself to myself' Connie Wicksteed,
a spinster from Brighton's Hove. Does she accept the hand
of slim, balding 'Just pop this in your offertory box' Canon
Throbbing, no dish it's true, but with a brilliant future on
both sides of the grave

or

does she give him the (*buzzer*) on the off-chance of
something more fetching coming along once her appliance
arrives?

CONNIE: Oh, Mr Right, where are you? Just give me a few
more days. Until Thursday.

THROBBING: Very well. After all, what is two more days in
Purgatory if it's followed by a lifetime in Paradise?

WICKSTEED: You silly man. You silly woman. Handcuffing
yourselves together. Don't do it. What for? I'd rather have
a decent glass of sherry any day. Of course, I despise the
body. Despise it. Stroking faces, holding hands, oh it all
looks very nice on the surface, but look inside: the pipes are
beginning to fur and the lungs to stiffen. We're all pigs,
pigs; little trotters, little tails. Offal. Show me a human

body and I will show you a cesspit.

(FELICITY *enters in a pool of rosy light and to shimmering music*.)

I eat every word.

FELICITY: I was passing the door and I came over rather faint.

WICKSTEED: I feel just the same. Is there anything I could offer you?

FELICITY: If I could just sit down.

WICKSTEED: Perhaps you would like some tea – or would you prefer me to clap my moist lips over yours and plunge my tongue again and again into your mouth sending you mad with desire – or would you prefer coffee?

FELICITY: Anything.

WICKSTEED: What is your name?

FELICITY: Felicity.

WICKSTEED: Felicity what?

FELICITY: The Hon. Felicity Rumpers.

WICKSTEED: Indeed? Connie, fetch in the delphiniums will you: I think we have a private patient.

FELICITY: I'm feeling much better now.

WICKSTEED: Are you?

FELICITY: I like it here.

WICKSTEED: Yes?

FELICITY: The atmosphere. The feel of the place.

WICKSTEED: I'm glad. It's . . . it's a bit untidy. It could do with smartening up a bit. Old, I suppose, without being old-fashioned. Carpets a bit thin . . . Plumbing's a bit noisy sometimes too. Bit smelly, even. Tobacco. Drink. But I tell you: it's a good deal better than a lot of these cheap gimcrack things you could pick up these days, even if it is a bit run down.

FELICITY: Yes?

WICKSTEED: Yes.

(*The telephone rings*.)

Excuse me, Miss Rumpers, one moment. Hello. Dr Wicksteed's surgery. Wicksteed speaking. Ah. Mr Purdue. Yes. One moment. This is an interesting call, Miss

Rumpers, and one that illustrates how vital a part we doctors play in the community. I have always made a point of making myself available for anyone who cares to call, anyone in trouble, in despair, anyone in particular who is contemplating suicide.

FELICITY: Suicide!

WICKSTEED: This patient, Mr Purdue, is on the brink of self-destruction. But before he actually attempts to take his own life, he calls me, his family doctor knowing I will be here.

FELICITY: The poor man.

WICKSTEED: A kind voice, a friendly word will often just tip that delicate balance between life and death, will turn back the patient from embarking on that journey to that far country from whose bourne, as Shakespeare so well put it, no traveller returns. So if you'll excuse me, I'll just have a word with him . . . strictly speaking of course I shouldn't, as you're a private patient and he isn't. . . .

FELICITY: No, no, not at all.

WICKSTEED: That's most magnanimous of you.

FELICITY: No. I'm quite happy.

WICKSTEED: Well I only wish Mr Purdue was. Hello, Mr Purdue. Mr Purdue, hello . . . He seems to have . . . hung up. I am wondering whether I ought to give you a little examination.

MRS WICKSTEED: (*Off*) Arthur!

WICKSTEED: Though now would not appear to be the best time. Excuse me one moment.

FELICITY: It used to be so flat. Can you tell?
(*To the tune of 'On the Isle of Capri'*.)
    'Twas on the A43 that I met him.
    We just had a day by the sea.
    Now he's gone, and he's left me expecting.
    Will somebody, please, marry me.

DENNIS: I didn't know anyone was here.

FELICITY: Hello.

DENNIS: I've got a disease called Brett's Palsy. I've only got three months to live.

FELICITY: Really?

DENNIS: Yes. At the outside.

FELICITY: But that's tragic.

DENNIS: I'm glad somebody thinks so.

FELICITY: You're so young.

DENNIS: Don't touch me. You're sure you haven't got any disease?

FELICITY: No, you have.

DENNIS: Yes, but I don't want any complications, do I?

FELICITY: You poor boy. Poor frightened boy.

DENNIS: Don't tell my father. He's a doctor.

FELICITY: Perhaps he could heal you.

DENNIS: Him? He couldn't heal a shoe.

FELICITY: This disease: you say there's no cure?

DENNIS: None.

FELICITY: And in three months you'll be dead?

DENNIS: I'm certain.

FELICITY: Look, I'd like to see you again. Can I?

DENNIS: Me? You must be peculiar.

FELICITY: I would, I would really.

DENNIS: When? I don't have much time.

FELICITY: Thursday 2.30. Where?

DENNIS: Here.

FELICITY: My name's Felicity. What's yours?

DENNIS: Dennis.

WICKSTEED: Trevor, what are you doing here. You've no business in the consulting room.

DENNIS: Goodbye, Penelope.

FELICITY: Felicity.

DENNIS: Yes.

WICKSTEED: My son, I'm afraid. Trevor.

FELICITY: He said his name was Dennis.

WICKSTEED: Did he? Then it probably is. Look, the doctor-patient relationship is such an important one, one of mutual trust and respect. And here are you such a young, shy innocent creature and I'm . . . somewhat older. It would be helpful, I think, it would help me, if we could

break the ice a bit and maybe perhaps sometime go for a
spin in the car sometime, anytime, say Thursday at 2.30?

FELICITY: My mother's very strict. I. . . .

WICKSTEED: Splendid, I'll meet you at the end of the West
Pier.

MRS WICKSTEED: (*Off*) Arthur!

WICKSTEED: You won't be late?

FELICITY: I'm never late.

WICKSTEED: Coming, my love.

> No. Not too old at fifty-three.
> A worn defeated fool like me.
> Still the tickling lust devours.
> Long stretches of my waking hours.
> Busty girls in flowered scanties
> Hitching down St Michael panties.
> Easing off their wet-look boots,
> To step into their birthday suits.
> No! I am abusing my position
> As their trusty old physician.
> Virtue be mine, I will not do it
> Just to pacify this lump of suet.

MRS SWABB: I see it all. His ruse I rumble:
> That spotless girl he means to tumble.

MRS WICKSTEED: Who was that?

WICKSTEED: Only a patient.

MRS WICKSTEED: Man or woman.

WICKSTEED: They're all the same to me.

MRS WICKSTEED: How old are we, Arthur?

WICKSTEED: You are fifty-one and I am. . . .

MRS WICKSTEED: Fifty-three.

WICKSTEED: Fifty-three. And it doesn't seem five minutes since
I was sixteen.

MRS WICKSTEED: When did the fire go out, Arthur?

WICKSTEED: What?

MRS WICKSTEED: Nothing. It isn't as if he's attractive. I'm
much more attractive than he is. If he would only stretch
out his hand and say my name.

204

WICKSTEED: Muriel.

MRS WICKSTEED: Yes.

WICKSTEED: It is your cake-decorating class on Thursday?

MRS WICKSTEED: Yes. Why?

WICKSTEED: Then you won't be wanting the car.

MRS WICKSTEED: No. Why?

WICKSTEED: I am going to the open session of the BMA Conference.

MRS WICKSTEED: Indeed? The house will be empty.

WICKSTEED: I'll put an end to this duplicity . . .

> But not before I've had Felicity.
> Then take, oh take this itch away
> Lest my ruin end this play.

(*The telephone rings.*)

MRS SWABB: Telephone. Telephone. Telephone.

MRS WICKSTEED: Hello, Dr Wicksteed's residence. Yes. Speaking. *Percy!*

MRS SWABB: That will be Sir Percy Shorter to whom some reference has already been made.

MRS WICKSTEED: After all these years! Longing to. Longing to. Well, why not here? Yes. Thursday afternoon. No. He's going out. Yes. How exciting. Yes. Mum's the word. Goodbye. Kiss, Kiss, Kiss.

MRS SWABB: It is the afternoon of the Thursday in question, and lunch, cooked by the fair hands of guess who is just over. I started them off with a little clear soup with scattered *croûtons*, followed by a fricassee of lamb with just a hint of rosemary. This I garnished with diced carrots and pommes duchesses. Then they had apple charlotte or the cheese board, followed by wafer-thin mints and a choice of beverages. I think they enjoyed it.

WICKSTEED: It was disgusting.

(MRS WICKSTEED *wears a dashing hat with perky feathers.*)

MRS WICKSTEED: I think this hat suits me. Of course, it needs someone who can carry it off. You can't skulk about in a hat like this.

CONNIE: (*In her cub mistress's uniform*) Has anyone seen my woggle?

MRS SWABB: When did you have it last?

MRS WICKSTEED: I should look in what is inappropriately in your case called your breast pocket.

MRS SWABB: Here's another picture of Sir Percy addressing the conference.

WICKSTEED: He hasn't grown an inch in twenty years.

MRS WICKSTEED: Size isn't everything.

(*The door bell rings.*)

DENNIS: (*Aside*) She's early!

MRS WICKSTEED: (*Aside*) He's early!

DENNIS: ⎱
MRS WICKSTEED: ⎰ I'll go.

MRS SWABB: Stand back! I am the door. It's not a person. It's a parcel.

WICKSTEED: A parcel?

MRS WICKSTEED: A parcel!

MRS SWABB: A parcel! For Miss Wicksteed.

CONNIE: For me?

MRS WICKSTEED: Yes.

CONNIE: I'm expecting it.

MRS WICKSTEED: Who's it from?

CONNIE: I don't know.

MRS WICKSTEED: You're expecting it and you don't know who it's from? I've never heard of that before.

WICKSTEED: I have. My surgery's full of girls expecting something and they don't know who it's from.

MRS WICKSTEED: Most mysterious. Not that I'm in the least bit curious. (*Exits.*)

CONNIE: I think it's them.

MRS SWABB: Open it.

CONNIE: I shan't dare wear them.

MRS SWABB: Come on.

CONNIE: But it's time for cubs.

MRS WICKSTEED: Mrs Swabb, you may take the afternoon off.

MRS SWABB: But I have an enormous backlog of dusting.

MRS WICKSTEED: I insist . . . all work and no play makes Jack
a dull boy. And talking of dull boys, what are your plans?

DENNIS: A long walk in the fresh air.

MRS WICKSTEED: Splendid. And you?

CONNIE: Cubs. Why?

MRS WICKSTEED: Just asking. I'm going to my cake-decorating
class. I don't really want to, but we're electing a new
secretary and it's like anything else: if the rank and file
don't go the militants take over. (*Exits.*)
(*They open the parcel.*)

MRS SWABB: 'I was a spinster for fifteen years,' writes Miss
P.D. of Carshalton. 'Three years ago I invested in your
appliance and since then I have been engaged four times.'

DENNIS: 'The Rubens, in sensitized Fablon, as used on Apollo
space missions.' Try it on.

CONNIE: No. It's too late.

MRS SWABB: It's never too late. Listen. 'In reply to yours. . . .
Etc., etc. . . . They are easily fitted without assistance but
to forestall any difficulties our fitter Mr Shanks will call on
Thursday May 29th.'

DENNIS: That's today.

CONNIE: But he can't. I'm not here. I'm at cubs.
(MRS WICKSTEED *claps hands offstage.*)

MRS SWABB: Look out. Heads down.

CONNIE: What shall I do?

MRS SWABB: Say you're ill.

MRS WICKSTEED: Still hanging about? You should have been at
the toadstool half an hour ago! A scout is punctual at all
times. That was the rule when I was a scout.

DENNIS: She's ill.

MRS WICKSTEED: She's late. Come along, clear the decks. Off,
off, off. Out, out, out.
Goodbye house, goodbye chairs . . . goodbye.

WICKSTEED: What's all the hurry? Anybody'd think you
wanted us out of the way.

MRS WICKSTEED: Wanted you out of the way? What a
ridiculous idea! What an absurd idea! Why, the idea is

absurd. It is ridiculous. relax. There's plenty of time. It's only 2.30.

WICKSTEED: 2.30. My God. 2.30. Plenty of time! Don't be ridiculous. There's not a moment to lose.

(*He rushes out and they all follow.*)

MRS SWABB: Quiet, isn't it? Gone quiet. It won't last. It will not last. Give them five minutes and they'll be in and out of here like dogs at a bazaar. Sniffety sniffety sniff. On the fruitless quest of bodily pleasures. And it is all a waste of time. After all as I tell my husband what is the body but the purse of the soul? What is the flesh but the vest of the spirit? Me, I don't bother with sex. I leave that to the experts.

(DENNIS *and* FELICITY *come in.*)

DENNIS: Hello.

FELICITY: Hello, Dennis.

DENNIS: You remembered my name, Penelope.

FELICITY: Felicity.

DENNIS: I'm supposed to be out for a long walk in the fresh air.

FELICITY: I'm supposed to be meeting your father. What are you staring at?

DENNIS: Nothing. You.

FELICITY: Me? What for?

DENNIS: You're so nice looking, firm and full whereas. . . .

FELICITY: Your poor hands. All those long thin fingers.

DENNIS: See all the veins. Horrible.

FELICITY: I don't mind.

DENNIS: Don't you honestly?

FELICITY: Girls don't. They don't expect all that much. That's the first lesson you've got to learn. Most men don't bear close examination.

DENNIS: You seem to know a lot about it. I know nothing. I've got such a lot to learn.

FELICITY: And so little time to learn it.

DENNIS: And nobody to teach me. I was wondering . . .

FELICITY: Yes?

DENNIS: Could we go for a walk?

FELICITY: It's too hot for walking.

DENNIS: Yes. I suppose it is.

FELICITY: Of course, we could walk a little . . . then throw ourselves down in some lush warm summer-scented meadow.

DENNIS: I get hay fever.

FELICITY: Or pause by a sparkling stream and perch together on some cool moss-grown rock.

DENNIS: I get piles.

FELICITY: Nature is hard.

DENNIS: I could take my raincoat.

FELICITY: What a brilliant idea.

DENNIS: Felicity.

FELICITY: What?

DENNIS: I feel very peculiar. I think I may be catching something.

(*They take hands and go.*)

MRS SWABB: Bless them! I think they've clicked. Scorpio and Sagittarius. Lovely combo. Well, I think I'll just have a glance at the *Lancet*.

(*Enter* MRS WICKSTEED.)

MRS WICKSTEED: You!

MRS SWABB: The mistress of the house! I wasn't expecting your return.

MRS WICKSTEED: No, I have returned unexpectedly. An unforeseen hitch at my cake-decorating class! A shortage of hundreds and thousands put paid to the proceedings. Anyway, I thought I gave you the afternoon off.

MRS SWABB: I am an indefatigable worker.

MRS WICKSTEED: You are a Nosy Parker. If you're so anxious to be doing something, there's one or two groceries waiting to be picked up.

MRS SWABB: Where?

MRS WICKSTEED: Sainsbury's, where else? That takes care of her for the next two hours.

(*Exit* MRS WICKSTEED *and* MRS SWABB.
Sea sounds.)

WICKSTEED: (*Alone*) Break, break, break
    On thy cold grey stones, O Sea
    And would that my tongue could utter
    The thoughts that arise in me.
Would that it could, but you see Felicity I'm rather a shy
person.
Are you Doctor?
Don't call me Doctor. Call me Arthur.
Are you Arthur?
Now you mention it, Felicity, I suppose I am. But you
Felicity . . . you somehow restore my faith in human kind,
remind me of what perfection the human body is capable.
And spirit, oh yes, and spirit, Felicity. To think I was
already qualified when you were born. I might have
brought you into the world, felt the first flutter of your
fragrant life. I could have cradled you in my arms, touched
your little face. . . .
Arthur.
Yes, Felicity?
Arthur, you could still.
Could I? Oh, Felicity. (*Exits.*)
(*The door chimes go.*)
(*Enter* MR SHANKS.)

MRS WICKSTEED: Percy. . . . Oh, good afternoon.

SHANKS: I'm looking for someone by the name of Wicksteed.
    W-I-C-K-S-T-E-E-D. Wicksteed. Yes.

MRS WICKSTEED: Yes?

SHANKS: And I think I've found her. Mr Shanks is the name.
    Full marks. Ten out of ten. They are wonderful. *Wonderful*.

MRS WICKSTEED: You think so?

SHANKS: They are outstanding. Out-standing.

MRS WICKSTEED: Golly. Appreciation after all these years.

SHANKS: What a charming home, and my goodness, don't they
    enhance it. The balance, dear lady, almost perfect. Almost,
    but not quite. Still, that's what I'm here for. May I?

MRS WICKSTEED: This is what they must mean by the
    Permissive Society.

SHANKS: I believe this one is a fraction bigger than the other.

MRS WICKSTEED: To hell with symmetry. How that touch revives me.

SHANKS: It will not have escaped your notice that the customer, Miss Wicksteed, is becoming a little excited.

MRS WICKSTEED: At last! A tenant for my fallow loins.

SHANKS: However, rest assured. This excitement is not mutual. I am an expert. A crash course at Leatherhead, the firm's training centre, set in the heart of Surrey's famous rural surroundings, lays down a standard procedure for every eventuality. Mind you, these are exceptional. I've only seen one pair to rival these, and she's now the manageress of the only cinema in Fleetwood. Look, you're such an outstanding example, we often compare notes, my colleagues and I . . . and since I've got my little Polaroid handy. . . .

MRS WICKSTEED: I was wondering when you were going to mention that. Your Polaroid, your lovely little Polaroid. . . .

SHANKS: Some snaps . . . just for the record. . . .

MRS WICKSTEED: Yes, yes, a record. Music!

(*The stage is flooded with sensual music.*)

Muriel Wicksteed, what are you doing? Can this be you? Yes. Yes, it is me. The real me. The me I've always been deep down. Suddenly the body reasserts itself, breaks through the dead crust of morality, and from the chrysalis convention bursts the butterfly, freedom.

(*The telephone rings.*)

I will see to that. Dr Wicksteed's residence. Oh, it's you Mr Purdue. No, you cannot speak to Dr Wicksteed. This is his afternoon off. You're about to commit suicide? I see. If you must choose to commit suicide on doctor's afternoon off, that's your funeral. *Au revoir.* Or I suppose I should say goodbye. Now where was I . . . Oh yes.

(*She embraces* SHANKS.)

SHANKS: I repeat there is nothing to be ashamed of. This is all in a day's work to me.

MRS WICKSTEED: I don't think he should throw his promiscuity in my face. One doesn't like to think one is simply a convenience.

SHANKS: A client not a convenience.

MRS WICKSTEED: Client? I'm not going to have to pay you for this?

SHANKS: It's all included in the five pounds.

MRS WICKSTEED: Five pounds! That's wicked.

SHANKS: There's nothing more I can do.

MRS WICKSTEED: He comes in here, goes for my bust like a bull at a gate and then says there's nothing more he can do. There is more. 'The bust is but the first port of call on the long voyage of love.'

SHANKS: I have other ladies to see.

MRS WICKSTEED: Other ladies. The idea!

SHANKS: Stop. Take them off. They are a sacred trust. You are not fit to wear them.
(*He slaps her bust.*)

SHANKS: It's the . . . it's the real thing, isn't it? Flesh.

MRS WICKSTEED: Of course it's flesh. What did you think it was – blancmange?

SHANKS: Is there anywhere I could wash my hands?

MRS WICKSTEED: Time enough to wash your hands when we've been to Paradise and back.

SHANKS: No!

MRS WICKSTEED: No. That means yes. So much at least Freud has taught us.
(*She drags* SHANKS *off.*
Sea sounds.)

WICKSTEED: It shocks you, I'm afraid, me a respectable, middle-aged doctor waiting like a fool on the end of Brighton Pier. Ludicrous? But listen.

Say nobody saw and nobody heard
Say no one at all would breathe a word
Say nobody knew the you that was you
And your secret dreams could all come true.
Picture the scene, figurez-vous,

You could have whoever you wanted to:
Felicity Rumpers, Omar Sharif,
Julie Andrews, Mr Heath.
Orgies of swapping, five in a bed.
You, me and Omar, Julie and Ted.
Don't tell me you wouldn't, given the choice
Old men with schoolgirls, ladies with boys
If she's what I fancy you really can't quarrel,
'Cos given the chance you'd be just as immoral.
Nobody's perfect: I'm fifty-three.
And the tide's going out, Arthur Wicksteed, M.D.
    (*Exits*.
Enter SHANKS *pursued by* MRS WICKSTEED.)

SHANKS: No, no, please, no.

MRS WICKSTEED: I am Diana. You are my quarry. I am stalking you with all the lithe grace of a panther.

SHANKS: Does anyone know the dialling code for Leatherhead?

MRS WICKSTEED: I close in for the kill, my haunches taut, my flanks rippling. . . .

SHANKS: No, no.

MRS WICKSTEED: My head goes down and I pounce.

SHANKS: Yee-ow.
    (SHANKS *makes a run for it, straight into the arms of* SIR PERCY.)

SIR PERCY: I'm looking for Mrs Wicksteed.

MRS WICKSTEED: Percy! Don't you recognize me?

SIR PERCY: Muriel. You haven't changed. She's enormous.

MRS WICKSTEED: Do you know each other?

SIR PERCY: No.

SHANKS: How do you do.

SIR PERCY: How do you do. I was wondering whether. . . .   } *together*

MRS WICKSTEED: I suppose I ought to. . . .

SIR PERCY: Perhaps you would tell me. . . .   } *together*

MRS WICKSTEED: In case you're wondering. . . .

SHANKS: Er. . . .

SIR PERCY: Yes?

SHANKS: Nothing.

SIR PERCY: Muriel, this man isn't your husband?

MRS WICKSTEED: Yes! No.

SIR PERCY: Ah. I saw no resemblance but twenty years is a long time.

MRS WICKSTEED: It is, it is.

SIR PERCY: If he is not your husband, what is he doing in his shirt tails?

MRS WICKSTEED: He's a patient.

SIR PERCY: A patient.

MRS WICKSTEED: What did you think he was . . . my lover, ha ha ha.

SIR PERCY: Ha ha ha.

SHANKS: Ha ha ha.

SIR PERCY: What are you laughing at? You've got no trousers on.

SHANKS: I can explain that.

SIR PERCY: Did anyone ask you?

SHANKS: No.

SIR PERCY: Are you a private patient?

SHANKS: No.

SIR PERCY: Then shut up. Unbalanced?

MRS WICKSTEED: Mad. He only called for his tranquillizers.

SIR PERCY: Don't worry. I have some with me.

SHANKS: You have to padlock your underpants when she's around, I can tell you.

SIR PERCY: Really?

SHANKS: She's man mad.

MRS WICKSTEED: Me. Ha. She laughed her scornful laugh.

SIR PERCY: Here, take these.

SHANKS: No.

SIR PERCY: I am President of the British Medical Association. Take them.

SHANKS: No.

SIR PERCY: Very well Muriel, we must go intravenous.

(MRS WICKSTEED *prepares a hypodermic*.)

SHANKS: She took my trousers off.

SIR PERCY: What for?

SHANKS: What for? What do people usually take other people's trousers off for?

SIR PERCY: You tell me.

SHANKS: She wanted my body.

SIR PERCY: Your body. Your body? Thank you Muriel. In case of doubt, just knock them out.

SHANKS: What?

SIR PERCY: When hackles rise, I tranquillize.

MRS WICKSTEED: They do less harm if you keep them calm.

SIR PERCY: Hold him, Muriel.

SHANKS: No. No. All I want is to telephone Leatherhead. (SIR PERCY *injects him*.)

SIR PERCY: This is the way we generally telephone Leatherhead. That's it. Up you get.

SHANKS: Please. Does anyone know the dialling code for Leatherhead?
(SHANKS *collapses*.)

SIR PERCY: Typical of your husband.

MRS WICKSTEED: Arthur?

SIR PERCY: Leaving a patient running loose about the place.

MRS WICKSTEED: It wasn't really his fault.

SIR PERCY: Slapdash. Inconsiderate. Don't suppose he's changed.

MRS WICKSTEED: You haven't changed either. Have I?

SIR PERCY: I never liked him. He once said I was small. You were a fool, Muriel.

MRS WICKSTEED: What?

SIR PERCY: To throw yourself away on that little nobody. Still I suppose he makes you happy.

MRS WICKSTEED: Arthur? He falls asleep as soon as his teeth hit the glass. Oh Percy.

SIR PERCY: Is he about, your husband? I'd quite like to see him. The years have doubtless taken their toll?

MRS WICKSTEED: No. He's gone to the conference. The open session.

SIR PERCY: What open session? There is no open session today.

MRS WICKSTEED: You're certain?

SIR PERCY: Of course. I am the President. How else could I be here.

(MRS SWABB *enters with a wheeled basket of groceries*.)

MRS WICKSTEED: You've been quick.

MRS SWABB: I had a following wind.

MRS WICKSTEED: Where is Dr Wicksteed?

MRS SWABB: Dr Wicksteed? He's on the Pier. (*Exits*.)

MRS WICKSTEED: I fear the worst.

SIR PERCY: Death?

MRS WICKSTEED: Sex. And if I know him, he's with a patient.

SIR PERCY: A patient? Indeed! First item on the agenda – get your things on. Second, a visit to the Pier. Come on, buck up. And third, the ruin of a certain general practitioner.
(*He lifts the semi-conscious* SHANKS, *who hangs like a dummy in his arms*.)
Take careful note of all you see.

MRS WICKSTEED: I will, I will, and who knows. . . .

SIR PERCY: Yes?

MRS WICKSTEED: This may be a blessing in disguise.

SHANKS: Disguise.

MRS WICKSTEED: I shall be free.

SHANKS: Free.

MRS WICKSTEED: And together the future will be ours. (*Exits*.)

SHANKS: Ours.

SIR PERCY: No fear. But revenge, ha ha.

SHANKS: Ha ha.

SIR PERCY: After all these years.

SHANKS: All these years.

SIR PERCY: I think we need a booster.

SHANKS: Booster.

(SIR PERCY *exits carrying* SHANKS.
Sea sounds.)

WICKSTEED: As the sun went down on that long afternoon, a lean, distinguished figure might have been observed standing all of an hour at the end of the Pier. Several times he made as if to greet solitary ladies as they approached, but

each time he fell back, disappointed and alone. (*Exits.*)
(*Enter* SIR PERCY.)

MRS SWABB: Ah, I know who this is. I'll call her down, Mr Shanks. She's upstairs. Miss Wicksteed, your visitor. (CONNIE *enters, wearing her appliance.*)

CONNIE: Well? What do you think of them? Aren't they wonderful.

SIR PERCY: This must be what they mean by the Permissive Society.

CONNIE: They've been held up by the rail strike.

SIR PERCY: Is that what it is? You *are* Miss Wicksteed, aren't you?

CONNIE: Yes, why?

SIR PERCY: Her boldness rouses me strangely.

CONNIE: Touch them if you like, they're very firm. But I suppose you know that. (*As* SIR PERCY *touches her, his trousers fall.*) I don't think you ought to get excited.

SIR PERCY: No?

CONNIE: Tell me, if someone were stroking them would they be able to tell the difference?

SIR PERCY: I don't follow.

CONNIE: Would they be satisfied?

SIR PERCY: In due course, I hope, yes. Suspenders, Miss Wicksteed, how nice to find someone keeping up with the old ways. Oh God, think of all the years I've wasted. This is the sort of woman I've been waiting for. Bold, provocative with an ardour equal to mine. Come, let me clasp your urgent young body. Kiss me. Again. You earth maiden, will you marry me?

CONNIE: And I've only had them on five minutes! This is what they must mean by the Permissive Society. Could I ask you something?

SIR PERCY: Yes.

CONNIE: Are you supposed to wash them?

SIR PERCY: You mean, you don't?

CONNIE: No. Not yet.

SIR PERCY: You mad Lawrentian Creature.

CONNIE: I'd thought of brushing them. I've got a wire brush
    that might do.
    (SIR PERCY *follows her off.*)

THROBBING: Ah, a pair of trousers. Oxfam! Zambia will be so
    grateful.
    (*Enter and exit* CONNIE *and* SIR PERCY *tangoing across*
    the stage.)
    But what is this? My bride to be in the arms of another
    man, and before we're even married.
    (CONNIE *and* SIR PERCY *return, still tangoing,* CONNIE
    leaves SIR PERCY *and joins* THROBBING *at the end of the*
    dance.)

CONNIE: My fiancé.

SIR PERCY: She has fainted. Stand back. I am a doctor.

THROBBING: You don't look like a doctor to me. You haven't
    any trousers on. You look like a cad and a loose fish. Get
    away, bending over the prostrate body of my fiancée in your
    underclothes, that is my privilege.

SIR PERCY: Poor fool. She thought she could seduce me.

THROBBING: Seduce? Her? I have been engaged to Miss
    Wicksteed for ten years and she has never so much as laid a
    finger on me.

SIR PERCY: King Sex is a wayward monarch.

THROBBING: Come on, come on. Stand up and fight. Stand up.

SIR PERCY: I am standing up.

THROBBING: You'll probably want some handicap on account of
    your size.

SIR PERCY: What did you say?

THROBBING: I'm bigger than you are.

SIR PERCY: What gives you that idea?

THROBBING: One doesn't exactly have to be a quantity sur-
    veyor. Little squirt.

SIR PERCY: (*He lands a blow*) LITTLE.

THROBBING: Ooh. Ahh. Look. Can't we just talk this over? I've
    known quite a lot of small people in my time.

SIR PERCY: Small. Small.

THROBBING: I don't hold anybody's size against them. We

don't know how big Shakespeare was, do we? And look at Hitler. Mind you, he's a bad example. Connie, are you all right?

CONNIE: Yes.

THROBBING: Has this man been interfering with you?

CONNIE: Yes. Yes oh yes. I'm going to marry him.

THROBBING: *Him?*

SIR PERCY: Why not, sailor?

CONNIE: Yes, why not? He found in me something I never knew was there.

THROBBING: Connie. What are those?

CONNIE: They're a recent development.

THROBBING: What is his name?

CONNIE: I haven't asked.

THROBBING: You're going to marry him and you don't even know his name?

CONNIE: Yes, I do know his name. His name is curtains billowing wide on a summer night. His name is a special secret rose pressed in an old book. His name is the name of all lovers down the ages who have cried their challenge to the wild night and dared to cast themselves away on the frail bark of love. What is your name, by the way?

SIR PERCY: Sir Percy Shorter.

(CONNIE *screams and exits.*)

It's not my fault if I send women mad.

THROBBING: Mad? You? You Mickey Mouse. Why don't you marry someone your own size? Goodness! It's time for Evensong.

SIR PERCY: That settles it. You're a clergyman. Start saying your prayers!

(DENNIS *and* FELICITY *come in with* MRS SWABB.)

MRS SWABB: Canon Throbbing, I don't think you know Miss Rumpers, newly returned from Addis Ababa.

THROBBING: Welcome to our shores.

(SIR PERCY *primes his hypodermic.*)

FELICITY: What are you doing?

SIR PERCY: The balance of his mind is disturbed. I am about to redress it.

(*Exit* THROBBING *pursued by* SIR PERCY.)

FELICITY: How do you think it will happen, then?

DENNIS: I imagine you just sort of fade away really. Don't lets talk about it.

FELICITY: How tragic. A widow at twenty-two.

DENNIS: I don't want to think about it any more.

FELICITY: No. I too will be brave. I will be more than brave. I will be plucky. 'Felicity, his plucky young wife, survives him.'

DENNIS: All the germs will flee before the greatest medicine of them all.

FELICITY: Love?

DENNIS: Sex.

(*To the tune of 'Shuffle off to Buffalo'*.)

DENNIS: We've been going rather steady.
So it's time to go to beddy
Turn the lights down low.

FELICITY: Oh, oh, oh.

DENNIS: You know which way we're heading
We're heading for a wedding.

MRS SWABB: Oh no, no, no, no NO?

DENNIS: ⎫ 'Some day the stork will pay a visit
MRS SWABB: ⎭ and leave a little souvenir.

DENNIS: Just a little cute what is it.

FELICITY: We'll discuss that later, dear.'

DENNIS: You go home and get your knickers
And I'll race you to the vicar's
And it's ends away.

FELICITY: ⎫
DENNIS: ⎭ Mm, mm, mm.

MRS SWABB: Don't anticipate it
Wait to consummate it
Not every day's a wedding day.

(DENNIS *kisses her passionately*.)

DENNIS: You put your tongue in my mouth. Are you supposed to do that?

FELICITY: It's optional.

DENNIS: This is what they must mean by the Permissive Society. Penelope.

FELICITY: Felicity.

WICKSTEED: Ah! Is this your long walk in the fresh air?

DENNIS: It's all right.

WICKSTEED: All right? you lay your acned face in Miss Rumpers' lap (Good afternoon, Miss Rumpers) and you say it's all right.

DENNIS: She doesn't mind. It's mutual.

WICKSTEED: Mutual! HA! It is never mutual. Get off. Get off. Be careful, I implore you, Miss Rumpers. That head is riddled with dandruff. Get out, you lounge lizard. You're not fit to hold a candle to Miss Rumpers, let alone anything else. My dear young lady, how can you forgive me? In my own house. . . .

FELICITY: Dennis and I. . . .

WICKSTEED: Stop! Stop! Do not couple your name with his. That he should even contemplate touching your fresh, clean, innocent, young body fills me with such shame, such loathing. Filth, filth. Forgive me.

FELICITY: No. Do not touch me.

WICKSTEED: No. How can I approach you? How can I even speak to you? The least thing about you, the spent cartridge of your lipstick, the dry bed of your compact, the fluff in your handbag's bottom, all the fragrant clutter of your loveliness, I am as dirt and vileness beside it. *But*. . . .

FELICITY: But?

WICKSTEED: But speaking thus I speak as a man. And as a man I cannot touch you, but as a doctor . . .

FELICITY: Does that make a difference?

WICKSTEED: Oh yes. As a man I see you as a fresh, lovely, passionate creature. As a doctor, you are to me a machine, an organism, a mere carcass. Feeling does not enter into it. As a doctor I am a eunuch: I touch you . . . without passion, and without desire.

FELICITY: Yes.

WICKSTEED: Now I touch you as a man.

FELICITY: Yes.

WICKSTEED: Now I touch you as a doctor.

FELICITY: Yes.

WICKSTEED: You see the difference? So have no fears, my dear
   young lady when in a few moments I shall ask you to
   remove your clothes in their entirety. Because I shall be as
   far from desire as is a plumber uncovering a manhole. Off.
   Off.

   (FELICITY *goes off*.)

   How well I understand your fears. Life is such a dirty
   business these days. Everyone trying to grab what he can.
   What is the poem. . . .

FELICITY: I don't know.

WICKSTEED: A young Diana golden haired,
      Stands dreaming on the verge of strife,
      Magnificently unprepared.
      For the long littleness of life.
      Are you prepared for that, Felicity?
      The long littleness . . . sometimes longer,
      sometimes littler
      It comes as quite a shock to some girls . . .
      others just take it in their stride.

   (FELICITY *enters in her slip*.)

   Hello.

   (*He kisses her*.)

      Hello ears.
      Hello eyes.
      Hello nose.
      Hello mouth.
      Hello fingers.
      Hello knees.
      Hello Percy.

   (SIR PERCY *has come in and is watching aghast*.)

SIR PERCY: So.

WICKSTEED: I was just giving this young lady an aspirin.

SIR PERCY: In her underclothes?

FELICITY: It's very hot in here.

WICKSTEED: Don't worry. I have a diploma in tropical medicine. Felicity, Miss Rumpers, I don't think you know Sir Percy Shorter.

WICKSTEED:
SIR PERCY: } President of the British Medical Association.

SIR PERCY: Is this young lady a patient of yours?

WICKSTEED: The idea that a doctor of my reputation would meddle with a patient is repugnant to me. Leave my ears alone will you dear. And if not a patient, what?

SIR PERCY: You tell me.

WICKSTEED: A friend. Of the family. The whole family. Like you. Strange, because she's not a bit like you. Come out of there, Miss Rumpers. Nothing in my trousers pocket of any interest to you. Humbugs, you know. She knows I keep them there.

SIR PERCY: You're old enough to be her father.

WICKSTEED: So are you.

SIR PERCY: She wasn't tickling my ears.

WICKSTEED: That's true, Miss Rumpers, why don't you tickle Percy's ears. I don't think she wants to. I'm not surprised.

SIR PERCY: Enough of this. Shall I tell you what I think?

WICKSTEED: No.

FELICITY: Yes.

SIR PERCY: I think this young woman is a patient. That you were abusing your position to interfere with her. That it is a scandal. That you are a blackguard. That it is my duty to bring your little games to the notice of the Medical Disciplinary Committee. That I will do all in my power to have you struck off.

WICKSTEED: No.

SIR PERCY: What have you to say to that?

WICKSTEED: You little pratt.

SIR PERCY: WHO ARE YOU CALLING LITTLE?

(MRS WICKSTEED enters.)

MRS WICKSTEED: Arthur!

WICKSTEED: Muriel!

SIR PERCY: I have just discovered your husband with his tongue down this young lady's throat.

MRS WICKSTEED: Kissing. Kissing. You slut!

SIR PERCY: I fear kissing was just the tip of the iceberg.

MRS WICKSTEED: Of course I've known for years our marriage has been a mockery. My body lying there night after night in the wasted moonlight. I know now how the Taj Mahal must feel.

WICKSTEED: Listen. I can explain everything.

MRS WICKSTEED: No. Save it for the decree nisi.

WICKSTEED: Divorce? We can't get divorced. Think of our son, Trevor.

MRS WICKSTEED: DENNIS.

WICKSTEED: He will be the child of a broken home. He will probably turn to juvenile delinquency.

MRS WICKSTEED: He is too old for juvenile delinquency.

WICKSTEED: Thank God for that.

MRS WICKSTEED: Mention of divorce and avenues open up all round. Think of it, Percy: a hostess, perhaps at one of our leading London hotels, catering for an international clientele, where my knowledge of languages can be put to good use.

WICKSTEED: You have no knowledge of languages.

MRS WICKSTEED: A smile knows no frontiers. Thank goodness I'm not alone.

WICKSTEED: And now, suddenly, at this moment of rejection, she goes knock, knock, knock at the door of my heart, and through a gap in the chintz I see the ghost of an old passion.

SIR PERCY: Come, Muriel, lean on me.

(*Enter* PURDUE *with a ready noosed rope.*)

PURDUE: Excuse me, Doctor. . . .

WICKSTEED: I'm sorry, Mr Purdue. It's my afternoon off. I have lost my career. I have lost my wife. You are all I've got left.

FELICITY: Me?

WICKSTEED: Yes. But we can be happy together, you and I.

Together we can defy the world. Snap our fingers at public opinion. What do you say, Felicity?

(PURDUE *is meanwhile preparing to hang himself.*)

DENNIS: Can I help, Mr Purdue?

PURDUE: Nobody can help me.

DENNIS: Oh, don't say that.

SIR PERCY: I won't mention my engagement for the moment. She'll understand, of course. Sensible girl. Never been the clinging type.

PURDUE: I'm going to do it.

MRS WICKSTEED: Come, Percy. Come into the house of my body. Shelter from the storms of life under the eaves of my breasts.

PURDUE: I am going to do it.

WICKSTEED: What do you say?

FELICITY: Actually, I'm already spoken for.

WICKSTEED: Spoken for? By whom?

FELICITY: Dennis.

WICKSTEED: Dennis? Who's Dennis?

FELICITY: Your son, Dennis.

WICKSTEED: Leonard! O my God!

PURDUE: I'm going to do it. I am really.

MRS WICKSTEED: What are you doing standing on my best chair?

PURDUE: Oh, sorry.

(MRS WICKSTEED *removes the chair, leaving* PURDUE *hanging.* DENNIS *and* FELICITY *are clasped in each other's arms as. . . .*)

MRS SWABB: (*Announces*) Delia, Lady Rumpers.

LADY RUMPERS: Felicity!

CURTAIN

225

No time at all has passed.

MRS WICKSTEED: We were just going to have a glass of sherry.

LADY RUMPERS: So I see.

WICKSTEED: You are Felicity's mother?

LADY RUMPERS: I am.

(LADY RUMPERS *looks fixedly at* PURDUE *who is still swinging.*)

WICKSTEED: Take no notice. Some people will do anything for effect.

(*He swings* PURDUE *on to a chair where he stands with his head still in the noose.*)

PURDUE: I don't really want to commit suicide. It's just a call for help.

LADY RUMPERS: So. I see I got here in the nick of time. Felicity, put that young man's hand back where it belongs and get some clothes on.

FELICITY: Yes, Mother.

LADY RUMPERS: Who is that depressing youth?

WICKSTEED: My son. He depresses me too.

LADY RUMPERS: Not too depressed to take my daughter's clothes off.

WICKSTEED: No, you worm.

MRS WICKSTEED: He didn't.

WICKSTEED: Take no notice of my wife. She is his mother.

LADY RUMPERS: And you are his father.

WICKSTEED: Don't remind me.

SIR PERCY: Wicksteed did it. He is the culprit.

WICKSTEED: Yes. Yes. I did it. I am his father. I turned him into this, this snivelling, loathsome little lecher. Where did I go wrong, where do we go wrong, we parents, generation after generation?

SIR PERCY: It's all lies. I can tell you what happened. I don't believe we've had the pleasure.

MRS SWABB: Allow me. This is Delia, Lady Rumpers.

SIR PERCY: Another titled person. What a breath of fresh air. Lady Rumpers, I am a doctor.

LADY RUMPERS: Another doctor. Then I don't want to hear another word. I've had a bellyful of doctors.

PURDUE: I want a doctor: I'm depressed.

MRS WICKSTEED: So would I be if I had my head in a noose.

PURDUE: I only want to put *one* foot in the grave.

LADY RUMPERS: Oh, this is intolerable. Felicity. It shouldn't take all day for you to get your skirt on.

WICKSTEED: Can I help?

LADY RUMPERS: Don't touch her.

WICKSTEED: (*To* DENNIS) No, get back. You've done enough damage.

DENNIS: Me?

WICKSTEED: Control yourself.

LADY RUMPERS: Daring so much as even to look at a girl like Felicity.

WICKSTEED: Yes.

MRS WICKSTEED: No.

LADY RUMPERS: You are dirt.

WICKSTEED: Dirt.

LADY RUMPERS: Filth.

WICKSTEED: Filth.

FELICITY: Mother. He's sick.

WICKSTEED: Yes, sick; sick, sick. You toad.

SIR PERCY: If you'd allow me. . . .

WICKSTEED: Shut your face.

DENNIS: Dad. Dad.

WICKSTEED: Don't 'Dad, Dad' me.

LADY RUMPERS: To think we've only been in this country three weeks. Everywhere it's the same. Sex, sex, sex. Well I'm not having any.

MRS SWABB: I'm not surprised.

LADY RUMPERS: When I get you back to our suite at the Claremont, you're going straight into a hot bath and I shall personally scrub you all over with carbolic.

WICKSTEED: Ah, the privileges of motherhood.

LADY RUMPERS: Perhaps you will believe me now, Felicity.
Men will touch you, rob you, rifle you of all you possess.

SIR PERCY: Flesh isn't property, you know.

LADY RUMPERS: Yes it is. What is one's body but property?
What is one's own flesh and figure but the most precious
inheritance? When that is spent one is indeed bankrupt of
everything. From this moment on I shall not let her out of
my sight. Haile Selassie was right. We should never have
left Addis Ababa.

(*Exit* LADY RUMPERS *and* FELICITY.)

MRS WICKSTEED: You slid out of that very well.

WICKSTEED: I did rather.

MRS WICKSTEED: I want you out of this house in half an hour.

WICKSTEED: Yes. I must collect my thoughts and pack.

MRS WICKSTEED: And we must have a little talk, Percy. About
the future.

SIR PERCY: Yes.

MRS WICKSTEED: Our future.

(*Exit* SIR PERCY *and* MRS WICKSTEED.)

PURDUE: Has everybody gone?

MRS SWABB: Everybody of any consequence.

PURDUE: Marvellous!

MRS SWABB: It's all self, self, self in this house. Locked in our
tiny domestic tragedies only I, Amelia Swabb, can take the
wider view. What seems to be the trouble?

PURDUE: I'm depressed.

MRS SWABB: Pisces is in the second quarter of Saturn: naturally
you're depressed.

PURDUE: (*Getting down*) I am Pisces.

MRS SWABB: Why don't you look on the bright side? Next week
the sun'll be in Saturn and Pisceans will be laughing.

(*Exit* MRS SWABB *and* PURDUE.)

SIR PERCY: I have no sympathy with him at all. None.

MRS WICKSTEED: He *is* my husband.

SIR PERCY: I do not understand how he could betray such a fine
body. . . .

MRS WICKSTEED: Nor do I.

SIR PERCY: As the British Medical Association.

MRS WICKSTEED: What more does he want.

(*Enter* WICKSTEED.)

WICKSTEED: Not more. Different. (*Exits.*)

SIR PERCY: And a doctor. Entrusted with the bodies of his patients. Caught red-handed.

MRS WICKSTEED: Red-handed, yours so plump and white.

SIR PERCY: Please, Muriel. Of course we have all been tempted. Every doctor has. The lowliest locum in the back streets of Liverpool can take advantage of a patient, if he allows himself. Because the doctor-patient relationship is itself a kind of seduction. But one says, 'No. No, body, I will not do this. No, hands, keep to your appointed task. No, eyes, stick to the affected part.' That is what Professionalism means. Yes?

MRS WICKSTEED: Have you. . . .

SIR PERCY: Never, NEVER. Though I've had my chances. Discerning women seem to find me attractive, God knows why. . . .

MRS WICKSTEED: Yes.

SIR PERCY: Look, Muriel, there's something I have to tell you. Walk tall, Percy.

MRS WICKSTEED: Yes?

SIR PERCY: This afternoon . . . I met the woman of my dreams.

MRS WICKSTEED: Oh Percy. (*Kisses him.*)

THROBBING: Good evening.

MRS WICKSTEED: Canon Throbbing! I want you to be the first to know, Arthur apart. And it will be Arthur apart. Separation City, I'm afraid. You must congratulate us.

THROBBING: You and him? I think you must be mistaken. This man is engaged to my fiancée, Miss Wicksteed.

MRS WICKSTEED: No, you are mistaken. You are engaged to your fiancée, Miss Wicksteed.

THROBBING: That's what I thought until this afternoon.

MRS WICKSTEED: This afternoon. What happened this afternoon?

THROBBING: I was present when he proposed.

MRS WICKSTEED: Percy and Connie?

THROBBING: *He* proposed. She accepted. I protested. Then I had to get my skates on for Evensong.
(*Enter* WICKSTEED.)

WICKSTEED: Evensong on ice? The Church must be desperate.
(*Exits.*)

MRS WICKSTEED: Percy. Are you or are you not engaged to my sister-in-law?

SIR PERCY: Is your sister-in-law a woman with a nondescript face, but an outstanding figure?

MRS WICKSTEED: Certainly not. She has a bust like a billiard table.

THROBBING: She is as slim and graceful as a boy. Perhaps that is what attracted me to her in the first place.
(*Enter* WICKSTEED.)

WICKSTEED: Sometimes I think Freud died in vain. (*Exits.*)

SIR PERCY: Certainly a person purporting to be Miss Wicksteed thrust herself on me this afternoon. I can still feel her urgent young body rippling beneath my fingers.

MRS WICKSTEED: It's unlike Connie to thrust herself, even slightly.

THROBBING: He must have led her on.

SIR PERCY: It's animal magic.

THROBBING: It's being little. They have to assert themselves.

SIR PERCY: Watch it, Vicar. I gave your sister-in-law no encouragement at all.

THROBBING: Then kindly explain, Lofty, how you came to be without your trousers.

MRS WICKSTEED: Percy, is this true?

SIR PERCY: No. Yes. President of the BMA, physician to the Queen: I can have any girl I want.

MRS WICKSTEED: Connie. Come here this minute.
(CONNIE *enters, but without her appliance.*)

CONNIE: Yes, Muriel.

MRS WICKSTEED: Don't Muriel me, you minx. You seem to have been busy this afternoon. Now Percy. Is this the lady?

SIR PERCY: In some respects, yes. But what has happened to

her urgent young body? I have been deceived. Terribly
deceived. I don't want her either.

MRS WICKSTEED: Now Connie. Perhaps you can throw some
light on the proceedings. Canon Thing here has got it into
his head that you are all washed up. Is this true?

CONNIE: Yes.

THROBBING: No. Oh Mowgli, my wild jungle child, say it's not
true.

CONNIE: It is true.

MRS WICKSTEED: Then who are you engaged to?

CONNIE: To this gentleman here. He proposed to me.

SIR PERCY: Lies. LIES, LIES, ALL LIES.

MRS WICKSTEED: Are you sure he proposed?

CONNIE: Quite sure: he took his trousers off.

SIR PERCY: May I speak. MAY I SPEAK.

MRS WICKSTEED: Percy.

SIR PERCY: MAY I?

THROBBING: No.

SIR PERCY: Look here. I am Sir Percy Shorter, FRCS, FRCP.

CONNIE: How do you do. I'm sure we're going to be very
happy.

SIR PERCY: We are not. WE ARE NOT. WE ARE NOT
GOING TO BE HAPPY AT ALL. I deny it. I deny
everything. And I will go on denying everything. You
believe her? Her unsupported . . . and I mean unsupported
word against mine. And you Muriel. Think of the times
we've had together. Do they mean nothing to you?
NOTHING? This cringing, flat-chested, dowdy little
spinster. I am not going to throw myself away on that. It's
all fantasy. A fantasy of frustration and loneliness and
sadness and despair. And as such entirely DESPICABLE. I
think you owe me an apology.

MRS WICKSTEED: Percy. How could I have ever doubted your
word.

SIR PERCY: And do you agree her talk was fantasy?

MRS WICKSTEED: A tissue of lies.

SIR PERCY: Very well. I am big enough to overlook it.

THROBBING: Just one moment. Am I right in thinking you deny anything untoward occurred this afternoon?

SIR PERCY: Absolutely. Absolutely.

THROBBING: What time did you come here this afternoon?
(*The next sequence must be like a cross examination, very gentle and slow, then gradually increasing in speed leading to the fatal slip of the tongue.*)

SIR PERCY: About three.

THROBBING: About three?

SIR PERCY: About three.

THROBBING: About three. You came into this room?

SIR PERCY: I came into this room.

THROBBING: You're sure of that?

SIR PERCY: Of course I'm sure. Look here. . . .

THROBBING: Miss Wicksteed came in?

SIR PERCY: That is correct.

THROBBING: And you say you arrived about three?

SIR PERCY: That is correct.

THROBBING: And then you . . . what . . . talked?

SIR PERCY: Talked, chatted, made conversation.

THROBBING: She was wearing a blue dress, is that right?

SIR PERCY: That is correct.

THROBBING: So you arrived about three, came into this room, talked, chatted, made conversation. . . .

SIR PERCY: Talked, chatted, made conversation. . . .

THROBBING: And she was wearing a blue dress?

SIR PERCY: A blue dress.

THROBBING: She sat on the sofa?

SIR PERCY: She sat on the sofa.

THROBBING: You stood?

SIR PERCY: That is correct.

THROBBING: And you say you arrived about three? And came into this room?

SIR PERCY: Arrived about three, came into this room.

THROBBING: Talked, chatted, made conversation?

SIR PERCY: Talked, chatted, made conversation.

THROBBING: And she was in her blue dress?

SIR PERCY: And she was in her blue dress.

THROBBING: And what colour were her knickers?

SIR PERCY: Blue . . . no pink. Argh!

THROBBING: Thank you Sir Percy. That's all I wanted to know. I'm sorry Miss Wicksteed. Your witness.

MRS WICKSTEED: So. You big story.

SIR PERCY: Muriel.

MRS WICKSTEED: Don't Muriel me, you four foot Casanova.

SIR PERCY: You see, you see. It always has to come back to that.

MRS WICKSTEED: All those years I've dreamed of you, the man I might have married.

SIR PERCY: All right, I wanted you once, but you spurned me and why? Because I was small. And your husband laughed. Well when I've finished with you you'll both be laughing on the other side of your faces. Little, small. So I'm small am I? Well I'll tell you something Muriel. You are not small. Not small at all. You are HUGE. ENORMOUS.

MRS WICKSTEED: Stop it.

SIR PERCY: You think I fancied you? You!

MRS WICKSTEED: You did, you did.

SIR PERCY: You great wardrobe. That model went out years ago.

MRS WICKSTEED: Stop it. I'm ageless, do you hear, ageless.

SIR PERCY: And don't think you're going to trundle back to your snivelling little husband, and live happily ever after in your nice little provincial backwater. Because I am going to break him. BREAK HIM, do you hear? I've broken bigger men than that. And I'll do it again. Professional misconduct. Professional incompetence, interfering with patients . . . a list of charges as long as my arm.

THROBBING: Well that's not very long.

SIR PERCY: Watch it, Vicar.

CONNIE: Please don't do it. For my sake.

SIR PERCY: For your sake? What did you ever do for me, except pull the wool over my eyes?

CONNIE: It was nice while it lasted.

SIR PERCY: It was an illusion.

CONNIE: It always is.

SIR PERCY: No. I shall break him. He's had his chips.

MRS WICKSTEED: No. No.

SIR PERCY: The party's over, Doctor. Curtains. This is the end of the line for you, Arthur Wicksteed, a general practitioner from Brighton's Hove.

MRS WICKSTEED: The shame! The disgrace! The POVERTY!

SIR PERCY: Finita La Commedia, Arturo.

> (*Exit* SIR PERCY, *followed by* MRS WICKSTEED.)

CONNIE: So you see now, marriage is out of the question.

THROBBING: Is it?

CONNIE: Oh yes. What I have done, you can't forgive. This foul, foul thing.

THROBBING: It was only kissing.

CONNIE: No. One kiss and he could have had anything. It would always lie between us. No I am Damaged Goods.

THROBBING: I forgive you.

CONNIE: You mustn't. He mustn't.

THROBBING: I must. It is my principles.

CONNIE: I am a harlot. A Jezebel.

THROBBING: I know, I know.

CONNIE: A whore.

CONNIE: Oh Connie, how infinitely more desirable you are now. Can't you see, Connie, what vistas are opening up?

CONNIE: I think I can. Oh God.

THROBBING: Sin with him you can sin with me. I wanted you before. I want you twice as much now.

CONNIE: No, please, Harold, no.

THROBBING: Gently we can lead each other on as together we explore all the alleys and pathways of the body. Just think of it.

CONNIE: I'm trying not to.

THROBBING: Together we shall be in the forefront of Anglican sexuality. Perhaps I might even write a frank and fearless account of our activities for the *Church Times*. Oh such sin. Only it won't be sin because we shall be married, married

234

and allowed to do what we want. Married and FREE.

CONNIE: Free?

THROBBING: (*To the tune of 'Shuffle off to Buffalo'*)

    I must go and tell the verger

    That there'll shortly be a merger

    And it's some day soon.

CONNIE: No, no, no.

THROBBING: Can't believe my luck.

    Because I'm going to break my duck

    Upon a honey, honey, honeymoon.

(*They exit as* MRS WICKSTEED *and* MRS SWABB *enter*.)

MRS SWABB: It's kiss 'n' make up time. I'm glad to see somebody's doing the sensible thing. (*Exits*.)

MRS WICKSTEED: Now, Muriel old girl. You're going to have to play your cards pretty carefully, or you will end up on the discard pile. I don't know. And me with the menopause just shoving its nose above the horizon. As if I didn't have enough on my plate.

(*Enter* WICKSTEED, *bags packed*.)

WICKSTEED: I fold up my twenty-five years in the medical profession. I put in twenty-odd years of marriage, plus a slightly threadbare respectability. And that's it. All in ten minutes. Ten minutes and the world turns. Our world. In Memphis, Tennessee, fourteen babies have been born since this play began. In Hobart, Tasmania, a flower turns to the sun. In Lima, Peru, an old man is dying, and in Birmingham, England, two lovers turn to each other in the silence of the night . . . and somewhere out there in the singing silence of space, a tin flag flutters. Our world. Somewhere between the loving and the lying and the kissing and the crying and the living and the dying and the fishing and the frying is that something we call life. Our world.

MRS WICKSTEED: All packed, I see.

WICKSTEED: A few things I've thrown together.

MRS WICKSTEED: Where are you going?

WICKSTEED: Relatives.

MRS WICKSTEED: Close relatives?

WICKSTEED: Stevenage. I think I have an aunt there.

MRS WICKSTEED: You're a stinker, Arthur Wicksteed. Do you know that?

WICKSTEED: Oh yes.

MRS WICKSTEED: A rotter.

WICKSTEED: It's funny. . . . Having you I didn't want you. Losing you, I want you again.

MRS WICKSTEED: Hard cheese.

WICKSTEED: 'His wife has promised to stand by him.'

MRS WICKSTEED: What?

WICKSTEED: I was just thinking, it would look better if you stood by me. Maybe I wouldn't be struck off.

MRS WICKSTEED: It would *look* better. Of course I should have to dress the part: one thing I've learned in life is that few right thinking people can withstand a really good twin-set and pearls. But what about my feelings?

WICKSTEED: I was forgetting those.

MRS WICKSTEED: As usual. After all she wasn't just something on the side, was she? There've been others.

WICKSTEED: A few.

MRS WICKSTEED: A few?

WICKSTEED: Quite a few.

MRS WICKSTEED: I am fed up.

WICKSTEED: I think I am too. Muriel. I suppose it's too late to start again.

MRS WICKSTEED: Much too late. All those women lie between us.

WICKSTEED: And in your life, no one?

MRS WICKSTEED: No one. Nothing. Never.

WICKSTEED: Percy?

MRS WICKSTEED: A dream. A fantasy. No one has ever laid a finger on me except you. And you it's so long. I've almost forgotten. Suppose I were to overlook your disgraceful conduct.

WICKSTEED: My shameful, shameful conduct. Filthy conduct.

MRS WICKSTEED: Yes.

WICKSTEED: If only you could be big enough.

MRS WICKSTEED: Then there'd have to be a different going on.

WICKSTEED: How different?

MRS WICKSTEED: No more twin beds.

WICKSTEED: I sleep so badly.

MRS WICKSTEED: Then we shall sleep badly together.

WICKSTEED: Yes, Muriel.

MRS WICKSTEED: Perhaps in the long watches of the night I shall bring you comfort.

WICKSTEED: Perhaps you will.

MRS WICKSTEED: I will. There is no perhaps about it. You see, you have no rights, Arthur. They have been forfeited over the years. Whereas innocence has kept mine intact. Kiss me.

WICKSTEED: Here?

MRS WICKSTEED: Yes. No. Hard.

WICKSTEED: If you insist.

(WICKSTEED *puts his arms round her and kisses her*.)

MRS WICKSTEED: And that's how it's going to be. But I am not forcing you. You may take it or leave it.

WICKSTEED: This or my aunt in Stevenage. I suppose I'd better take it.

MRS WICKSTEED: A wise decision. Now I think we might retire for a little nap.

WICKSTEED: But I'm not tired.

MRS WICKSTEED: Excellent. Neither am I.

WICKSTEED: Muriel. I . . .

MRS WICKSTEED: What?

WICKSTEED: Nothing.

MRS WICKSTEED: You see, innocence will always triumph in the end.

WICKSTEED: Though if there was anybody I'd forgive you. I know.

MRS WICKSTEED: No need. There was nobody. Nobody at all. Now, what were we talking about? The future.

WICKSTEED: No. The past.

MRS WICKSTEED: Then we must listen to the voice of the future.

(*Enter* SHANKS.)

SHANKS: Has anybody seen my trousers?

WICKSTEED: Who is this?

MRS WICKSTEED: Probably a patient left over from surgery.

WICKSTEED: He is not my patient.

SHANKS: I'm not anybody's patient.

MRS WICKSTEED: Then you've no business here. Get out.

SHANKS: You again. No. Please don't touch me. No. No. Keep off.

WICKSTEED: Odd. He seems to know you.

MRS WICKSTEED: In my voluntary work I rub shoulders with all sorts. . . .

SHANKS: Don't let her touch me. You'll protect me won't you?

WICKSTEED: Against what?

SHANKS: Against her.

MRS WICKSTEED: I don't want to touch you.

SHANKS: You did before.

MRS WICKSTEED: Hold your tongue.

WICKSTEED: Before? Before what, Muriel?

MRS WICKSTEED: I don't know. How am I supposed to know?

SHANKS: She's a monster.

WICKSTEED: She is not a monster. She is my wife.

SHANKS: She's sex mad.

MRS WICKSTEED: Listen, I wear the corsets in this house, so shut your cake-hole, before I give you a bunch of fives.

WICKSTEED: Muriel. Is there something between you and this man?

MRS WICKSTEED: Arthur. I am not friends if you say things like that. It's quite plainly a delusion.

SHANKS: A delusion? Is this a delusion?

(*He shows him the Polaroid snaps.*)

Or this? The camera cannot lie.

WICKSTEED: What wonderful pictures. Who is it?

SHANKS: Who? It's her.

WICKSTEED: Good God. So it is. Muriel, what have you got to say?

MRS WICKSTEED: Damn. Damn. I am ruined.

WICKSTEED: Is this your clear conscience? *Qu'est-ce que c'est que ça, madame?* Not to mention *que ça?*

MRS WICKSTEED: Silliness, silliness. That was all it was.

WICKSTEED: Is this your innocence?

(*He plucks at* SHANKS' *shirt-tails.*)

Or this?

SHANKS: Stop it.

WICKSTEED: So. Now it's my turn.

MRS WICKSTEED: No. Arthur, please.

WICKSTEED: Don't touch me. Don't touch me. You're not fit to touch me.

MRS WICKSTEED: It was a mistake.

WICKSTEED: And don't grovel. I can't abide a groveller. You see, I always thought no one else fancied her. I've always had this sneaking feeling that if I hadn't married her, no one else would. But (*he looks at the snaps*) my goodness me! It's *Forever Amber* all over again. Flower arrangements, cake decorating. All those long suburban afternoons. . . . It was lovers, lovers from all walks of life, like you. How long has this been going on?

MRS WICKSTEED: This afternoon. Ten minutes. That's all.

WICKSTEED: I don't believe it. I believe it's been going on for years. Sex isn't something that happens overnight, you know.

MRS WICKSTEED: You're wrong, so wrong.

WICKSTEED: Go to your room. Pack one or two things, just in case. You may have to go to your mother's. (*To* SHANKS.) And you, get out.

SHANKS: I'd like to ex. . . .

WICKSTEED: Get out.

MRS WICKSTEED: (*Returning*) Arthur.

WICKSTEED: Yes.

MRS WICKSTEED: Am I to be turned out of my own house?

WICKSTEED: I was.

MRS WICKSTEED: Can't we forgive and forget? We can live on our memories.

WICKSTEED: I have no memories, only scars.

MRS WICKSTEED: Arthur, please.

WICKSTEED: No, Muriel.

(*She exits.*)

WICKSTEED: The eyes, cool but kindly, looked back unflinchingly from the glass. There was pain in those eyes, a hint perhaps of some secret sorrow. He ran his lean brown fingers through his thinning hair and sighed. And yet, at the corner of his firm, yet sensitive mouth, there hovered the merest suspicion of a smile. 'I'm still in the game' he thought. (*Exits.*)

(*Enter* SHANKS.)

MRS SWABB: I see you're still in your underpants. And the same pair too. Have you never heard of the dictum: undies worn twice are not quite nice?

SHANKS: No. (*Exits.*)

MRS SWABB: And they talk of comprehensive education.

(*Enter* PURDUE.)

PURDUE: That is the dirtiest gas oven I've ever put my head in.

MRS SWABB: It's not gas, it's electric. (*Exits.*)

(FELICITY *and* DENNIS *enter.*)

DENNIS: Felicity.

FELICITY: I gave her the slip. I had to see you again.

DENNIS: Yes. I feel the same way. Except. . . .

FELICITY: Except what?

DENNIS: Could you love me if I wasn't going to die?

FELICITY: But you are.

DENNIS: I mean we all die sooner or later. So say it was later rather than sooner.

FELICITY: How much later?

DENNIS: Roundabout the time you're supposed to die, three score years and ten.

FELICITY: How much is that?

DENNIS: Seventy.

FELICITY: Another fifty years. No, my love, we must resign ourselves, there is no hope.

DENNIS: No. I don't think there is.

SHANKS: At last.

MRS SWABB: Oh no. Not again.

(SHANKS *approaches* FELICITY.)

SHANKS: I had rather an unpleasant experience earlier, so you'll forgive me if I'm cautious.

FELICITY: How do you do.

SHANKS: I thought I must be losing my touch. But no. One look at you and I realize, those could never be real.

(MRS SWABB, DR *and* MRS WICKSTEED, DENNIS, FELICITY, CANON THROBBING *and* CONNIE *have come on to the stage and are watching, fascinated.*)

SHANKS: The line so crisp, the silhouette so pert. If that's not our product I'll go back to chicken farming.

(*He touches* FELICITY'S *breast and she slaps his face.*)

MRS WICKSTEED: I second that. (*Fetches him another.*)

SHANKS: I can't understand it. On the training course they teach you to tell blindfold.

WICKSTEED: What are you doing here, anyway?

SHANKS: I'm looking for my client.

(FELICITY *slaps him again.*)

DENNIS: Without your trousers?

THROBBING: Is he a commercial traveller?

(CONNIE *slaps* THROBBING.)

SHANKS: In a sense.

DENNIS: If he's a commercial traveller, he must often be without his trousers.

(WICKSTEED *slaps* DENNIS.)

MRS WICKSTEED: Arthur!

THROBBING: What do you travel in?

(CONNIE *slaps* THROBBING, MRS WICKSTEED *slaps* WICKSTEED, SHANKS *slaps* DENNIS, WICKSTEED *slaps* MRS WICKSTEED *as* LADY RUMPERS *enters.*)

MRS SWABB: Delia, Lady Rumpers.

LADY RUMPERS: Out of my way, you pert slut. Is this what we were promised when we emerged from the Dark Ages? Is this Civilization? I'm only thankful Kenneth Clark isn't here to see it.

MRS SWABB: I'm not actually sure he isn't.

LADY RUMPERS: (*To* SHANKS) You.

SHANKS: Good evening.

LADY RUMPERS: Good evening. What has happened to your trousers?

SHANKS: I don't know.

LADY RUMPERS: Well you'd better find them. If I'd wanted to see people running about in their shirt-tails I should have stayed in Addis Ababa.

CONNIE: Good evening.

LADY RUMPERS: Good evening.

THROBBING: Good evening.

LADY RUMPERS: Good evening. Why should your face be familiar? Have you ever been called to serve the Lord in heathen parts?

THROBBING: Well, I was for a short time a curate in Leeds.

MRS WICKSTEED: Good evening.

WICKSTEED: Good evening.

LADY RUMPERS: All in all I can say quite confidently I have seen nothing like this even in the cesspots of Mespot. And Felicity, leave that dismal boy alone.

WICKSTEED: Hear, hear.

LADY RUMPERS: Shut up. Do you hear?

FELICITY: No. I won't. I love Dennis.

DENNIS: We want to get married.

LADY RUMPERS: Love, Madam. I do not want to hear that word. You talk of love with a body like yours. Time enough to fall back on love when the bloom begins to fade. I didn't slave away bringing you up in a temperature of 115 in the shade for you to talk of love as soon as my back is turned.

WICKSTEED: I quite agree.

LADY RUMPERS: Shut up.

MRS WICKSTEED: Hear, hear.

LADY RUMPERS: You too. The word marriage has been mentioned. It is out of the question. Felicity is far too young for a start. . . .

FELICITY: But Mother.

LADY RUMPERS: And the young man.

WICKSTEED: Keith.

MRS WICKSTEED: Dennis.

LADY RUMPERS: . . . far too ugly.

WICKSTEED: True. A boy like that proposing marriage to a girl the strap of whose bra he is not worthy to undo.

LADY RUMPERS: Don't touch her.

THROBBING: Could I say something?

LADY RUMPERS: }No.
CONNIE:

MRS WICKSTEED: May a mother have a voice?

LADY RUMPERS: }No.
WICKSTEED:

LADY RUMPERS: A girl like Felicity and a shrivelled thing like him. Think of the stock. Why you wouldn't do it to a hyacinth.

MRS WICKSTEED: Hyacinths don't fall in love.

WICKSTEED: If you ask me, he wants a kick up the arse.

LADY RUMPERS: Come, Felicity. It's time we were going. When I hear the word arse I know the way the wind is blowing.

MRS WICKSTEED: Lady Rumpers. Arthur. One moment. May a mother speak? Fair dos. We're all of us pretty well headed for the sere and yellow. It's times hurrying footsteps all round these days, isn't it? Now Dennis, he's not a glamour puss. Never will be. Even though he is the fruit of our loins. Partly our fault. Funny boy. Difficult to love. Never liked touching him very much and quite frankly it makes a difference. Touching, looking, loving . . . without it which one of us would thrive? Look at your girl, Felicity. Stroked and cherished all her life. Lovely girl.

LADY RUMPERS: Lovely girl.

WICKSTEED: Lovely girl.

MRS WICKSTEED: But that's because she's been worn next to the heart. Result: she blooms. Dennis, shoved away at the back of the drawer, result: drab, boring, spotty, nobody wants him.

243

CONNIE: But that's me too.

MRS WICKSTEED: But I say this: love him, as your girl seems unaccountably to love him, and he'll blossom.

MRS SWABB: I think he's looking better already.

LADY RUMPERS: No, never. It's quite right you should be kind to him. You are his mother. I am under no such handicap.

CONNIE: Please.

LADY RUMPERS: No.

MRS SWABB: Please.

LADY RUMPERS: No.

DENNIS: Please.

LADY RUMPERS: No.

FELICITY: Please.

LADY RUMPERS: No. My daughter. . . .

WICKSTEED: Oh, stuff your daughter.

MRS SWABB: (*Indicating* DENNIS) He already has.

LADY RUMPERS: What?

(LADY RUMPERS *gives a great cry and swoons.*)

MRS SWABB: Did I strike a wrong note?

WICKSTEED: Excuse me, I'm a doctor.

MRS WICKSTEED: We know you're a doctor.

WICKSTEED: She has fainted.

MRS WICKSTEED: Dennis, is this true?

MRS SWABB: Quite true. Between 15.10 and 15.25 this afternoon they carried out the docking procedure.

WICKSTEED: You mean, you and her, her and you?

DENNIS: Yes.

THROBBING: What was it like?

LADY RUMPERS: After all my precautions. Gone. Tossed away on him.

FELICITY: No. It was love.

LADY RUMPERS: Love. You don't understand. No one understands. The shame. The waste. My own shameful story all over again.

MRS WICKSTEED: Oh crumbs!

LADY RUMPERS: Many years ago, when I was not much older than Felicity is now, I had just arrived in the colonies . . .

I . . . you have to know this Felicity. I should have told you before. I had just arrived in the colonies when I found I was P-R-E-G-N-A-N-T.

THROBBING: PRAGNANT?

MRS WICKSTEED: Pegnat.

LADY RUMPERS: PREGNANT. I was not married at the time.

MRS WICKSTEED: What about General Rumpers?

LADY RUMPERS: Tiger and I met soon afterwards. He loved me . . . I . . . respected him. We married. He was a gentleman but shy. He only went into the Army in order to put his moustache to good purpose. He was glad of a child for his life too had its secrets: a passing-out party at Sandhurst had left him forever incapable of having children. He threw the blanket of his name over Felicity and together we achieved respectability. Call me fool, call me slut, call me anything you like. But I vowed at that time that the same thing should never happen to Felicity. And now it has. My poor child. Oh Felicity, Felicity.

WICKSTEED: And where is he now, her real father?

LADY RUMPERS: Do you think I have not asked myself that question? Lying under mosquito nets in Government House do you think that question has not hammered itself into my brain?

WICKSTEED: Have you any clues?

LADY RUMPERS: One and one only. He was a doctor. Yes. That is why I despise your profession.

MRS WICKSTEED: His name. Do you not know that?

LADY RUMPERS: No. I suppose that shocks you.

MRS WICKSTEED: Nothing could shock me any more.

LADY RUMPERS: Picture the scene. Liverpool. The blitz at its height. I am bound for the Far East. Our convoy is assembled ready to go down the Mersey on the morning tide. Suddenly I am told I cannot sail.

WICKSTEED: Yes?

LADY RUMPERS: No. I had no vaccination certificate. The black-out. An air raid in progress. The docks ablaze. I set off alone to find a doctor. Buildings crashing all round me.

Crash, crash, crash. Bombs raining down on the street.
Boom, boom, boom. I see a brass plate. The surgery in
darkness. The doctor under the table. He writes me a
certificate. I am grateful. Think how grateful I was. We
talk.

THROBBING: Yes, yes, go on.

LADY RUMPERS: Two voices in the darkness of the surgery as
the storm rages outside. His hand steals into mine. . . .

THROBBING: Yes, then what did he do? . . .

LADY RUMPERS: We cling to each other as the bombs fell.

THROBBING: Yes?

LADY RUMPERS: I need not tell you the rest.

THROBBING: They always miss out the best bits.

LADY RUMPERS: The All Clear sounds as I stumble back on
board. Came the dawn we slipped out of the Mersey and
headed for the open sea. Do you know the Atlantic at all?

MRS WICKSTEED: No.

LADY RUMPERS: It is very rough. I thought I was sea sick. Only
when we docked did I realize I had a bun in the club.

MRS WICKSTEED: Tragic.

WICKSTEED: Wonderful.

LADY RUMPERS: I blame the War.

WICKSTEED: Ah the War, that was a strange and wonderful
time.
    Oh Mavis and Audrey and Lilian and Jean
    Patricia and Pauline and NAAFI Christine
    Maureen and Myrtle I had you and more
    In God's gift to the lecher the Second World War.

MRS SWABB: In shelters and bunkers on Nissen hut floors,
    They wrestled with webbing and cellular drawers.
    From pillbox on headland they scoured the seas
    While pinching our bottoms and stroking our knees.

LADY RUMPERS: Echoes of music drift into the night.
    Never in peace will it all seem so right.

WICKSTEED: Oh Lost Generation where are you now?
    I still see Lemira, Yvonne's in Slough.
    Mothers like you, with girls in their twenties.

Fathers like me: we all share such memories.

LADY RUMPERS: One mad magenta moment and I have paid for it all my life. Felicity ruined.

MRS SWABB: We don't know she is, do we? One swallow doesn't make a summer.

FELICITY: Never mind, Mummy. After all he wants to marry me.

LADY RUMPERS: Yes. Go Felicity. Be happy.

FELICITY: Happy. Oh Mummy, if you only knew.

WICKSTEED: Such a waste.

MRS WICKSTEED: At least somebody's happy.

WICKSTEED: Is she happy?

MRS SWABB: She looks happy to me. But then I'm a behaviourist.

MRS WICKSTEED: You're a busybody.

MRS SWABB: And I can make her happier still.

FELICITY: Nobody can make me happier.

MRS SWABB: I can. I want to explain about Dennis.

DENNIS: No, Mrs Swabb, no.

FELICITY: Such a short time we have together.

MRS SWABB: But it isn't.

FELICITY: It's three months.

MRS SWABB: No.

FELICITY: No?

DENNIS: No.

FELICITY: Longer?

MRS SWABB: Yes.

DENNIS: No.

FELICITY: Much longer?

MRS SWABB: Much, much longer.

FELICITY: You mean . . . he's not going to die at all?

MRS SWABB: Strong as a horse.

DENNIS:
FELICITY: } Oh, no.

MRS SWABB: It's all in the mind.

WICKSTEED: This doctor in Liverpool, I'm interested. What did he look like?

LADY RUMPERS: As I say there was a black-out. I saw his face only in the fitful light of a post-coital Craven A. He was small, but perfectly proportioned. In some respects more so. I don't suppose I shall ever find him.

MRS SWABB: Who knows. One day the doorbell will go and he will walk back into her life.

(*Bell.*)

THROBBING: Isn't that the doorbell?

WICKSTEED: Don't lets jump to conclusions. It could be the man next door taking his first tentative steps on the xylophone.

MRS SWABB: Sir Percy Shorter.

SIR PERCY: I wish to speak to your daughter.

LADY RUMPERS: My daughter has been spoken to by at least four people this afternoon, one of whom has proposed marriage. Naturally, she is exhausted.

SIR PERCY: I wish to take down her evidence.

MRS WICKSTEED: You've taken down quite enough this afternoon.

SIR PERCY: LIES, LIES.

LADY RUMPERS: What sort of evidence?

SIR PERCY: She has this very afternoon been assaulted.

MRS WICKSTEED: Haven't we all.

LADY RUMPERS: Suffice it to say that my daughter is to marry the person who assaulted her.

SIR PERCY: But he is married already. To this lady. (*Indicating* MRS WICKSTEED.)

LADY RUMPERS: Indeed. She has been masquerading as his mother. These are new depths.

WICKSTEED: Understandably Sir Percy is a little confused.

SIR PERCY: Little!

WICKSTEED: He is over-excited. You are over-excited.

SIR PERCY: That is not true. I was never more calm in my life. I am the only person here telling the truth. Unclean, unclean. I'll break you. Under cover of a medical examination this man assaulted your daughter.

LADY RUMPERS: You? My daughter appears to have been

248

assaulted by the whole family.

MRS WICKSTEED: No. Not me.

WICKSTEED: No. Not you. You confined yourself to our friend in the shirt-tails. You're the prey of any tom-cat that knocks at the door.

SIR PERCY: (*To* WICKSTEED) You can talk.

MRS WICKSTEED: (*To* SIR PERCY) You can talk.

SHANKS: (*To* MRS WICKSTEED) You can talk.

THROBBING: I seem to be the only one with nothing to be ashamed of.

LADY RUMPERS: Now I remember you. You are the Beast of the 10.26. Just because you're a clergyman you think you can look up girls' legs.

CONNIE: Is this true?

THROBBING: One has to look somewhere.

CONNIE: Harold! Don't touch me.

FELICITY: Don't touch me. Don't touch me.

DENNIS: Penelope.

FELICITY: FELICITY. I despise you. You lied to me.

DENNIS: Not really.

FELICITY: I thought it was only going to be for three months.

DENNIS: But you said you loved me.

FELICITY: All your faults . . . the stuff you put on your hair, your awful trousers, your terrible terrible feet. For three months yes, I could swallow it all, string vests, everything. But not for *life*.

DENNIS: What if I promised to commit suicide at the end of three months?

FELICITY: It's very nice of you, but it wouldn't be the same. Don't touch me.

MRS WICKSTEED: Arthur.

WICKSTEED: Don't touch me.

FELICITY: (*To* DENNIS) Don't touch me.

WICKSTEED: (*To* SIR PERCY) Don't touch me.

CONNIE: (*To* THROBBING) Don't touch me.

SIR PERCY: All in all, I can say quite confidently that I've seen nothing like this since I was a locum in Liverpool.

(*All come on slowly, and stand in a great circle round* SIR
PERCY.)

MRS SWABB: And now, suddenly the air is black with the wings
of chickens coming home to roost.

WICKSTEED: You did say Liverpool?

SIR PERCY: Liverpool.

LADY RUMPERS: Liverpool?

MRS WICKSTEED: Liverpool.

MRS SWABB: Liverpool.

SIR PERCY: Yes, Liverpool. What of it. I did a locum there. In
the War.

WICKSTEED: Yes, of course, the War.

LADY RUMPERS: That would be the Second War, the one to
make the world safe for democracy?

SIR PERCY: That was how it was advertised.

WICKSTEED: When the enemy was always listening, and
cigarettes were two a penny. (*He lights a cigarette lighter.*)

MRS SWABB: Put that light out.

(*Darkness, the sounds of an air raid.*)

LADY RUMPERS: That's him! That's him!

SIR PERCY: Who?

LADY RUMPERS: My seducer.

SIR PERCY: Are you all mad?

WICKSTEED: Liverpool. The War. The docks. Yes?

SIR PERCY: No.

WICKSTEED: Buildings crashing down. Whole streets ablaze.
Yes?

SIR PERCY: No. No.

WICKSTEED: A doctor's surgery. Yes?

SIR PERCY: I don't remember.

WICKSTEED: Your surgery.

SIR PERCY: No.

WICKSTEED: And then, a knock comes at the door. It is a
patient. A woman.

SIR PERCY: It could have been anybody.

WICKSTEED: But it wasn't anybody.

SIR PERCY: It was nobody.

LADY RUMPERS: Nobody! It was me!
  (*Lights up.*)
SIR PERCY: You!
LADY RUMPERS: Don't you remember how we clung to each
  other in the darkness of the surgery?
THROBBING: Yes. Yes. Tell it like it is.
SIR PERCY: No.
LADY RUMPERS: And then you took me.
THROBBING: Yee-ow.
SIR PERCY: I took *you*? You took *me*. Your Land Army
  breeches came down with a fluency born of long practice.
LADY RUMPERS: It is immaterial.
THROBBING: Could we go back over that bit in more detail?
SIR PERCY: No.
THROBBING: They've missed it out again.
LADY RUMPERS: There was a child. She lived and found
  powerful friends. She is living now. She is a lady and very
  beautiful.
DENNIS: And I love her.
  (FELICITY *weeps*.)
SIR PERCY: What's the matter with her.
WICKSTEED: It must be something of a shock to find she's got
  you for a father.
SIR PERCY: Father? Me? Bless her. To think, all these years
  denied the chance of lavishing on her fatherly affections.
  Those little services of love which are a father's right.
  Stroke her hair, wipe away her tears, bath her.
LADY RUMPERS: Bath her?
SIR PERCY: Well, perhaps no. But help her choose her dresses,
  rub on her suntan lotion . . . those one hundred and one
  things only a father can do. You can see she needs a father's
  hand.
WICKSTEED: Not down her blouse.
LADY RUMPERS: I see you haven't changed. No word of regret.
SIR PERCY: The incident had vanished from my mind.
LADY RUMPERS: You funny little man.
SIR PERCY: Don't say that.

LADY RUMPERS: Rumpers was a little man too. He made no
    secret of his height. Strange, I've been looking for you all
    my life and now I've found you I don't know what to do
    with you.
SIR PERCY: You've got nothing to do with me.
LADY RUMPERS: You don't even seem sorry.
SIR PERCY: Why should I be sorry? I didn't know there was a
    child.
WICKSTEED: And are you in the habit of seducing every patient
    who comes into your surgery?
SIR PERCY: It was the War.
WICKSTEED: And Lady Rumpers was your patient?
SIR PERCY: No.
LADY RUMPERS: You were the doctor, I was the patient and
    Felicity was the outcome. (*Exits.*)
WICKSTEED: Tut, tut, tut. Hard lines, Perce.
SIR PERCY: Don't call me Perce. I am Sir Percy Shorter,
    President of the BMA.
WICKSTEED: Not for much longer.
SIR PERCY: You wouldn't dare.
WICKSTEED: I would. Unprofessional conduct. Interfering with
    patients. A list of charges as long as your arm, no, my arm.
    And the chief witness your own illegitimate daughter. I
    think it's sleeping dogs time, Percy. Otherwise one word
    and it's curtains, finito.
SIR PERCY: It's not fair. Why is it always me?
WICKSTEED: How extraordinary! So even you, Percy are
    human. Just like all the rest of us, the world over. Each one
    of us walking the world because someone somewhere
    happened to bring their body and lay it against another
    body. Everyone. Every person you see in the street, read
    about in the newspaper. All the names in the births
    column. All the names in the deaths column. Chinese
    swimming rivers with guns in their mouths, the Ryder Cup
    team. The Pope on his balcony. Everybody. Everywhere.
    All the time.
MRS SWABB: (*Bowing deeply*) Sir Percy. Could I crave a boon?

SIR PERCY: She's mad too. They're all in the plot.

MRS SWABB: Examine Dennis. Tell her he's dying. Pretend.

SIR PERCY: Pretend? Tell her, who? Why?

MRS SWABB: Felicity.

SIR PERCY: My daughter? Pretend? I couldn't pretend that. I
   couldn't. You don't know what you're asking. My position.
   Jeopardizing my professional integrity.

MRS SWABB: You haven't got any. Not now.

SIR PERCY: Nobody knows that.

MRS SWABB: They could always find out.

SIR PERCY: LIES. LIES. Blackmail. It's a PLOT. I WILL
   NEVER DO IT. NEVER NEVER NEVER. Where is he?

MRS SWABB: Follow me, Sir Percy. I will conduct you thither.

   (*Enter* CONNIE *and* FELICITY *each looking at themselves.*)

CONNIE: It used to be so flat.

FELICITY: It used to be so flat.

CONNIE: Can you tell?

FELICITY: You can tell.

   (SHANKS, *in Purdue's trousers, comes upon* CONNIE *still trying
   to adjust her bust.*)

SHANKS: Something tells me you're the person we're looking
   for. Miss Wicksteed?

CONNIE: Yes.

SHANKS: Allow me. There. Striking without being indiscreet.
   Full but not vulgar. What a day. Would you like to take a
   walk?

CONNIE: In the street? Won't people stare?

SHANKS: At a striking woman. Yes. People will stare.

CONNIE: I shall need different clothes, a larger fit. My hair
   ought to be different. My whole style.

SHANKS: Come. The world is waiting.

   (*Exit* SHANKS *and* CONNIE.
   Enter SIR PERCY, *with* DENNIS *and* MRS SWABB.)

SIR PERCY: There is no doubt about it. Brett's Palsy.

MRS SWABB: Brett's Palsy. How terrible. How terrible, Felicity.

DENNIS: Don't overdo it.

SIR PERCY: In its tertiary stage.

MRS SWABB: Tertiary. That's good. Tertiary is good. Tertiary is very good.

DENNIS: How long have I got?

SIR PERCY: Do you really want me to tell you?

DENNIS: For the sake of the my fiancée, yes.

FELICITY: Your former fiancée. I gave you back the ring.

SIR PERCY: In the circumstance a wise precaution. Your engagement would have been broken off anyway.

FELICITY: You mean. . . ?

SIR PERCY: I'm afraid so. Three months. Four at the outside.

FELICITY: You're sure?

MRS SWABB: President of the BMA. Physician to the Queen, 'course he's sure. A man in his position can't afford to make mistakes, can you.

SIR PERCY: No.

FELICITY: Oh Dennis. Forgive me.

DENNIS: So I do have Brett's Palsy after all. I knew I had Brett's Palsy. I always said I had Brett's Palsy. Felicity, how could you ever have doubted I had Brett's Palsy. Time is short. We must be married this minute. (*They exit.*)

MRS SWABB: That was very sporting of you, Sir Percy.

SIR PERCY: Not difficult. Really rather sad.

MRS SWABB: Sad? Why?

SIR PERCY: He has three months to live. He thought he had Brett's Palsy. He has got Brett's Palsy. As paranoids sometimes have enemies, so hypochondriacs sometimes have diseases. It isn't always in the mind.

MRS SWABB: But he's so happy.

SIR PERCY: So what are you weeping about. He's happy. He's got his lady love. She's happy. She thinks he's going to die. He is going to die. Everybody's happy. Except me.

MRS SWABB: Well we're into injury time now.
  There's no time to make a rhyme up.
  Just the wedding and the line up.

MRS WICKSTEED: Dear Dennis, I hope he's making the right decision.

WICKSTEED: What does it matter? He's in love.

MRS WICKSTEED: And we're back where we started.

WICKSTEED: I say love. That great conglomerate. Affection and attraction, envy and desire. All marketed under the same label. A father's love, a daughter's love, love of wives for husbands and mothers for children. It's love all right. But which department . . . the headquarters in the heart or the depot between the legs?

MRS WICKSTEED: Do try not to be vulgar, Arthur, or we shall never get on.

WICKSTEED: Only time will tell.

MRS SWABB: Delia, Lady Rumpers.

LADY RUMPERS: From youth and from desiring
    From love and passion free
    Old with too much regretting
    My future's plain to see.
    A small hotel in Eastbourne
    A nightly game of whist.
    An old colonial lady
    Who'll die and not be missed.

SIR PERCY: But Delia I too am lonely
    For lonely are the brave
    Come. Why do we not go together,
    In step towards the grave?

MRS SWABB: So as the shadows lengthen
    Across the lawns of life
    They walk into the sunset . . .
    Sir Percy and his wife.

    (CONNIE *sweeps on, transformed, with* SHANKS.)

    These flashing legs
    This smile so regal.
    I know that face.
    Dame Anna Neagle!

CONNIE: No, no. You fool. It's me, it's me.
    Got up like an awful tart,
    But ready now to pay to Life
    The debt I owe to Art.
    My new fiancé, Denzil here,

Is keen on heavy petting.
He wants to go too far with me
And by God I'm going to let him.

THROBBING: (*To* CONNIE) Your future hopes, your married bliss
On firm foundations rest.
Who knows, one day, I just might be
A guest upon that breast.
My life I squandered waiting
Then let my chance go by.
One day we'll meet in Heaven.
That Matlock in the sky.

MRS SWABB: That's a refreshing change. The first time this evening everyone has had their trousers on.
(*Enter* PURDUE *without trousers.*)
I might have known. Where are your trousers?

PURDUE: I gave them to him. You don't need trousers where I'm going. I've just taken fifty sleeping pills. The pink ones.

WICKSTEED: Those aren't sleeping pills. They're laxatives.

MRS SWABB: He's right. You don't need trousers where he's going.
(THROBBING *presides over wedding of* DENNIS *and* FELICITY.)

DENNIS: Yes, I take this woman.
For my lawful wedded wife.

FELICITY: To honour, love and cherish.
The remainder of his life.

DENNIS: It will be longer than she thinks.

MRS SWABB: And shorter than he knows.

FELICITY: My breast is filled with happiness.

CONNIE: And mine with cellulose.
(*All dance.*)

MRS SWABB: The body's an empty vessel,
The flesh an awful cheat,
The world is just an abattoir,
For our rotting lumps of meat.

So if you get your heart's desire,
Your longings come to pass,
Remember in each other's beds
It isn't going to last.
The smoothest cheek will wrinkle
The proudest breast will fall.
Some sooner go, some later
But death will claim us all.

WICKSTEED: No, no, no. Well, yes . . . but. . . .

MRS WICKSTEED: But what?

WICKSTEED: But on those last afternoons in the bed by the door.
On the Clement Attlee Ward,
When you mourn the loss of energy
Even Lucozade cannot replace
And Sister Tudor thinks you may go any time,
Do you think that you think
Of the things that you did
Or the things that you didn't do?
The promise broken, the meeting you missed,
The word not spoken, the cheek not kissed.
Lust was it or love? Was it false or true?
Who cares now?
Dying you'll grieve for what you didn't do.
The young are not the innocent, the old are not the wise,
Unless you've proved it for yourselves,
Morality is lies.
So this is my prescription: grab any chance you get
Because if you take it or you leave it,
You end up with regret.

(*All go, leaving him.*)

Put it this way.

A VOICE: Arthur.

WICKSTEED: Whatever right or wrong is
He whose lust lasts, lasts longest.

(*He dances alone in the spotlight until he can dance no more.*)

CURTAIN

ENJOY

CHARACTERS

WILFRED CRAVEN (DAD)
CONNIE CRAVEN (MAM)
MS CRAIG
LINDA CRAVEN
HERITAGE
ANTHONY
GREGORY
MRS CLEGG
ADRIAN
SID
HARMAN
CHARLES
ROWLAND

Enjoy was first presented on 15 October 1980, at the Vaudeville Theatre, by Michael Codron with the following cast:

WILFRED CRAVEN	Colin Blakely
CONNIE CRAVEN	Joan Plowright
MS CRAIG	Philip Sayer
LINDA CRAVEN	Susan Littler
HERITAGE	Roger Alborough
ANTHONY	Julian Ronnie
GREGORY	Steven Flynn
MRS CLEGG	Joan Hickson
ADRIAN	Graham Wyles
SID	Michael Hughes
HARMAN	Marc Sinden
CHARLES	Simon Painter
ROWLAND	Gareth Price

Directed by Ronald Eyre

Playgoers who find that this text does not coincide with what they heard in the theatre may assume that the cast just did not know their lines. They will (I hope) be wrong. The text here printed is that of the play prior to rehearsal and production.

The chorus 'For unto us a child is born' from Har.del's Messiah.
*The music is cut off sharply in full flow, there is a brief silence and
the curtain rises on the living-room of a back-to-back house in the
North. The outside door opens directly on to the street and other
doors lead to the scullery and the upstairs. It is neat and ordinary
and some effort has been made to improve the place. There should be
something not quite right about the room . . . Is it that the furniture
is too far apart (as it is, for example, in opera)? Or is it islanded in
the centre of the stage with space round it . . . a stage upon a stage?
Perhaps it's just that the room is too real.*

MAM *and* DAD *are a couple in their sixties. They are discovered in
the middle of their marriage.*

DAD *sits in the easy chair by the fire.* MAM *stands.*

DAD: (*Answering a question, with controlled anger*) Sweden.

MAM: Sweden?

DAD: Sweden.

> (MAM *goes into the scullery and* DAD *roots in the depths of the
> chair for a magazine, which he holds close to his face as his
> eyes are bad.*
>
> MAM *starts singing 'Fly Home Little Heart' (Novello,* King's
> Rhapsody). *She sings well and knows all the words. She stops
> singing, abruptly, comes back, whereupon* DAD *puts the magazine
> away.*)

MAM: This room's upside down. (*Pause*) Where? Dad.

DAD: Sweden.

MAM: Sweden. It's news to me is that. (*Pause*) What if anybody
comes?

DAD: Feel my arm.

MAM: It's like a tip.

DAD: Two minutes.

MAM: It's where they commit suicide and the king rides a
bicycle, Sweden.

DAD: Mam.

MAM: I don't want to feel your arm. What do I want to feel your
arm for? I'm always feeling your arm. Feel your own arm.
(*She feels his arm.*) You use this arm, you.

DAD: That's the point: I don't use it. I can't use it. I can't feel
it.

MAM: It's an excuse. You curry sympathy. Do you feel that?
(DAD *shakes his head.*)
This?
(DAD *shakes his head again.*)

DAD: Don't stop.

MAM: I'm bored.

DAD: You've nothing better to do.

MAM: I have. I've the milk bottles to put out.
(MAM *goes back into the scullery.*)

DAD: It wants a different environment. The new flats have this
underfloor central heating.

MAM: (*Off*) You've let it beat you, that arm. You want to make it
a challenge, something to be overcome. That's today's
philosophy with handicaps. You see it on TV all the time.
There's people with far worse than your arm gone on to not
bad careers.

DAD: I've no feeling in one arm; I've got a steel plate in my
head; I can hardly see and you talk about a career. I thought
I was retired.

MAM: (*Off*) I wish women could retire. (*Pause*) What have I
come in here for?

DAD: I haven't lost my gift for responsibility. That's something
you never lose, the ability to command respect. Milk bottles.
I had six men under me.

MAM: (*Returning with the bottles*) Well it's not a bad little biscuit
barrel. Women don't get biscuit barrels choose how long
they work.

DAD: Once we get shifted I plan to take an active part in the
community association; I was thinking in bed last night I
might take up French.

MAM: As the victim of a hit-and-run driver I think you're
entitled to put your feet up. (*She is at the door putting the
milk bottles out.*) Smoke rising from the Grasmeres. The toll
of destruction goes on. I've no tears left. (*She sits down
again.*) Where did you say Linda's gone?

(DAD *groans.*)

I felt your arm.

DAD: Sweden. Sweden. Linda has gone to Sweden.

MAM: I won't ask you again.

DAD: You will.

MAM: I won't. I'll think about something else. (*Pause*) My
mother lost her memory. I think.

(*Pause*)

(*Looking at a magazine.*) They're bonny curtains. Only
they're nylon. I wouldn't have nylon. Smells, nylon. I
wouldn't have any man-made fibres. Wool, cotton, you can't
go wrong.

'Try these easy to make prepared in advance menus and be
a relaxed and carefree hostess when the doorbell rings.'

(*Pause*)

Have I asked you where Linda has gone?

DAD: Yes.

MAM And have you told me?

DAD: Yes.

MAM: I know then? (*She looks miserable.*)

DAD: Sweden, Sweden, Sweden, Sweden. Sweden.

(*Pause*)

MAM: We're under siege here. Pulling down good property. It's
a sin.

DAD: I think of the future.

MAM: When I was a girl there were droves and droves of houses
like these. You'd see them from the railway, streets of them,
the stock of every town and city in the country. What's
become of the old estates? Streets were played in when we
were little, courted in when we were young . . . Harringtons,
Hawkesworths, Gilpins, Grasmeres . . . groves deserted,
drives emptied, terraces reaped of every house. Rubble.

DAD: Light! Air!

MAM: We're a relic. An ancient monument. We are living in the last back-to-backs in Leeds. (*She goes into the scullery singing 'Bless This House' (Brahe).*)

DAD: I have high hopes of the maisonette, Mam. I mean it to be a new start. A different going on.

(MAM *sings on.*)

I'm looking forward to the chrome-plated handles on the bath. That'll transform my life. And non-slip vinyl. Vinyl throughout. There's even vinyl in the lifts.

MAM: (*Returning*) It's best not to expect too much. The worst is the most I intend to expect. Then I shan't be disappointed.

DAD: No more trailing to the bin. Just chuck it down the chute. It's the last word in waste disposal.

MAM: They pee in those lifts. It takes more than a bit of vinyl to alter human nature.

DAD: It's south facing so I was thinking in bed last night I can go in for a few tomatoes.

MAM: They found a baby down one of those chutes.

DAD: We could be self-sufficient where tomatoes are concerned. I shall sit out on that bit of grass.

MAM: Another mecca for dogs.

DAD: It's a new life beginning! (*He opens his arms wide in an expansive gesture.*) Come, bulldozer, come!

MAM: What's she doing going to Sweden? I bumped into her in the scullery last night and I don't remember anything about Sweden. She didn't look like someone going to Sweden. I wonder where she does go sometimes.

DAD: She's a personal secretary. She goes where she's told. That's the nature of her employment.

MAM: She's just this minute come back from some other place abroad. West Germany was it? Now it's Sweden.

DAD: That's the contemporary world.

MAM: She didn't have any luggage. You have luggage if you're going to Sweden.

DAD: Not in this day and age. It's like popping across the road. A new world. And don't go calling our Linda.

MAM: I'm not calling her. I'm only saying you don't waltz out of the house empty-handed last thing at night saying, 'I'm going to Sweden', even if it is the twentieth century.

DAD: What do you know about the twentieth century? I know one thing. She'd feel my arm. She loves me does Linda.

MAM: If we're talking of love I know somebody else who'd have liked Sweden, somebody else with whom it'd 've struck a chord.

DAD: Guide-books, street-plans: she'll have Stockholm at her fingertips.

MAM: I admit the person in question generally made a bee-line for the Mediterranean, but given the right circumstances he wouldn't have said No to Scandinavia. Talking of love.

DAD: If I know her boss it'll be one long round of conferences, our Linda there at his elbow. Still she'll generally manage to snatch an hour or two from her gruelling schedule to take in the principal sights. She might even get to a sauna. It's where saunas originated, Sweden.

MAM: They've spread to Leeds now, talking of love.

DAD: Sweden boasts some fine modern architecture plus a free-wheeling attitude towards personal morality. But our Linda's a sensible girl: she won't be bowled over by that.

MAM: He always had a level head. Only he was quite happy to stay at home. He was the stay-at-home type. Talking of love.

DAD: Then why didn't he?

MAM: Why didn't he what?

DAD: Stop at home.

(*Pause*)

MAM: Dad.

DAD: What?

MAM: How will anybody find us when we move?

DAD: Who?

MAM: Anybody anxious to locate us. With the house pulled down where will they start?

DAD: Who?

MAM: A casual visitor, say. A one-off caller. Anybody.

DAD: You send out cards. They give you cards to send out.

MAM: That's nice.

(*Pause*)

Dad. What if it's someone you can't send a card to because

you've lost touch?

DAD: Too bad.

MAM: The Corporation's bound to keep a schedule. You'll be able to walk into the Town Hall and find out where we've been put. They'll keep track—we pay rates.

DAD: It won't happen. He'll not come.

MAM: Who?

DAD: I won't say his name.

MAM: How do I know to whom you're referring then? Who, Dad?

DAD: You won't get his name out of me.

MAM: I wonder if he's famous: he went to London.

DAD: Yes, we know what for.

MAM: Its institutions and libraries. Its public buildings, the concerts, art galleries and places of interest.

DAD: Not forgetting its superb toilet facilities. The dimly lit charms of its public conveniences. Purlieus of that nature. Talking of love.

(*Silence*)

MAM: Sweden was where Mr and Mrs Broadbent went last year. One of these winter-break things. Very reasonable apparently: they couldn't get over the public transport.

DAD: You want to forget about him.

MAM: Who?

DAD: You're losing your memory, capitalize on it and forget him. Because I do not want his name mentioned. You will never see him again. He is dead. He does not exist.

MAM: Why am I sitting on this chair? I never sit on this chair. I don't remember ever sitting on this chair before.
(*A knock on the door.*) That must be Linda. She can't have gone to Sweden. She must just have forgotten her key.
(MAM *looks out of the window.*)
It's not Linda. It's a young woman.

DAD: What sort of young woman?

MAM: A young woman. She looks like a total stranger.

DAD: They tell you not to open the door. They put out leaflets.

MAM: Professional type. Little grey costume—blondeish.

DAD: There's all sorts now. The women are worse than the men.

They're devoid of conscience. She'll go away.

(*A loud knock.*)

MAM: Very slim. Looks as if she keeps off the carbohydrates.

DAD: Be still.

(*They wait.*

Another knock.

DAD *gets up. Looks. Goes to the door. Shouts through the letter-box.*)

DAD: Listen. We're on the telephone and there's an Alsatian within earshot. So get lost.

(DAD *is coming away from the door when there is another knock.*)

Be told. You have come to the wrong house.

MAM: She may be from the Corporation, it's a smart little costume. (*Shouting through the letter-box.*) If it's about the new flat we're waiting to be allocated; we're an oldish couple; we don't have that many visitors.

(*A piece of paper is put through the letter-box.*

They let it lie for a moment, looking at it, then MAM *picks it up.*)

(*Reading*) 'This neighbourhood is shortly to be demolished.' Well, we know that. 'In the past, redevelopment has often ignored many valuable elements in the social structure of traditional communities such as this. Their sense of identity has been lost and with it the virtues of self-reliance, neighbourliness and self-help.' This is going to take some studying out. 'Your council is anxious to avoid the mistakes of the past and preserve those qualities.' What qualities? Oh, self-reliance, neighbourliness and self-help. 'It is therefore undertaking a social study of selected families in this area . . .' They do this sort of thing now. It's the sort of thing they do. 'This card will be shown to you by a qualified sociologist. Kindly admit him/her to your home as an observer. The observer will not speak.' (Oh.) 'Try not to engage him/her in conversation as this may falsify the true picture of your home life he/she needs if this project is to succeed. The name of your observer is Ms Craig. Your co-operation is appreciated. R. S. Harman. Projects Director.' I've seen his picture in the *Evening Post*, cutting a ribbon.

DAD: No.

MAM: We must have been selected; they've picked us out down at the Town Hall.

DAD: It's an intruder.

MAM: They couldn't go to twenty-six with him being black: they'll know we're a bit more classy. Fasten your trousers. (*Through the letter-box.*) We shan't keep you a moment. (*She tidies the already tidy room.*)

DAD: It's been on the wireless: don't open your door.

MAM: She's only going to observe us. They put a premium on consultation nowadays. We ought to be flattered. And she's a striking woman. Of course, it's a goodish salary now, local government.

DAD: She's come to kill me.

MAM: She's not above twenty-five.

DAD: She'll kill me.

MAM: Kill you? She's got one of these new briefcases, I've seen them in Schofields. She's from the Council. They don't kill you from the Council: what with social workers, meals on wheels and one thing and another all their efforts are the other way. They want to keep you alive. Come to kill you! Take one of your tablets.

DAD: There'll be murder.

(*Another knock.*)

I'm telling you. Don't open it.

MAM: Don't. Don't. It's always don't. The doors I could have opened if it hadn't been for you. My voice would have opened any door. I could have been in the Choral Society, sung on the stage of the Victoria Hall. I could have been rubbing shoulders with doctors' wives, solicitors, people with their own transport. I could have been going out to coffee mornings in select neighbourhoods, mixing with all sorts. I could have blossomed half a dozen times over. But no. Why? You. You, Dad, you.

DAD: Connie.

(DAD *rises from the chair.* MAM *pushes him back.*)

MAM: Sit down. We'll see if she kills you. Coming.

(*She unlocks the door.*

*There is a slight pause, long enough for one to begin to wonder
if there is still anybody there, then the door is pushed smartly
back and to the strains of 'Waltz of My Heart' (Novello, The
Dancing Years)* MS CRAIG *comes in, walks straight across the
room with no hesitation at all, sits on an upright chair down
stage, puts down her handbag at one side of the chair, takes out
a pad and waits, pen in hand.*

MS CRAIG *is a man. Not a man in outrageous drag, a man who
is a woman perhaps but nevertheless a man.*

Silence.

MAM *looks at him/her for a long time.*

DAD *keeps looking and looking away. He can't see* MS CRAIG *all
that clearly.)*

MAM: How do you do. Pleased to meet you.

(MS CRAIG *looks coolly at them with no response whatsoever.*)

This is my husband, Mr Craven. And I'm Mrs Craven.
We're The Cravens.

(*Pauie*)

DAD: I'm frightened, Mam.

MAM: Then have one of your tablets. He gets over-anxious. It's
not mental. He's the victim of a hit-and-run driver. Don't
start yet, this isn't typical yet. I'm sorry the place is upside
down, I haven't had a chance to get round this morning,
that's not typical either. Haven't we been having some
weather?

DAD: Mam!

MAM: She's starting.

DAD: Connie.

MAM: Shut up.

(*Silence.*)

Our visitor hasn't picked the most comfortable chair, has she,
Dad? (*Pause*) Though I've read that a straight back is better
for you. (*Pause*) Bad backs seem to be on the increase.
(*Pause*) It must be to do with sitting habits. One way and
another. (*Desperately*) My sister-in-law had a terrible back
and they put that down to lolling about in easy chairs, only
then it turned out that she had a progressive disease of the
spine. Which she died of. Unfortunately. (*Pause*)

DAD: It was a slipped disc.

MAM: It wasn't a slipped disc. It was a long-term illness.

DAD: How do you know? You can't remember.

(MS CRAIG *makes a note*.)

Mam. She's just made a note. What did I say?

(MS CRAIG *writes something else down*.)

Look, Mam.

MAM: I'm taking no notice. (*Whispering*) Dad, what is the survey about again?

(DAD *hands her the schedule and* MAM *reads it again*.)

I have a tendency to forget: one of the penalties of getting older. I take after my mother; she suffered with her memory. Is it to do with us being happy? Is that the gist of it? We are.

DAD: And if we're not, we shouldn't let on to you.

MAM: We are anyway, by and large. Put down happy. Not discontented.

DAD: We will be happy once we're out of this midden.

MAM: It used to be one of the better streets, this. You were always thought to be a bit more refined if you lived in this street. It was that bit classier. None of them are very classy now.

DAD: Course they're not classy. How can they be classy when they're flattened?

MAM: Mr Craven's always been on the side of progress: he had false teeth when he was twenty-seven. Notice too that this is an end house, giving us three downstairs windows as opposed to two in the other houses. I don't know whether that's relevant.

DAD: I had six men under me.

MAM: We've been very happy all in all. I'd offer you a cup of tea but if we're meant to behave as if you're not here I can't, can I?

(MS CRAIG *writes something down*.)

Don't put me on record as not having offered though. If you were an ordinary run-of-the-mill visitor I would.

DAD: We never have any visitors.

MAM: Only because we're not well served by public transport.

I'd like to have gone in for these coffee mornings. You read about them in magazines: functions in the home in aid of one thing and another. Like-minded people. Only Mr Craven's not keen on company. One of the big might-have-beens. I'll make some tea. You go on behaving normally, Dad.

(MAM *goes into the scullery singing 'I Can Give You the Starlight'* (*Novello*, The Dancing Years). *She calls from the scullery.*)

We're waiting for our Linda. (*Pause*) We think she may have gone somewhere. (*Pause*) Where is it we think she's gone, Dad?

DAD: *Sweden.*

MAM: Mr Craven worships Linda. (*Pause*) Tell her about Linda, Dad.

DAD: Shut up about Linda.

(MS CRAIG *writes something down.*)

She's a personal secretary.

MAM: She's a personal secretary. She's our only daughter.

DAD: Our only child. Goes all over. Last week it was West Germany. You've never been to West Germany, I bet. She spent Christmas in the Lebanon. A grand girl. Everything a father could wish for.

(MAM *returns.*)

MAM: She's quite at home in hotels; can choose from a menu without turning a hair. He's deeply proud of her. Where is it she's gone?

DAD: I said to her last time she was home: Did you ever dream you'd be in Beirut? But she's very modest: she just laughed.

MAM: Just laughed. Where was it she liked? Antwerp, was it?

DAD: Antwerp! *Hamburg.*

MAM: I forget, you see. My mother was like that. It's boys that generally travel. Daughters are more the stay-at-home type. Linda's different.

DAD: She was a wanderer, right from being a kiddy. It was always: Get out the atlas, Dad. Let me sit on your knee. Show me Las Vegas, Dad. Rio de Janeiro.

MAM: Sat on his knee. Las Vegas. Rio de Janeiro.

DAD: They advertised for a Girl Friday. Someone with the ability to arrange small private lunches and take creative decisions in a crisis. She's strong on both those points.

MAM: She takes air travel in her stride. It's a shame she's not here. You'd have had something in common.

DAD: What?

MAM: Both career women.

DAD: There's no comparison.

MAM: He idolizes Linda. Only she's not normal for girls round here.

DAD: Normal? She's exceptional. You won't find girls like Linda stood on every street corner. Girls with no advantages who are in a position to fly off to Scandinavia at five minutes' notice.

MAM: They've both done well.

(*At 'both'* MS CRAIG *looks up.*)

DAD: I can hear a kettle.

MAM: Right from the start we were determined neither of them should have to go through what we went through.

DAD: I can hear a kettle. Make the bloody tea, go on.

(DAD *makes some threatening move towards* MAM *with his stick as she goes.*)

Go with her. Go on.

(MS CRAIG *doesn't stir.*)

So it's me you're watching? Not her. What for? There's only me, sitting. (*Pause*) And that's not real, not accurate. Because you're here too. You spoil it. Go away and I might be natural. Me alone in a room. What's that like? You'll never know. Private, madam. My secret. (*Pause*) And don't think you're going to pick up any information about me and her either. Our so-called sexual relations. If that's the sort of gen you're after you go out of here on your arse. I make no apology for using that word. On your arse. I know you want to know. You're just the sort of casual caller that does. Well, no. No. No. (*He bangs his stick closer to her but she does not flinch.*) Write *that* down. (*She doesn't. Pause*) Still, I'm not an unreasonable man. You've got your job to do. And I don't want to give you the idea I'm trying to hide something, or that anything unorthodox goes on between my wife and me. It doesn't. Nothing goes on. Nothing at all. I don't know whether that's unorthodox. Judging from all these magazines it probably is. No foreplay. No afterplay. And fuck all in between. But don't expect me to expand on that. What made you do this job?

(MS CRAIG *makes a note.*)

So far as the formal sex act is concerned, in the actual performance of sexual intercourse, or coitus or whatever you were brought up to say, I start off at some disadvantage. I've no feeling in this arm and I can hardly see. Which knocks out at least three erogenous zones for a kick-off. I was run over down at Four Lane Ends.

(*In the scullery* MAM *is singing 'We'll Gather Lilacs'* (*Novello,* Perchance to Dream).)

I was on a crossing. I was within my rights. He came straight at me. It wasn't a genuine accident. I don't think it was an accident at all. It was a deliberate attempt at murder. The police kept the file open for months but they never found him. Do you drive? I expect so. They all have cars on the Council. I don't bear a grudge. I did bear a grudge for a long time, only now they've put me on tablets, since when the grudge has gone. But there's no feeling in that arm. I couldn't tell if this hand was wet or dry, if you understand me. It's numb. Grip it. Go on. Grip it hard. Listen, I'm old enough to be your father. You can't afford to turn your nose up at me. Bite it. Go on. Bite the bugger.

(*She doesn't.*)

No, you're like her. You're two of a kind. She won't either.

MAM: (*From scullery*) How do you like your tea, Dad?

DAD: We've been married twenty-five years. Strong. I like it strong. 'Dad.' You never asked me my name. It's Wilfred. Wilf. Only it never gets used. Always Dad. It's practically new, my name; it's hardly been used since we were first married. It's kept for best. She'll use it when I'm dying, you'll see. She'll fetch it out then.

(*Pause*)

Linda touches it. Linda strokes it. Linda wants the feeling

back. She's a saint is Linda. Only what good's that when she's in bloody Sweden?

(MAM *comes in with a nice tea-tray*.)

MAM: Who are you talking to?

DAD: I'm talking to madam.

MAM: There's nobody here, Dad. Nobody here at all. (*She winks at* MS CRAIG.) We're just having a normal day.

DAD: Where's my beaker? Which cups are these? We don't use these cups.

MAM: (*Sotto voce*) Dad.

(DAD *belches*.)

Pardon.

DAD: What?

MAM: Beg pardon. I don't know what sort of impression this young lady's getting. I'm trying to behave normally and you seem bent on showing us up.

(DAD *gets up*.)

Where are you going?

DAD: For a piss.

(MRS CRAVEN *is mortified*.)

MAM: He wouldn't say that normally. He'd say anything but that. Pay a visit. Spend a penny. There's half a dozen ways you can get round it if you make the effort. He's just trying to impress.

DAD: Well what about you?

MAM: What?

DAD: Normally every time I get up to go to the lav, you say 'Don't wet on the floor.'

MAM: I never do.

DAD: Without fail. She does 'Don't wet on the floor, Dad.' (*He goes*.)

MAM: I don't say that. I promise. Though he is very slapdash. He puts it down to his arm but frankly I think he doesn't concentrate.

(*Pause*)

We were the first couple in this street to install an inside toilet. You could say we were pioneers in that department. Then everybody else followed suit. (*Pause*) When we first came there was all that having to go down the street. I never liked that. (*Pause*) Mr Craven's not been well. He's on tablets. The aftermath of being run over. One of these hit-and-run drivers. Are you motorized? Practically everybody is nowadays. Without a car you're static. It was after his accident he started imagining things. Someone was trying to kill him. Dr Sillitoe's got him on tablets for depression. It's not mental, in fact it's quite widespread. A lot of better-class people get it apparently. I'm surprised I haven't had it because you're more at risk if you're sensitive, which I am. More than Dad anyway. Only it's not mental. Health is a great gift. He reckons he'll be better once we get into these horrible new flats but I have my doubts. They're not the high flats. Not the multis. They've discontinued those. It's a maisonette. They're built more on the human scale. That's the latest thing now, the human scale. Still I've no need to tell you that, if you're from the Housing.

(DAD *returns.*)

DAD: She's not from the Housing. She's doing a survey. She's seeing how we live. I put her in the picture *vis-à-vis* our sex-lives.

MAM: I think I'll just have a run round with the Ewbank.

DAD: I was telling her in graphic detail how nothing happens.

MAM: I wage a constant battle against dust.

DAD: I was hoping she'd be able to furnish me with some comparative statistics.

MAM: It's having an audience. Saying stuff. Ordinarily speaking we never have a wrong word.

DAD: We do.

MAM: We don't.

DAD: We fucking well do.

MAM: And he doesn't swear.

DAD: I do. I fucking do.

MAM: He doesn't use that word.

DAD: What word?

MAM: The word he just used.

DAD: Well say it. Say it.

MAM: NO. That isn't my husband. I forget your name. What is it you're from?

DAD: Read it. Read it. *Read it.* (*He hands* MAM *the paper.*) I'm telling her the same thing sixteen times over.

MAM: You'd better go.

DAD: Sit still.

MAM: You've changed your tune. You didn't want her in here. She was going to kill you. He's all over you now.

DAD: It's something fresh for me, having a witness. It's a change from suffering in silence.

MAM: It's all a performance. For your benefit. We don't live like this. Granted we have the occasional difference but when it's just the two of us we get on like a house on fire.

DAD: It's a hell-hole. I had six men under me.

MAM: He sits there. Never does a hand's turn. Always under my feet. I'm following him round picking up this, wiping up that. Retirement. Women don't retire, do they? When's our whip-round? I keep that toilet like a palace.

DAD: This is her number-one topic. Have you noticed? Have you got that written down? My wife is the world authority on toilets. She has an encyclopaedic knowledge. She could go on TV. One of these general-knowledge programmes, except where normal folks say they know about Wordsworth or Icelandic sagas, she'd opt for toilets.

MAM: Shut up. Don't listen.

DAD: Day in day out, you talk about nothing else.

MAM: I don't. I talk about all sorts. What were we talking about before she knocked at the door? Something. He has me this way, you see, because I can't remember. My memory's poor. My mother was the same. But we have proper conversations. It isn't just toilets. We really run the gamut sometimes. What were we talking about before?

DAD: We were talking about the new flats.

MAM: That's right. Well that's not toilets.

DAD: The chrome handles on the baths.

MAM: You see.

DAD: The vinyl flooring.

MAM: Vinyl flooring. That's right. We were talking about vinyl flooring. We were having a really good conversation about vinyl flooring.

DAD: The flats have vinyl flooring. Vinyl flooring throughout.

MAM: That's right.

DAD: Even in the lifts.

MAM: Yes. (*Absently*) They pee in those lifts.

(MAM *cries out in dismay and covers her face in her hands.* DAD *says nothing but stretches out his arms as if to say 'My wife.'*)

I forget.

DAD: It's not simply you forget. You forget that you do forget half the time. That's what I can't stand. If you could only remember that you forget it'd make it easier. For me.

MAM: Well I do forget. I know that.

DAD: And everything you've said, you've said before. Sixteen times. Every question you ask, you've asked before. Every remark you make, I've heard. I've heard it nineteen times over. Day after day after day.

MAM: We're married.

(*Long pause.*)

There's a couple down the street would do better than us. He's black but she always passes the time of day. They're more typical than we are.

DAD: Stay there.

MAM: If you wanted to go two doors down there's one of these single-parent families. And he's a problem child. That's quite typical of round here too. We're not typical.

DAD: We're not typical because of you. I'm the typical one.

MAM: You're depressed. You're on tablets. That's not typical. There's none of that on our side of the family.

DAD: I may be depressed, only I've still got hopes. This house depresses me. You say I don't help, I've given up trying. Because when I do it's 'Don't use that bucket, that's the outside bucket.' 'Don't use that cloth, I use that to do under the sink.' It's a minefield this house. She's got it all mapped out. The dirty bits and the clean bits. Bits you have to wash your hands after, bits you wash your hands before. And aught that comes into contact with me is dirty. I dirty it.

MAM: Well you do. You don't take care.

DAD: I pollute my own house. Me, I'm the shit on the doorstep.

MAM: That's a word he's heard other people say. He only says it to impress you. It's no crime, cleanliness.

DAD: I am clean.

MAM: You're not. They aren't clean, men. Except our Linda's the same.

DAD: Yes. She's like me is Linda. She's got her priorities right.

MAM: Linda. It's all Linda. Well I had somebody like me, once. He was clean.

DAD: Be quiet.

MAM: Sixteen. Clean. Quiet. Shy.

DAD: Shut up.

MAM: Your own son.

DAD: I haven't got a son.

MAM: You haven't got a son? Who is it I've got in my mind's eye then? A son. A clever son. A son who came top all through school. A lovely, lovely son.

DAD: Gone. Dead. No son.

MAM: No son, no son: no time for son, no room for son. All Linda.

DAD: Shut up about Linda. I love Linda. I love her.

MAM: Yes. I know you do.

(DAD *hits her.*

As he does so, MS CRAIG *involuntarily gets up. It is a startling departure, more startling than the blow, and it has the effect of stopping them dead in their tracks. They both focus on her.*

MS CRAIG *instantly recovers her composure, sits down again and makes a very small note.*

Pause)

MAM: She's written it down, that blow. It'll go on record down at the Town Hall. Next thing is we'll be pestered with social workers.

DAD: I didn't mean it, Connie.

MAM: They won't know that. They'll think that's the normal pattern of events. We should have sent her away.

DAD: We should never have let her in in the first place. We're too old for this guinea-pig lark.

MAM: He never hits me. He's not struck me in ten years!

DAD: It eggs you on, somebody sat there. It's all right her saying nothing but that eggs you on more. She wormed all sorts out of me while you were in the scullery, just sitting there.

MAM: Me and all.

DAD: We're in the computer now. Push a button and up will come the particulars. We can forgive and forget but not the computer.

MAM: What have we to be ashamed of? This is a happy marriage.

DAD: I'm turning her out.

MAM: We've done nothing but fratch ever since you arrived. We go for days and never have a wrong word. You aggravate matters, you distort things, watching, sitting there.

DAD: Having to pretend you're not here. You are here, taking it all in. So out, madam. Now. Come on. This is my house. It's my right.

(MS CRAIG *doesn't move.*)

MAM: Go on, love. If Dad thinks it's best you go. (*No response.*) For our sakes! You know what he's like. Dad knows best. It's not just him. We'd both like you to go. We've talked it over.

DAD: Not like. No like about it. I've told you. Get out. And take your notebook with you. (*He picks up* MS CRAIG's *handbag and hands it to her.*) We're fed up of being scrutinized. Condescended to. Criticized implicitly. We don't want somebody educated in this house. So off. Out.

MAM: Don't hit her, Dad. Not her head, Dad.

DAD: Looked at, made notes on. Sized up, pinned down. Assessed, cheapened, dismissed, ridiculed. Well it's over. Finished. Now. Right?

(MS CRAIG *slowly and deliberately rises, when the door opens suddenly and* LINDA *hops in, holding her ankle.*)

LINDA: Shit!

MAM: (*Brightly*) Hello, Linda!

LINDA: *Shit!*

MAM: We thought you'd gone somewhere abroad. Where was it we thought she'd gone, Dad? Somewhere.

LINDA: Shit shit shit.

MAM: Linda's a personal secretary.

(LINDA *isn't a personal secretary.* LINDA *is quite plainly a tart.*)

LINDA: Forty-five quid. Forty-five flaming quid. And the heel's snapped clean off.

MAM: You don't get the workmanship now. Everything's the same. Particularly electrical goods.

LINDA: Listen. These shoes cost nearly fifty quid. They were hand-stitched. Made in Rumania. You can't get better workmanship than that. They're Rumanian pigskin. Only they were designed for use on fitted carpets. Not obstacle courses. Not mountaineering. Have you been outside that door? It's a wilderness!

DAD: Come see your old Dad, Linda. Come give your Dad a kiss and tell us about Scandinavia.

LINDA: Shit.

DAD: Feel my arm.

LINDA: And who are we then? One silk-stockinged leg flung carelessly over the other?

MAM: She's a fellow businesswoman, Linda. It's a survey of some description. Happiness, friendship. It's all official.

DAD: Official trouble.

(LINDA *reads the form.*)

LINDA: Nice costume.

MAM: Linda always had taste. A dress sense came very early.

LINDA: What does 'traditional communities' mean?

MAM: The streets. These houses. Gilpins, Grasmeres, our overall environment.

DAD: The slums.

MAM: We were thinking you'd gone abroad somewhere.

DAD: Sweden.

LINDA: And neighbourliness means that cow next door?

MAM: Mrs Clegg has her good side, Linda. When Dad had shingles she was worth her weight in gold.

LINDA: Sweden? Swindon.

DAD: I had visions of Scandinavia. Swindon's Wiltshire.

LINDA: You just sit here? Is that all she does?

DAD: Yes, and we don't want it. On your way, you. Our Linda comes home to unwind. She's enough on her plate without you sat there annotating. What was the weather like in Swindon, love? Have it nice, did you?

LINDA: Stay if you want, sweeheart. I never object to onlookers, once in a while. It takes all sorts, that's my motto.

MAM: I agree.

LINDA: Brings out the actress in me, if you see what I mean. Course it's all acting really, isn't it?

DAD: She's wonderful, this girl. Got her philosophy of life worked out down to the last detail.

MAM: They might find they've got things in common. They've both got bags of poise.

DAD: Her legs aren't a patch on Linda's.

LINDA: I'm not staying long. It's only a flying visit.

DAD: Foreign parts again, is it, love? You and your boss. Another top-level conference. Feel my arm. All his travel arrangements at your fingertips. Every hitch anticipated by his unobtrusive Girl Friday. I love this girl. I live for this girl. Feel my arm.

LINDA: (*Still looking at the letter*) Preserve what?

MAM: A close-knit community. The society of the streets. They want to know why we're so happy.

DAD: Feel my arm. It's irrelevant to you, Linda. You triumphed over all that. You transcended it.

LINDA: Where's my suitcase? I'm leaving.

DAD: You don't need a suitcase, Linda. An overnight bag's all you want. A change of clothes and a few simple accessories. Europe these days, it's only like the next street.

LINDA: I'm leaving. How many more times?

MAM: Leaving? Why?

LINDA: I'm going to Saudi Arabia. (LINDA *goes upstairs.*)

DAD: Saudi Arabia! That's the way with Linda. One minute she's here, next minute she's flying over the Red Sea.

LINDA: (*Off*) Where's my suitcase?

MAM: Look on top of our wardrobe. She sounds to be leaving for good.

DAD: Business trip. Moment's notice. Rooms booked at the local Intercontinental Hotel. Prawn cocktail and steak diane in her room, followed by early bed so as to be fresh and alert at her boss's elbow for the first round of negotiations in the morning. It won't take her two minutes to pack. Always travels light does Linda. Got it down to a fine art. Toothbrush and briefcase, that's all she needs.

(*At this point* LINDA *comes in with a large suitcase and an equally large pink teddy bear or dog.*)

Planning to be away long, love? When is the duration of the conference?

LINDA: What conference? I'm going to Saudi Arabia. To live.

MAM: You live here, Linda. This is your home.

LINDA: This? It's a pigsty.

MAM: We're your parents.

LINDA: Yes. Fat Pig One and Fat Pig Two.

MAM: Ignore that, love. She's probably menstruating.

DAD: It's not very commodious here, I agree, but it'll be different once we're into the maisonette.

MAM: The bus service is tip top and you'll have your own room with washbasin *en suite*.

LINDA: I'm going to Saudi Arabia.

DAD: You can't. It's sons that migrate; daughters, they're supposed to live round the corner. You can confirm that. You're the sociologist.

(MS CRAIG *is blank.*)

Nod, you blank bugger.

LINDA: Who says I am your daughter anyway?

DAD: Linda!

MAM: Course you're our daughter: I bought you those slippers.

LINDA: They've brought me up, I grant you, but it would take more than that to convince me this is my mother and father. As such.

DAD: Linda. You've never voiced these doubts before.

LINDA: I've never had an independent witness before.

MAM: But we have pictures of you as a baby. On a rug. I should have kept the rug. That would have proved it.

DAD: You've staggered me a bit, Linda. I've to some extent idolized you. I must be your father. I've given you that much affection.

LINDA: I contemplated having a blood test, but I was told it wouldn't be conclusive, and even if it was it wouldn't

convince me. Though I could modify my position to this
extent: one of you may be my parent but definitely not both.

DAD: You're my daughter right enough. I recognize my dogged
determination. My optimism and will to win.

MAM: She's got my hair. Her hair's the split image of mine. Her
eyes are the same colour.

DAD: (*Contemptuously*) Blue.

MAM: She's got my skin.

LINDA: Your skin, lady? Is that your skin? I should know.

DAD: No, she's my girl, this one. Set her sights on something she
wants and she goes all out to get it. I was like that once. My
girl.

MAM: And mine.

(*Silence*)

And mine, Dad.

(DAD *doesn't answer.* MAM *weeps.*)

LINDA: Do you remember having me?

MAM: I remember having somebody. I had a lot of pain. I
remember the pain.

LINDA: What intrigues me is who the other person was. I imagine
it must have been somebody prominent in the world of
sport or entertainment. A tycoon possibly. Someone with
bags of personality at any rate. Quite frankly it wouldn't
surprise me if it was somebody extra-terrestrial.

DAD: Don't be so daft, Linda. What would I be doing with
somebody extra-terrestrial?

MAM: You must be our daughter: we love you.

LINDA: Love. You're always on about love. I don't want love. I
want consumer goods.

(LINDA *goes upstairs for a moment.* DAD *sits in flabbergasted
silence while* MS CRAIG *writes slowly.*

The ensuing conversation is partly shouted up the stairs.)

DAD: Why Saudi Arabia?

LINDA: (*Off*) It could be Kuwait. Plans aren't finalized yet.

MAM: You'd be a fool to leave Leeds. (*To* MS CRAIG.) It's a
tip-top shopping centre now they've secluded the traffic. A
pedestrians' paradise. There's some grand shops, people
come from all over. (*Pause. To* LINDA.) I saw a very

reasonable little costume in Lewis's. (*Pause*) The new precinct's gorgeous. It's all climate controlled. It's a godsend in inclement weather. Tell her, Dad. It has the biggest Boots outside Manchester.

DAD: There won't be a Boots in Kuwait.

LINDA: There will. There'll be everything there soon. Boots, Littlewoods. C. & A. They're queuing up.

MAM: Not climate controlled.

LINDA: No need to control it. It's hot.

DAD: Turning your back on all this love.

MAM: They have some right bonny little handbags in Schofields.

LINDA: I'm going to bury the past. And everyone that goes with it.

DAD: We're getting on, Linda.

MAM: Our idea was that you'd look after us in our old age. We thought you'd be bobbing in and out like daughters do. You can't do that from . . . where is it you're going? Sweden?

LINDA: I have my own young life to lead.

DAD: What will happen to us?

LINDA: You're going into the horrible new flats.

MAM: What if we can't manage?

LINDA: Contact your social worker.

MAM: We don't have a social worker. Do we?

(LINDA *should play whenever possible to* MS CRAIG.)

LINDA: Then do what everybody else does: go into a home.

MAM: We don't want to go into a home.

LINDA: Why? There's some nice homes now. Big places on the outskirts, standing in their own grounds. Drives, shrubbery, everything. One even has a lake. Feed the ducks.

DAD: Who'll come and see us.

LINDA: All sorts come. These voluntary groups. The Variety Club comes. Lions come. Unemployed school leavers come. Old folks in homes these days, they're inundated with visitors. You won't have a moment to yourselves. I can send you a postcard now and again to pin up on the door of your locker. (*To* MS CRAIG.) They provide them with lockers now. They've got much more enlightened in that respect.

MAM: I'll make a cup of tea. Oh Dad, Dad! (*She goes into the scullery.*)

DAD: Linda.

LINDA: What?

DAD: With all due respect to your mother, Linda, she is the imposter.

(LINDA *is in and out packing so* DAD *is talking to her and to* MS CRAIG.)

She doesn't take after her Mam for a start. Linda's not swilling and scrubbing and keeping the place straight. She's like me, devil may care. I'm the genuine parent. No question. But when it comes to who her mother was I'm a bit stumped. I think Linda's right, it's got to be someone who mirrors her qualities, someone with poise and bags of get up and go, somebody famous. And I have to admit my contacts with the famous have been few and far between. We had the Princess Royal down to the works once to open a new canteen. She half-paused at an adjoining table and expressed interest to some fellow workmates in the colour of the formica top, but that's as far as it went. Then I had some contact with Mrs Somebody-Something, a famous Dutch sprinter.

LINDA: A Dutch spinster?

DAD: No, love. Sprinter. She won the Olympics once before you were born. Not a particularly good-looking woman but the personality very well defined. She ran past the end of the street once in pursuit of some charity thing and I remember thinking 'Well, there's an opportunity here if I want to take it.' But to my mind the most likely candidate was one of the Rank starlets. You won't remember them. They were starlets for Rank, generally girls with large busts who'd been in films then went round the provinces officiating at functions. This one was Dawn something or something Dawn. She epitomized glamour.

LINDA: Glamour?

DAD: I met her when she was presiding over the gala opening of a discount warehouse in converted premises formerly a church. We went along for sentimental reasons . . . we'd got married there . . . and also because we were crying out for a bit of underfelt for the stairs. I know I engaged this Rank lady in conversation. I have her autograph on the back of a bill for felt underlay. It's upstairs somewhere if your so-called mother hasn't thrown it away. Whether anything actually transpired I can't say with any certainty. I have a very clear picture in my mind of something happening between us. The point is, Linda, I think you're right. That isn't your mother. That woman. You've no ties in that direction. Me, it's different. We're one and the same, you and me.

And the way I've been thinking is that with my experience in the Western Desert I'm actually cut out for Kuwait. I revel in the heat whereas your mother (her in there), she hates it. I've been begging her for years to go to Torquay only she says she was smothered at Scarborough. So where are you? Kuwait would suit my arm. The feeling would be back in no time. What do you say, Linda?

LINDA: I wasn't listening.

DAD: There's that many things I could do for you. Little jobs. I could keep your cosmetics ship-shape for instance. Not allow those nasty deposits to form round the top of your nail-varnish bottle . . . keep your mascara brushes soft and yielding . . . always have a point ready on your eyebrow pencils. Let me come, Linda.

MAM: (*Returning*) How will you make a living? You'll have to go out to work.

LINDA: Work? I shall never have to work again. I'm getting married.

MAM: Married! Oh, Linda. Why didn't you say? I'm so happy. She's getting married, Dad. Our Linda's getting married. I thought she was just going out there on spec but it's wedding bells!

DAD: I don't want her to get married. She's not ready for marriage. I've yet to meet the man that's good enough for our Linda.

MAM: Who will it be?

DAD: Kuwait? It will be one of these international oil men.

MAM: An oil man? You need a degree for that. Some form of higher education anyway. Our Linda's marrying somebody with qualifications.

(LINDA *returns*.)

When's the wedding?

LINDA: This afternoon. At least the civil ceremony. When we get to Saudi Arabia they have the religious ceremony where they slit the throat of a goat.

MAM: A goat. Oh. We've always been Church of England. Still it's nice when they believe anything at all these days. And I suppose the animals are more used to it out there. He's not an oil man then?

LINDA: Oil man? He's a prince.

MAM: A *prince*. Linda!

DAD: He's not coloured?

LINDA: Probably. I haven't seen him yet.

MAM: You haven't seen him? It's not love then?

LINDA: It might be. He's seen pictures of me.

MAM: Oh, well. It may ripen into love. These arranged things often do. Royalty it often ripens into love. You read about it. King Hussein married like that and his ripened into love. Even some of ours marry like that and it always ripens into love.

DAD: Where did he see these pictures of you?

LINDA: They were shown him by a business associate. He's sending a car.

MAM: A car, Dad! A prince is sending a car for our Linda!

LINDA: Only the bugger's late.

DAD: There won't be a car. They don't send cars for lasses who answer adverts.

LINDA: Who said I answered an advert? They're sending a car. They're sending a sodding car.

DAD: None of your secretary talk here. Who is he, then, this so-called prince? Why does he want to marry you?

LINDA: Why does anybody want to marry anybody? Why did you want to marry her?

DAD: I can't remember.

MAM: Love, wasn't it?

DAD: Candid photographs, were they? Full length?

LINDA: I was holding a bicycle and looking apprehensive. They were very tasteful.

MAM: Not taken at your desk, then? Sitting at your typewriter?

LINDA: No. I have been photographed at a desk. Sitting on a typewriter.

MAM: On it? How unusual.

DAD: Can I see them?

(LINDA *ignores this*.)

Getting all this down, are you?

MAM: I'd forgotten you. I was being utterly natural. Though this isn't normal. It's not every day Linda gets married and goes off to . . . where is it you're going, love?

LINDA: Saudi Arabia.

DAD: She's not going to Saudi Arabia.

LINDA: I bloody am.

DAD: Over my dead body.

MAM: You see. As soon as I draw their attention to you they start showing off.

DAD: You've been had. It's another con. You're always being conned. There won't be a car. Resign yourself. This is where you belong. At home with us. Feel my arm.

LINDA: No car? What's this then?

(LINDA *looks through one window*, MRS CRAVEN *with her*.)

MAM: (*Awestruck*) Is that it?

LINDA: That's just the bonnet.

MAM: Come look, Dad. It's that long, I can't even see the front of it.

(DAD *looks out of a different window*.)

DAD: I can't see the back.

LINDA: So now do you believe me?

MAM: I never doubted it. It's your Dad. He's been a sceptic ever since we were first married. What is he like, your fiancé? Quiet? Some of them can be very nicely spoken.

LINDA: I haven't *met* him.

MAM: He must have a good job, car like that.

DAD: Nobody has jobs in Saudi Arabia. They just sit over a hole in the ground and put it in cans. That's not a job.

MAM: What?

DAD: Oil, you flaming naffhead.

MAM: I'm more easy in my mind, now that I know that he's a prince and seen the car. You've done very well, Linda. The girl King Hussein married was only a shop assistant, though very vivacious apparently. Makes me wish we had a car.

LINDA: You wouldn't want a car like that. It's armour plated.

MAM: Vandals?

LINDA: Assassination.

DAD: I couldn't drive a car. Not with my arm. It'd have to be specially adapted.

LINDA: It is specially adapted: it's got a flame thrower.

MAM: Oh, that's unusual.

LINDA: One touch on the button and you're both dead. Burnt to a cinder.

MAM: Well there's all sorts of gadgets now, but if it gets you from point A to point B that's all you want.

LINDA: He's probably got it trained on you at this very moment.

MAM: Really? What will they think of next? (MAM *waves*.) That's not your fiancé driving it?

LINDA: That's the chauffeur.

MAM: He's English anyway.

LINDA: English? He's got a degree in mechanical engineering.

MAM: If he's got a degree why don't you fetch him in. He could perhaps do with a cup of tea.

LINDA: If I even looked at him they would have to chop his hands off at the elbow. Honour.

MAM: Your Uncle Graham was a bit like that. Someone looked at Thelma once and he threw them through a plate-glass window. But that wasn't religion. It was drink.

LINDA: I'll just go and have a word with him. (LINDA *goes out*.)

MAM: She'll probably have a swimming-pool.

DAD: In the car, possibly.

MAM: A cocktail bar.

DAD: Sauna.

MAM: I'd like a car with toilet facilities. W.C. Wash-hand basin. With facilities like that there'd be no need to get out of the car at all. The chauffeur looks nice. I've a sneaking wish our Linda was marrying him. Come and look at the car, love. (MS CRAIG *doesn't move*.)
It's all part of the picture. Happiness!
(MS CRAIG *gets up slowly and goes to one window and looks. Goes to the other. Sits down. Makes a slight note*.)

DAD: You don't ride in cars like that, madam.

MAM: I knew a cinema-manager a bit like him. Refined-looking. I can always pick out people who know what the word suffering means. He's coming in.

(LINDA *comes in with the handsome brute of a chauffeur,* HERITAGE.)

LINDA: Heritage wondered if you would like to look round the car and have a cocktail from the cabinet.

MAM: A cocktail. Why, what time is it? Thanks very much.

DAD: I'm stopping here with Linda. She'll be leaving us soon. Every minute is precious. (*He doesn't move.*)

MAM: You stunt me, Dad. Here's an unlooked-for opportunity for cocktails in the back of a Rolls Royce and you turn your nose up.

DAD: Linda.

LINDA: Go and have a flaming cocktail.

MAM: Are you coming, love, or are you staying to observe Linda? (MS CRAIG *doesn't move.*)

This isn't normal, of course. It's only once in a blue moon we have cocktails in the back of a Rolls Royce.

(MAM *and* DAD *go out, with* HERITAGE, MAM *singing 'Waltz of My Heart'* (*Novello,* The Dancing Years).)

LINDA: I shall be glad to see the back of this place. I can't wait to open the curtains in a morning and see minarets. (*She stands in front of* MS CRAIG.) Hello. Don't you have a little word for me then?

(*She laughs and is stroking* MS CRAIG's *face when* HERITAGE *returns. She leaves her hand on* MS CRAIG's *face for a moment before turning to him.*

She and HERITAGE *embrace passionately.*

This continues for a few moments. MS CRAIG *watches impassively.*)

LINDA: She's watching you, Brian. She's watching you kissing me. I can see her watching us. Can you?

HERITAGE No. I want to see her. I want to see her watching me.

LINDA: Get round in front of the mirror then. Get me in front of the mirror. Can you see her?

HERITAGE: Edge round.

LINDA: Oh, Brian. Can you see her?

HERITAGE: I can see her. The dirty bitch. She's just watching.
The dirty cow.

LINDA: Brian.

HERITAGE: What?

LINDA: I . . . I can't see her now.

HERITAGE: I want you to see her.

LINDA: I can't.

HERITAGE: I want to see you, seeing her, seeing me.

LINDA: We need another mirror. (*She looks round for one.*) That's
typical of this place: no amenities.

HERITAGE: I like her legs. Though she hasn't got much in the
way of tits.

LINDA: Course not. If you've got tits you don't work for the
Council; you get yourself into the private sector. Like me.
Brian.

HERITAGE: Linda.

(*They fall on the floor in front of* MS CRAIG *who moves very
slightly to accommodate them.*)

I can see right up her legs.

LINDA: You can see right up mine, if you want.

HERITAGE: Yes, only she doesn't want me to see up hers. Taking
it all in, aren't you? Watching my every move. Watching my
hands. Oh, yes.

(HERITAGE *starts to get* LINDA's *knickers down.*)

What's matter?

LINDA: I've gone off it.

HERITAGE: Well I bloody haven't.

LINDA: Well I bloody have. On the living-room floor? We're not
animals. Don't imagine this is the norm, coitus on the
carpet. I'm more on the shy side. You can't get me out of
my shell normally but it's with being on the eve of marriage:
there's a lot of unreleased tension. Mind you I knew he was
only after one thing when I saw him eyeing me in the
rear-view mirror. Kindly rejoin your vehicle.

HERITAGE: Sod you, madam.

LINDA: Don't you madam me. You're an employee.

HERITAGE: So are you.

LINDA: I am a personal secretary. I shall see my husband to be is informed of your conduct. It falls far short of the professional standards he is entitled to expect as a visitor to these shores and I hope he saws your scrotum off. He can, you know, in Saudi Arabia. They're a law unto themselves. And send them two inside, else there won't be a maraschino cherry left. And Heritage . . .

HERITAGE: Yes, madam.

LINDA: The luggage.

HERITAGE: Cow.

LINDA: Whatever happened to our tradition of service?

(HERITAGE *goes*.)

Nice of you to take an interest in the parents, so-called. I'm under intolerable pressure sometimes. I can't see what they have to live for, quite frankly. People do cling on, don't they? My problem is: I hate my loved ones. Folks do these days, I read it in *Readers' Digest*. They either love them, which means they hate them. Else they hate them, which means they love them. Of course most people keep up a façade. Only I can't, I'm just too honest. Smoke? Very wise. I'm going to give up when I get to Saudi Arabia. Do you believe in reincarnation? I do. I think that's why I can't get on with those two, they're so many turns behind me. They were probably insects last time round, whereas me, I get the feeling I'm quite advanced. I've been something Egyptian, I know that for a fact, some quite high-up handmaiden . . . I'm going back a few thousand years now. I know I was once waiting on in the temple in a ritual that culminated in human sacrifice. Another time I came over with the Vikings. As a man, of course. Sex is irrelevant in the great chain of being. Last time I think I was twins and died on the guillotine. It's fascinating when you go into it. I've read a great deal about it in paperback.

(MAM *and* DAD *are returning*.)

MAM: Nice car, Linda. The only comparable vehicle I've been in was at your Grandma's funeral. Only that didn't have a cocktail cabinet. I liked the absence of piped music. That was very tasteful. I shall save my cocktail stick as a memento.

LINDA: Right, I'm off.

MAM: Where are you going?

DAD: Linda. Aren't you going to kiss your father?

MAM: Aren't you going to kiss your mother? (Where is it she's going?)

LINDA: Saudi bloody Arabia.

MAM: Saudi Arabia. (*Weeping*) I never thought I'd have to kiss somebody goodbye who was going to Saudi Arabia.

DAD: You love us, don't you, Linda?

MAM: Course she loves us. Will it be Concorde?

LINDA: I expect so.

MAM: Fancy, Dad, our only daughter flying at twice the speed of sound plus as much champagne as she can drink.

DAD: You'll not like it. Women out there, they're rubbish.

MAM: That's their own women. They'll treat you like a goddess and if they don't you want to come straight back. With the customs being different I don't suppose they'll send out bits of wedding cake.

LINDA: No, but I'll send you some of the goat. (*She laughs.*)

MAM: Bless her. She's just trying to put a face on it, she'll be in floods of tears once she's round the corner. Maybe when you've settled in we could come out by the overland route and have a fortnight together somewhere at the seaside. Say goodbye to the young lady. Come on, Dad. Let's wave her off. (MAM *and* DAD *get up and go outside.*

MS CRAIG *remains sitting for a moment, then gets up and walks slowly round the room. She stops in front of the fireplace and looks at the mantelpiece.*)

MS CRAIG: One clock in light oak, presented to Mam's father after forty years with Greenwood and Batley. Stopped; the key lost.

A wooden candlestick that's never seen a candle. A tube of ointment for a skin complaint that cleared up after one application. An airmail letter, two years old, announcing the death of a cousin in Perth, Western Australia, the stamp torn off. Two half-crowns not cashed at decimalization because Mam read in the *Evening Post* that one day they would be priceless. Four old halfpennies kept on the same principle. A dry Biro.

Various reminders on the backs of envelopes. 'Pension, Thursday', 'Dad's pills', 'Gone down the road. Dinner on'. And, starkly, 'Gas'. A rubber band. Three plastic clips from the package of a new shirt, kept by Dad with the idea it will save wasting money on paper clips. Not that he ever does waste money on paper clips.

Three tuppeny-halfpenny stamps.

A packet of nasturtium seeds on offer with some custard powder. A newspaper-cutting recording the conviction for shoplifting of the wife of the local vicar, saved to send to relatives in Canada. Dad's last appointment card at the Infirmary and two grey aspirins.

Altar, noticeboard, medicine chest, cemetery. A shrine laden with the relics of the recent past and a testimonial to the faith that one day the world will turn and the past come back into its own and there will be a restoration. The coinage will make sense once more, letters again cost twopence halfpenny and life return to its old ways. On that day the nasturtiums will be planted, the half-crowns spent, the skin complaint will recur and the ointment be applied once more to the affected part. The Biro will flow again, the second cousin in Toronto will be informed at last of the conviction of the vicar's wife and on that day the key will be found and the clock strike.

(MS CRAIG *hears* MAM *and* DAD *returning and sits down.*)

MAM: She's gone. (*Pause*) Only us now.

DAD: Be off, you. We don't want you here now Linda's gone.

MAM: No, Dad. She's not to go. She's all right where she is. We shall be wanting a bit of company.

(*To the strains of 'Fly Home Little Heart'* (Novello, King's Rhapsody) MS CRAIG *slowly takes out a cigarette and lights it.* MAM *puts an ash-tray within range of her chair. Pause.*)

MAM: Where is it our Linda's gone? (*Pause*) Dad!

DAD: Feel my arm.

(MAM's *recorded voice is heard singing 'Fly Home Little Heart' as the curtain falls.*)

MAM's *voice is heard singing 'Love is My Reason for Living'* (*Novello*, Perchance to Dream) *as the curtain rises on* DAD *and* MS CRAIG *alone.*
Long pause.

DAD: The phrase 'no love lost' has always puzzled me. As in the sentence 'There was no love lost between me and her.' What does that mean? Does it mean that the love between the persons concerned was so precious they could not bear to spill a single drop? And thus no love went to waste. Taking love as some kind of liquid. I'm thinking of me and Linda. Or does 'no love lost' mean there was no love? None whatsoever. He didn't waste any love on her or she on him, so none was lost and they both hung onto their quota.
(*Pause*)
And 'Butter wouldn't melt in her mouth.' What the fuck does that mean? Somebody could be sat there looking as if butter wouldn't melt in her mouth and I wouldn't recognize it. I should miss it.
(*Pause*)
A woman came round with leaflets once. Special offer. Dry cleaning. Eiderdowns re-covered. Very reasonable. I had her on that table. Youngish woman. White boots. Butter melted in her mouth, one way and another.
(*Pause*)
She'll forget what she's gone for. She writes it down but she forgets she's written it down. She goes out for a bit of something tasty for the tea and comes back with toilet-rolls. We'll be found starved to death and the house stuffed with toilet-rolls.

299

(*Pause*)

I'm conversing but don't be misled. I'm still inconsolable over Linda. The bitch. My own daughter. I've invested so much love in that girl over the years. Saudi Arabia. Well, I'm writing it off. As from today. It was a bad investment and I'm disappointed. But I'm not going to let it get in the way of my new life. I'm going to start mixing again. I haven't mixed properly since my accident. Now there's going to be an alteration. Once we get into the flats I shall make a point of getting to know the other occupants. Get on dropping-in terms. Drop in on them, have them drop in on me. For coffee, for instance. I shall have a real shot at being the life and soul of the party and live more like you see in the adverts. I've never been a good mixer but I've discovered the secret now. It's to take an interest in other people. That's what makes people like you. If you take an interest in them. I've read several articles in different magazines and they all say the same: 'Take an interest in other people.' I tell you I'm going to be a changed man.

(*Pause*)

Have you any hobbies?

Do you do anything in your spare time?

You're probably a person of wide interests.

Those are questions normally guaranteed to break the ice.

(*The ice remains unbroken.*)

Remember I asked anyway. Make a note. (*She doesn't.*) I can't tell you how much I welcome this opportunity of talking to you alone. She confuses matters. I hope you noticed that as soon as she went we really started to hit it off. It was like that with the boy. My son so-called. He was in perpetual partnership with his mam. I never got near. I would have liked to have put my stamp on him but I never even got to take him to a football match. We would very likely have got on like a house on fire on our own only she was always putting her spoke in, making out she and him were the big duo. He'd have loved me, given the chance, I know. I don't see how he could have stopped himself.

(*Pause*)

Are you tall?
(*A moment, then* MS CRAIG *stands up.*)
I can't see.
(*She approaches.*)
You are tall.
(*She stands in front of him.*)
Show me your hand.
(*She slowly holds out her hand.*)
It's a smooth hand. It's a big hand. It's smooth only it's big.
He'd never hold my hand when he was little. Always her
hand. I had to force him. What would you say if I asked to
hold your hand? (*He takes her hand.*) It's a father's right.
It's normal.
(MS CRAIG *looks down at him and he up at her at which point
there is a loud bang on the door.*
She unhurriedly sits down again.
*A voice comes through the letter-box. It is young, wheedling
and intimidating.*)

ANTHONY: Hello, Grandad. It's me, Grandad.
DAD: I'm not your Grandad. Go away.
ANTHONY: I want to come in, Grandad.
DAD: You can't come in. I've got somebody with me.
ANTHONY: Grandad's lying. She's gone shopping. Grandad.
　　　Grandad.
DAD: I'm not his Grandad. How could I be his Grandad? What?
ANTHONY: I've a new book to show you.
DAD: I'm not in the mood.
ANTHONY: It's a good one.
DAD: He gets these books out. War books mainly. Rommel,
　　　Monty. The war in the desert seen in terms of overall
　　　strategy.
ANTHONY: Pictures of twat. Grandad.
DAD: I'm not his Grandad.
ANTHONY: You'll like this one. (*He kicks the door.*)
DAD: He'll get bored in a bit. They do get bored his generation.
　　　We never got bored.
　　　(MR CRAVEN *takes a zinc bath from behind the door and puts it
　　　across the threshold.*)

He's a hooligan. He's been sent away once or twice but he persistently absconds. He's out of control. He sometimes has green hair.

(*The letter-box opens and* ANTHONY *proceeds to piss through it into the zinc bath.*)

That's one of his favourite tricks, pissing through the letter-box. It's another thing that makes me look forward to the new flats. They're a different class of people there. And the letter-boxes are much higher up.

(*Another bang.*)

ANTHONY: A book, Grandad.

DAD: At school they're not interested in books. The teachers can't get them to look at books. I can't let him in on your account. He has these boots somebody bought him. Steel-tipped. They don't function as boots. They don't buy them for boots, because they're hard-wearing, they buy them to kick people to death with. The manufacturers want reporting.

ANTHONY: Books.

(MS CRAIG *gets up.*)

DAD: Where are you going? Sit down. Where've you got to? Come away from that door. You'll have him inside. Leave that.

(MS CRAIG *unlatches the door and sits down again, unhurriedly. The door opens and* ANTHONY *comes in slowly, calm and smiling.*)

ANTHONY: Hello, Grandad.

(*He is about sixteen.*)

DAD: His hair's generally dyed.

(ANTHONY *has left the door open and a youngish man* (GREGORY) *comes in, notebook in hand, and leans against the wall watching.*)

Who's this? Who're you?

ANTHONY: It's Gregory, Grandad. It's my friend Gregory. He's attached to me. I'm being studied.

DAD: Studied? You've just pissed through our letter-box!

ANTHONY: I had to do that. I have to act normally. I'm not supposed to behave. It's not like probation. I do what I want. Unless I do just what I want, it's useless. Isn't it, Gregory?

(GREGORY *is impassive as is* MS CRAIG.)

DAD: Does yours talk?

ANTHONY: He says 'fuck' now and again, but in a very natural way.

DAD: That's an earring he's got. In my day it was tattooes. Now it's earrings and coloured hair. Some of them dress up in smart little suits: they're the worst of all.

ANTHONY: I want to show you a book.

DAD: I don't want to see no book. A lad of your age. You ought to be outside playing football instead of stuck inside reading books. He's not a bad boy. He's run me no end of errands in the past. When they've done dyeing their hair and putting earrings in they're just lads same as we were. See, get yourself one or two crisps. (*He tries to snatch the book.*)

ANTHONY: I hope you're taking note of this carry-on. Under ordinary circumstances he would have no hesitation. This isn't the real him. You're making him shy.

DAD: You bugger.

ANTHONY: Dad and I share a common interest in the female figure, nude for preference.

DAD: It's a lie.

(ANTHONY *puts* DAD's *stick out of reach.*)

ANTHONY: There's genuine affection here though that may be hard to credit. It is not a lie.

DAD: Young man, help me.

ANTHONY: Gregory can't help you. It's not a part of his brief. Gregory's brief is to watch me. Stay with it, Greg. What say we adhere to our usual practice, Dad. I browse through until we hit upon something of mutual interest, fair enough? She's boring for a start. You're not looking, Grandad. You've got to look.

DAD: Go away. Showing me up.

ANTHONY: You should see us, Greg. These publications are our constant study. Not looking, Grandad.

DAD: It's true I do see them now and again. But they come from a very respectable newsagent's. There are sometimes articles about people's philosophies. How they got started in life. That's what interests the discerning reader.

ANTHONY: I don't think we like her, do we? Nor the usual

Portuguese waiter with his obligatory slack dick. No thanks.

DAD: Footballers give their thoughts. Prominent businessmen discuss free enterprise. Famous novelists tell you about drinks. There's a whole world here if you know how to acquire it.

ANTHONY: Nothing so far, but I am about to turn the vital page. *Watch*, you old sod. Look. (*He covers the face of the model.*) Now. Those tits ring a bell? You're not looking. Look. *Watch*.

DAD: No. No.

ANTHONY: (*Reading*) 'When it comes to changing a wheel our Norma can beat a man hands down.'
'Norma, who hails from Southport has no trouble putting her hand on the jack but is a bit puzzled what to do with it.'
'Ah, well, next time we have a blow-out we hope Norma's in the vicinity.'
Who's that, then, Grandad?

DAD: I don't know.

ANTHONY: They've got her name wrong. Her name's not Norma. Her name's Linda.

DAD: It never is. Our Linda's got brown hair. That one's a blonde. And Linda doesn't come from Southport.

ANTHONY: A wig, Dad. She's wearing a wig.

DAD: Our Linda knows nothing about cars.

ANTHONY: It's Linda.

DAD: Linda's a personal secretary.

ANTHONY: You old tosser. Your own daughter and you don't recognize her.

DAD: It's not her. I'd know if it was her.

ANTHONY: There's something wrong with your brain, Dad, if you don't recognize your own daughter. I'm going to have to lift up your steel plate and find out.

DAD: No. Leave my head alone. Stop him. Help me.
(GREGORY *and* MS CRAIG *rise.*)

ANTHONY: Now, Greg. Remember your brief. Knock, knock. Anybody there.
(*He bangs on* DAD's *head.* DAD *slumps in the chair.*)
Shit. He's passed out. Dad? Come on, Dad. Come on. Joke over.
Well whose fault was that? You saw what happened. I was

making this big effort to behave normally and he wasn't even trying. He was allowing his conduct to be influenced by the presence of onlookers. He gets bashful, resists and naturally he gets hurt. I'm really depressed now. I like him. Up to a point we're intimate friends, only when somebody's watching the barriers go up. Though why I can't imagine. What is there to be ashamed of? We're all human basically. (ANTHONY *shows* GREGORY *the magazine then goes back.*) He's not coming round. Wake up, Wilfred! He doesn't look well. What about it, Greg?

(GREGORY *comes over slowly, looks at* MR CRAVEN *and says nothing. He is back in his position when* MAM *comes in with her shopping.*)

MAM: I'd forgotten we'd got company. I couldn't remember what it was I went for but I got one or two things that'll come in. Our usual greengrocer's been knocked down. It was a pleasant little parade: butchers, confectioners, ladies' knitwear shop. Catered for just about everything and made a nice little outing. Now there's one shop selling used office furniture and the rest is a garden centre. They want their heads examining. Has Anthony been behaving himself? Hello, Anthony. (What's happened to your green hair?) Hello? (*To* GREGORY.) The bulldozers are knocking on. No trace of the Grasmeres. Dad asleep? You asleep, Dad?

(MAM *takes the shopping, toilet-rolls, into the scullery.* ANTHONY *jerks his head to* GREGORY *and goes.* GREGORY *pauses.*)

GREGORY: (*To* MS CRAIG) That bugger looks dead to me. Something anyway.

(GREGORY *shakes his head and maybe ruffles* ANTHONY's *hair as they go.*)

MAM: (*From the scullery*) I've just remembered I went for a tin of salmon. My mother went like this, you know. She lost her memory. I didn't see anybody I knew. I got a bit of a smile from one woman but that's all; there weren't many people about. They're curtailing the buses now. Scarcely a building as far as the eye can see and then they say we're short of open spaces. (*Coming in.*) Are you all right, Dad? You haven't been having an argument? He's not sulking again?

Sat there with your mouth open. Dad. *Dad.* DAD. I think he's had a funny do. Dad. Wake up. He's had a turn. Have you noticed anything?

(MS CRAIG *is impassive.*)

Say something. There must be a case for waiving the rules now and again. Dad. Dad. It's Mam. Wilf! Wilf!

(*Pause.* MAM *goes out hurriedly.*

MS CRAIG *gets up slowly and goes over to* MR CRAVEN. *She looks at him without touching him, then picks up* ANTHONY's *magazine and glances at it. She hears* MAM *returning and goes back unhurriedly to her chair.*

MRS CRAVEN *returns with* MRS CLEGG, *her next-door neighbour, a woman of the same age and some pretensions to refinement.*

MRS CLEGG *takes in* MS CRAIG *and listens to* MR CRAVEN's *chest. As she is doing so another observer* (ADRIAN) *comes in, pad and pencil in hand and hovers about watching her.*)

MAM: Has he gone?

(MRS CLEGG *listens to* MR CRAVEN's *chest, while watching* MS CRAIG *to whom she addresses sotto voce remarks.*)

MRS CLEGG (*Mouthing*) How do you do?

MAM: He's not gone, Nora?

MRS CLEGG: Mrs Clegg. From next door.

MAM: He was right as rain when I went out. Has he gone?

MRS CLEGG: (*Still addressing* MS CRAIG) They always turn to me. First sign of a crisis, it's 'fetch Nora'.

MAM: I'd call Dr Sillitoe but I'd want to change him first. And this place is upside down.

MRS CLEGG: You don't want him trailing all the way over here on a wild-goose chase. And you can't ring up. The kiosk's been vandalized. The insides have been ripped out again. I'd rip their insides out. He's got a good colour and he's not cold. If he has gone we've only just missed him. Was he constipated at all?

MAM: I'm not sure. It's not something he'd ever discuss.

MRS CLEGG: Is he dead, that's the question? We could burn some feathers under his nose, that's a traditional method. Have you got a pillow?

MAM: Yes, but they're all foam filled.

MRS CLEGG: With polystyrene? Burn that and it gives off a deadly poison.

MAM: Nora, what's happening to the world?

MRS CLEGG: I don't know. I'd castrate them.

MAM: Would he help? (*Indicating the new observer.*)

MRS CLEGG: Out of the question.

MAM: Mine won't even converse.

MRS CLEGG: Nor mine. But if he did I've a feeling he'd be very nicely spoken.

MAM: But Nora is he dead? Till I know I'm not sure what to do. Should I be showing grief? Do I mourn or what? I don't want to jump the gun. Isn't there somebody at the Council we could ring?

MRS CLEGG: No. (*Sotto voce.*) Not with them watching us. We've got to manage. Not fall back on outside agencies.

MAM: Is this death? I'd like an official view.

MRS CLEGG: Be brave, Connie. I think you must resign yourself to the fact that your beloved hubby has passed on.

MAM: Oh, Wilf. Are you sure?

MRS CLEGG: Ninety-nine per cent.

MAM: Wilf! Wilf! He never used to call me by name. Never Connie. Always Mam. Never my name except one stage when he used to call it out when ejaculating. I think I was meant to be touched. When he saw it cut no ice he desisted. I don't think he's said my name since.

MRS CLEGG: Now. The first thing to do is to lay him out in the customary manner, wash the body and dress it in the clean clothes traditionally set aside for this purpose. (*All this is directed towards the observers.*)

MAM: Can't Chippendales do that? The undertakers.

MRS CLEGG: Chippendales has changed hands. It's now a patio-paving centre. There is no Chippendales.

MAM: No Chippendales? Oh, Nora.

MRS CLEGG: I know. I'd bastinado them.

MAM: I'm not sure he's got a clean vest. I was going to wash it. That was one of the jobs I'd got lined up for today. What must they think? My mother could have done all this by instinct.

MRS CLEGG: You'll have the coffin here, of course. Not at the Chapel of Rest. So impersonal. You want to be grateful it happened at home. I had Clifford at home.

MAM: It's a good job we haven't got into the horrible new flats. They wouldn't get coffins into the lift.

MRS CLEGG: Another example of shortsighted planning. I'd strangle them at birth.

MAM: I keep forgetting what it is they're looking for.

MRS CLEGG: Survivors, that's what they're looking for. People who haven't gone under. I don't think I disappointed them. It's a nice change for me. I haven't had somebody dogging my every footstep since Clifford died.

MAM: Will it get written up?

MRS CLEGG: I imagine in the form of a report.

(MAM *goes into the scullery for some water.*)

I know I shall figure, albeit anonymously. We're a dying breed, women like me. I could probably deliver a baby if I was ever called upon and I can administer an enema at a moment's notice. Birth or death I'm an asset at any bedside. I don't dislike this carpet.

MAM: (*Returning*) I forget, you see, that's my trouble. I think I'd have more of the qualities they're looking for if only I could remember. My mother was like that.

They're writing all this down and none of it's normal. Cocktails in a Rolls Royce. Linda flying off in Concorde and now Dad dead. None of it run of the mill.

MRS CLEGG: You're lucky to have had such an action-packed day. I had some baking to do and one or two things to rinse through but nothing dramatic. Nothing to stretch me, nothing that demanded the whole of my personality.

MAM: You're getting some spin-off from this though.

MRS CLEGG: And that is what they're looking for, of course. Coping, mutual support. The way this cheek-by-jowl existence brings out the best in us.

MAM: I wish I could show more grief. I don't want you to think I'm heartless. We were inseparable, only I've got lots to do. Poor Dad. He had everything to live for, basically. I'm sorry I'm not crying. I feel grief-stricken even though I don't show it.

MRS CLEGG: A brave face. They'll understand.

MAM: I do care, deep down.

MRS CLEGG: It'll mean an increased pension.

MAM: Will it?

MRS CLEGG: Plus the death grant.

MAM: Do they give you a death grant?

MRS CLEGG: Provided there's been a death. I put Clifford's towards some loose covers.

MAM: And I suppose I'll still get his disability pension.

MRS CLEGG: What with one thing and another the horizon's far from gloomy.

MAM: He used to have a fine body, right up until his accident. He'd no feeling in this arm.

MRS CLEGG: He's no feeling in it now.

MAM: I suppose we've got to wash him all over.

MRS CLEGG: Of course.

MAM: His eyebrows want cutting.

MRS CLEGG: Never mind his eyebrows. Let's get his trousers off. Do you find this distasteful?

MAM: I'd find it more distasteful if he were alive, bless him! You're such a help, Nora. You should have been a nurse. So calm.

MRS CLEGG: I try to be warm, but clinical. It's a fine line. I'll loosen his trousers.

MAM: I haven't seen some of this for years. (*She weeps.*)

MRS CLEGG: Let it come, love. Let it come.

MAM: I did love him, Nora. I did. I loved him like a child. Only now it's too late.

MRS CLEGG: What's the best way to get his trousers off? You get his legs, and I'll pull.

MAM: Nora.

MRS CLEGG: What?

MAM: Would you be bitterly offended if I took his trousers off by myself?

MRS CLEGG: You can't do it without help.

MAM: I've got to try. He was a shy man, Nora.

MRS CLEGG: Connie. He's not here. He's gone. This is just the

shell. The husk. If you're not conscious you can't be
self-conscious. I'm thinking of your back.

MAM: You've been so good. So understanding.

MRS CLEGG: I've just been a neighbour, Connie. It's what
neighbours are for. Anyway, please yourself. Give us a shout
if there's anything you can't manage.

(MS CRAIG *approaches*.)

You don't want her watching if you don't want me.

MAM: But isn't she official? She's got to be here.

(MRS CLEGG *talks quietly to her observer while* MAM *gets on
with washing* DAD.)

MRS CLEGG: You'll probably think I'm old-fashioned, Adrian, but
my view is that when death occurs in the home, tragic
though it is, we should try to think of it as a privilege. So
many of the fundamental experiences of our lives have
passed beyond our personal control. Passed into the hands
of doctors, social workers, nurses and the like so we are
denied that contact with birth, sickness and death, with
poverty, with suffering and all those areas of human
experience. . .

MAM: Nora! (*Awestruck*)

MRS CLEGG: . . . which were the birthright of our parents . . .

MAM: Nora! (*Alarm*).

MRS CLEGG: . . . and gave their lives meaning and nourishment . . .

MAM: NORA!

(MRS CLEGG *goes over*.)

Look.

MRS CLEGG: Good garden rhubarb! What's that? Oh, Connie.

(*They cling to one another, gazing at* MR CRAVEN'*s body and at
one part in particular*.)

MAM: And you said he was dead.

MRS CLEGG: He may still be dead.

MAM: That's not dead. That's alive. That's life, that is.

MRS CLEGG: It may not be. It may just be a side effect. The
muscles contract. The body plays tricks. The dead often
seem to grin. This doesn't mean they are happy.

MAM: One touch of the flannel. The sly bugger. And me
thinking he was all dead and decent.

MRS CLEGG: Don't leap to conclusions.

MAM: I don't know where to look. And of course we would have company.

MRS CLEGG: Adrian. You'll have been to university. Would you say he was dead?

(ADRIAN *takes a look but says nothing.* MS CRAIG *has gone back to her chair.*)

MAM: I blame you.

MRS CLEGG: Me?

MAM: You would wash him. You would make out that's what it is we do. Traditionally. Normal procedure. For their benefit. Folks don't wash the dead and lay them out. Not in this day and age. It's what my mother used to do. This is the twentieth century. You call in an expert.

MRS CLEGG: She's forgotten. You see how it is. Love, Chippendales has changed hands. It's a patio-paving centre.

MAM: The Co-op hasn't changed hands. That's not a patio-paving centre. The Co-op does a perfectly adequate funeral. I've attended several and they couldn't be faulted. Besides which they'd come along with all this at their fingertips. They'd know if it was normal or not. Tie it down. Tether it. They'll be past masters, with diplomas. They wouldn't turn a hair. But oh no. It had to be Do It Yourself. We're supposed to behave normally.

MRS CLEGG: It's no problem for you. You can behave normally. You forget they're there half the time and when you remember you don't know what it is they're there for.

MAM: Well what are they there for? I don't know.

MRS CLEGG: What difference does it make. It's an unlooked for situation, this. Stuck in a room with a corpse that's not fit to be seen. I know one thing. If it were in my house I could rise to it magnificently.

MAM: You keep saying corpse. Corpse. We don't know if he is a corpse. I've only got your word for it. And all the evidence points the other way. The blighter. It's the same as when he was alive. Always trying to spring it on you. And don't keep looking at him. That's my husband. Saying you bake. You never bake. She never bakes. It's all bought stuff in her house.

It always has been. You were always running on to the end,
you, when there was an end to run on to. That's what killed
your Clifford. Chips and bought cakes. What do you do for
your dinner now they've pulled down the chip shop?

MRS CLEGG: She's under stress. Only you see what I have to put
up with. I don't think we can do any more good here, Adrian.
I'll see if I can find you a few home-made scones and some of
my own preserves. And perhaps when he's made up his
mind whether he's coming or going I'll bob in again. It's no
joke being a tower of strength round here, I can tell you.

(MRS CLEGG *and* ADRIAN *leave.* MAM *and* MS CRAIG *are alone.*)

MAM: Give me that towel. I said give me that towel.

(MS CRAIG *does so.*)

Thank you. Now. I'm not leaving him stuck here. We'd better
get him back in the chair. Come on. Frame.

(MAM *and* MS CRAIG *move him on to the chair.*)

Watching. Not feeling. And what if anybody comes? This is
what children are designed for, this. Buckling to. Rallying
round. And where are they? One's marrying a blackie and
I don't know where the other is. Our Terry. I loved him.
He can't have loved me, I've never had a postcard. I had a
record played for him on Family Favourites on the off-
chance he was in Australia. There's a limit to what you
can do.

I had visions of him going to university. I can just see him
in a scarf opening a bank account.

He's married probably now. Kiddies. I could be stood here
and all the time I'm a grandmother with cartloads of snaps
to catch up on. Instead of which I'm alone. Nobody to turn
to. No kids. Nobody. ('*I Can Give You the Starlight*'
(*Novello*, The Dancing Years) *begins quietly and it seems as if*
MS CRAIG *is about to speak when there is a bang on the door.*)
Oh, company!

(*She opens the door and* LINDA *comes in, lugging two suitcases,
exhausted.*)

(*Brightly*) Hello, Linda love. Have you come back?

LINDA: No. This is a mirage. I'm at this moment sitting under a
palm tree in one of the OPEC countries. (*She goes to the*

door which she has left open.) Come in if you're coming.
(*There is a pause and a large man* (SID) *in working clothes
enters*.)

MAM: Hello. Are you another one? They seem to be doing a
very thorough job. Sit down. Make yourself at home.

SID: Thank you.

MAM: Oh, quite talkative. What happend to your fiancé, love?
Did you not hit it off?

LINDA: I never saw him.

MAM: You were all set to marry him.

LINDA: Well I didn't, did I?
(*Pause*)
Though I got shortlisted.

MAM: Shortlisted? For his bride? How many of you were there?

LINDA: Twenty-five.

MAM: Twenty-five prospective brides? What sort of a man is that?

LINDA: It wasn't him. He wasn't even there. He'd had to fly off
to Vienna. It was his agent, somebody from Lloyds Bank.

MAM: Lloyds? That's one of the classier banks. I'd go there if I
had any money.

LINDA: I got as far as the last six then got eliminated.

MAM: What did you fall down on? Your shorthand?

LINDA: No! My tits!

MAM: Don't be bitter. I'm sure that's not the kind of thing he
was looking for, not if he was from Lloyds Bank.

LINDA: Listen, we had to parade up and down the Wharfedale
Room in our bra and panties!

MAM: At the Queen's Hotel? And it's where Sir Malcolm
Sargent used to stay!

LINDA: He said that although I'd done very well in the oral
examination my tits fell short of the standard required.

MAM: Fell short?

LINDA: He said they were small and a bit on the old side.

MAM: The cheek.

LINDA: What do they know about tits at Lloyds Bank?

MAM: Quite. Still I'm glad you've come back because we've had
a bit of bad news about your father.

LINDA: I thought he was quiet. Is he dead?

MAM: Possibly. It's not completely clear. There's evidence on both sides. I'd welcome your opinion.

(LINDA *lifts the towel covering* DAD.)

LINDA: Blood and sand!

MAM: Exactly.

LINDA: I don't know much about death. Is that what it looks like?

MAM: Yes and no.

LINDA: If he's dead what's he doing in the house?

MAM: Nowadays it is unusual. It was much more the thing when we were younger.

LINDA: Get him out of here. This is the twentieth century.

MAM: Linda, he's your father.

LINDA: Yes. I want to show some feeling and get him into the fridge. I can't understand. You were always so houseproud. What's Sid going to think.

SID: Don't mind me. I've got a family of my own.

MAM: This is a departure: gab, gab, gab.

LINDA: Have you notified the authorities?

MAM: I don't think so. I can't remember.

LINDA: Why not?

MAM: I'm beat, Linda. I'm weary. I'm just at the far end.

LINDA: You can't leave him stuck there. Notify somebody.

MAM: I will once I've got him washed.

LINDA: No. Now. Write it down so you don't forget. (*She does so.*) Dad dead. Burial required.

MAM: Why can't you do it?

LINDA: You're his wife.

MAM: We reckon to be a family.

LINDA: Family nothing. All you need do is tell them and they'll be round to fetch him like a shot. It's bread and butter to somebody is that. Stuck there. Life is for living, that's my motto.

MAM: I'll get me washed and go up to the Co-op.

LINDA: Why can't she go?

MAM: It's not her place. Why can't he go?

LINDA: What's it to do with him?

SID: My wife's in a steel collar. She had one of these accidents in the home. The home is more dangerous than the roads apparently. In terms of statistics.

MAM: That's fascinating. I wish she'd take a leaf out of your book.

LINDA: You'd better come upstairs.

MAM: Yes. Go upstairs. Have a meander round. Show him your room, love. Your home environment. All part of the picture.

LINDA: (*Wearily*) Mam.

MAM: And Linda.

(LINDA *pauses*.)

Don't be upset about Saudi Arabia. Plenty more fish in the sea.

(LINDA *and* SID *go upstairs*.)

She's a resilient girl. She'll soon bounce back. (*Pause*) Only I shall have it all to do, I can see that. The death and all the donkey work. He'd have taken all this in his stride. But then he'd been educated.

(*Music starts*.)

Did I tell you I had a son?

Terry his name was.

He loved music. Adored music. Dad was tone deaf. I had perfect pitch. So where are you? I could have been in the Philharmonic Chorus, you know.

Asked round to these coffee parties after rehearsals, cocktails, little savoury things. There's no telling where I could have ended. Another Kathleen Ferrier possibly. She had a northern background. It didn't stop her.

(*During this last speech* MAM *and* MS CRAIG *have begun to dance and* MAM *sings* 'I Can Give You the Starlight', *the music swelling under her singing as they dance*.)

You're light as a feather.

(*They dance in great style. When they stop they continue to hold one another for a moment*.)

MS CRAIG: Mam.

MAM: About bloody time! Got up in that costume. It doesn't suit you. It doesn't suit you one bit. Navy's your colour. You always looked lovely in navy. Give your Mam a kiss. I think on the whole I preferred you in sportscoat and flannels.

MS CRAIG: Those days are over.

MAM: Terry. Are you still Terry?

MS CRAIG: I spell it with an 'i'.

MAM: You didn't have far to go then?

MS CRAIG: My friends call me Kim.

MAM: Kim. That's a nice name. I prefer Kim to Terri. Kim's more classy. I never thought I'd have a son called Kim. Let alone a daughter. You wouldn't recognize Leeds. It's all pedestrianized now. The traffic's been secluded. And one way and another all your Aunties have died. Mrs Metcalf's had a stroke and their David now works in computers in Kettering. Has anything much else happened apart from you changing your name? Are you rich?

MS CRAIG: To some extent.

MAM: That's good. Though money isn't everything. Did you get a degree?

MS CRAIG: Yes. At Cambridge.

MAM: Cambridge. That's nice. You get all that from me. Your father never opened a book in his life, bless him. (*She goes and looks at him.*) No change. His thing's still there. Shocking except he wasn't all that bad. Considering you were his only son he didn't really dislike you. I shall miss him in other ways. I've missed *you*.

MS CRAIG: I've missed you too.

MAM: Linda hasn't changed, has she?

MS CRAIG: She has a bit.

MAM: She's a personal secretary, you know.

(MS CRAIG *nods.*)

She goes all over. She won't be here long before she's setting off. Stockholm. Kuala Lumpur. If it's not one place it's another. (*Pause*) Actually I don't believe that. Your Dad did. He thought she was a personal secretary. I didn't disillusion him. I don't think she's a personal secretary at all. You don't wear them hairy pink jumper things if you're a personal secretary. No, she lets us think she's a secretary but do you know what I think she is? A policewoman: that would account for her odd hours, bobbing in and out. I wouldn't put it past her to be on detective work. What do you think, Kim?

MS CRAIG: It's possible, Connie.

MAM: That shows you've gone up in the world, using my name. Better-class children do that. Treat their parents like people. Oh, Kim.

MS CRAIG: I'm going to take you away, Connie.

MAM: Where, Kim? London? I've always dreamed about going to London. Most people have made at least one visit by the time they reach my age. Let's have a day or two in London and it will remove the stigma.

MS CRAIG: I'm going to take you away for good! You're going to be protected.

MAM: What from? Not your Dad? He's dead.

MS CRAIG: Everything. Life. You're going to be looked after, Connie. Sheltered. Cared for.

MAM: It's a home, isn't it? You're going to put me in a home. You've come back just to put me in a home. Well, I'm not ready. I'm not silly. My memory's bad but I'm not incontinent. I don't want to go into a home. I want to go into the horrible new flats. Oh, Terry Craven, what a trick to do.

MS CRAIG: It's not a home, Connie. I wouldn't put you in a home.

MAM: Children always say that. That's what I said to my mother. And we did. We did. She lost her memory and we put her in a home.

MS CRAIG: Connie, I promise you. It's not a home. Listen.

MAM: No, you listen. You can't just put me in a home the way I put my mother in a home. It's not as simple as that now. There's people on the Council can stop you. Wardens, social workers. Old people now, they have to be treated with imagination, it's the law. And I'm not old. It's just that I forget. You and me were such pals.

MS CRAIG: Mam, how many more times, I don't mean a home.

MAM: Will you promise me? Promise me over the body of your father you will not put me in a home.

MS CRAIG: I promise you over the body of my father I will not put you in a home.

MAM: (*Pointing*) It's gone. Look, it's gone. Oh, Terry. It must just have been his way of saying goodbye. Oh, Wilf, forgive me, Wilf.

DAD: Wilf? What's this Wilf? What's happened?

MAM: Dad? Are you not dead? We thought you were dead.

DAD: You were wrong then, weren't you? You were premature. What's been the matter with me?

MAM: You passed out.

DAD: What am I like this for? Tied up?

MAM: You're not tied up.

DAD: I'm bound hand and foot.

MAM: You never are.

DAD: I can't move. I'm in water.

MAM: No.

DAD: I'm in water up to my neck.

MAM: You're at home. Look.

DAD: How look? I can't look. I'm in plaster from head to foot. I'm paralysed.

MAM: You weren't paralysed a minute ago. Sit for a bit and it'll go off.

DAD: Sit? I can't move.

MAM: It may be nerves. Nervous paralysis. People go for years thinking they can't move a muscle and it's nothing but their imagination.

DAD: It was that youth. Banging my steel plate, and her just sat there.

MAM: No.

DAD: She sat there and watched.

MAM: You're confused.

DAD: He was banging it up and down like a coal-hole lid while she never lifted a finger.

MAM: She'd never do that. Another human being. We thought you were dead.

DAD: I bet.

MAM: I was just learning to accommodate. You do lead us a dance.

DAD: I can't bloody move. Feel me. See if there's any feeling left.

MAM: I won't. I'm not starting on that game again.

DAD: Light me a cig.

MAM: I won't light you a cig. Light your own cig.

DAD: I can't move.

MAM: Use it as a challenge.

DAD: Our Linda'd light me one. Our Linda'd care.

MAM: Our Linda. Our Linda. You're going to have to change your tune a bit. There's going to have to be less of our Linda now.

(MS CRAIG *lights* MR CRAVEN *a cigarette, putting it in her mouth then his.*)

MS CRAIG: Changed your brand, Dad? These give you a more satisfying smoke, do they?

DAD: What do you know about a satisfying smoke. You're not man enough to know about a satisfying smoke. That's how I knew you were a nancy: you never smoked.

MAM: He smokes now, don't you love. Can't criticize him on that score.

DAD: Coming in all dolled up. I knew you straight off.

MAM: I would have done if it hadn't been for my memory.

DAD: Frocks. I caught him in one of your frocks once. While you were out. I was physically sick. My own son. He'd be fifteen then. I thought it was just a phase. I ought to have known. There were other signs. Most lads would have at least one unwanted pregnancy to their credit by the time they got to that age. Not our Terry.

MAM: His name's Kim, now, isn't it, love? I'm very happy for him. Her.

DAD: A bit of beef skirt, that's what he is. He wanted me killed. He looked on while I was assaulted.

MAM: Only as part of his job. He was conscientious even as a boy.

DAD: I can't *move.*

MAM: That's not Kim's fault. She's come to take us away, haven't you, Kim?

MS CRAIG: Yes, Connie.

DAD: *Connie?* Who the fuck's Connie?

MAM: Me, I'm Connie.

DAD: Don't you Connie, her, madam. I'm the one who Connie's her. She's Mam to you. Mam. Dad. Connie.

MAM: I'm Mam to you too. You never say my name.

DAD: I choose my moments. I say it when it's appropriate. Kim. Connie. Have you both gone mad? You dirty sods. You dirty stinking sods. Using your names. You disgust me.

MAM: Dad.

DAD: You wanted me dead. You thought I was dead. 'Wilf'.

MAM: We had begun to bank on it a bit, I must admit, however, let's change the subject. Kim's got a proposition to make.

MS CRAIG: I've come to take you away, Dad.

MAM: Where is it you're taking us, love?

MS CRAIG: It's on the outskirts.

MAM: Does that mean the Green Belt? It's been one of Dad's ambitions to live on the outskirts.

MS CRAIG: It's in a park.

MAM: I never dreamed I would end up in a park.

DAD: What sort of park? Homes are in parks. The outskirts are where all the homes are. He's going to put us in a home. Your son, stroke daughter.

MAM: It's not a home. Terry has promised me faithfully it's not a home.

DAD: You told your mother it was a hotel. A private hotel.

MAM: No.

DAD: She was just going there for the weekend while we went to Scarborough.

MAM: No.

DAD: She couldn't speak when we saw her next. She'd gone silly.

MAM: No.

DAD: Yes. It's a home.

MAM: God forgive you, Terry. Your own mother.

(GREGORY *opens the door and comes inside, waiting.*
ADRIAN *follows and waits, the other side.*
HARMAN *enters. The same age as* GREGORY *and* ADRIAN, *but with more authority. He is followed by two more young men,* CHARLES *and* ROWLAND, *who wait in the background, holding clipboards.*)

HARMAN: And if there is a problem get on to Maintenance and let them sort it out. It's what we pay them for. Now. What have we here?

(HARMAN *walks round the house and round* MAM *and* DAD

320

without speaking. GREGORY *and* ADRIAN *follow,* GREGORY *with a notebook,* ADRIAN *with a Polaroid camera.*)

(*After an excessive silence*) The mantelpiece is perfect. Pity they ruined the fireplace.

(GREGORY *makes a note.*)

The curtains are good.

(ADRIAN *snaps the curtains.*)

All this is beautiful.

(HARMAN *maybe frames a section of the room in his hands and* ADRIAN *then photographs it.* HARMAN *opens the staircase door.*) Get a sample of that wallpaper. It's terrible. (*He sees the bath.*) I like the bath. The bath comes over loud and clear.

(HARMAN *now looks very closely at* MAM *and* DAD, *without speaking. He maybe runs his hand over* MAM's *face absently.*) Hello, love.

MAM: Hello.

DAD: Who the fuck are you?

HARMAN: Hello! Are you the man of the house?

MAM: My husband's not himself at the moment.

(HARMAN, GREGORY, ADRIAN *and* MS CRAIG *now confer.*)

HARMAN: My feeling is we should take this place. As it stands. In fact don't let's piss around. We should take the whole street.

MS CRAIG: I thought so.

DAD: Who is this joker? Lay off.

(HARMAN *is standing by* DAD, *massaging his arm.*)

HARMAN: You're understandably intrigued, Mr Craven. Your home invaded . . . are you totally paralysed? . . . habits documented by strangers . . . do you feel that? . . . your everyday life subject to scrutiny . . . no? . . . the flesh is so good: white, white, *white.*

(GREGORY *makes a note.*)

DAD: Mam.

MAM: It's all right, Dad. He's from the Council. It's to do with all-round happiness. We had the explanatory letter.

DAD: Happiness nothing, I require medical attention.

HARMAN: When Kim mentioned her family to me, Mrs Craven, I was quite frankly surprised. I never knew you had a family, Kim, I said. I had you down as an independent sort of

person. And here you are. A queen. (I love the face, Kim.)
We send out expeditions to Brazil. We plunge through the
rain forests of the Amazon to protect a few lost tribes. But
it's here, Mrs Craven, now. This is the disappearing world.
Leeds, Bradford, Halifax. A way of life on its last legs.
Women like you . . .

MAM: I'm old-fashioned, I know . . .

HARMAN: This house . . . this street.

MAM: They're grand houses. I've always said so. It's a crime to
knock them down.

HARMAN: Absolutely. Show her, Adrian.

(ADRIAN *takes* MAM *to the door*.)

DAD: Slums.

HARMAN: No.

MAM: They've gone. The bulldozers have gone.

DAD: They'll be knocking off early, the buggers.

MAM: (*And possibly she goes outside the house so we just hear her
echoing voice*) There isn't a bulldozer to be seen.

HARMAN: No. I had them withdrawn.

DAD: Then unwithdraw them. We're waiting to get into the new
flats.

HARMAN: He's such value.

MS CRAIG: I know. I hate him.

HARMAN: Naturally.

MAM: Are we not going to be knocked down then?

HARMAN: Yes, but very lovingly and by qualified experts. Each
brick numbered; a chart made for every slate, the whole
house, the entire street to be re-erected on the outskirts in a
parkland setting.

DAD: It's a home.

MAM: It's not a home, Dad. These are all refined young men.

HARMAN: A park people will pay to go into. A people's park.

MAM: We shan't be with zebras and kangaroos. We went to one
of those once and they were all asleep. It was money down
the drain.

HARMAN: Visitors will alight from one of a fleet of trams to find
themselves in a close-knit community where people know
each others' names and still stop and pass the time of day.

322

There will be a cotton mill, steam engines and genuine hardship.

MAM: This park, is it in a clean-air zone?

HARMAN: Unfortunately yes, but on certain appointed days soot will fall like rain, exactly as it used to.

MAM: But will I be able to keep the place spotless?

HARMAN: Only by working your fingers to the bone.

DAD: Will there be a fireside?

HARMAN: A coal fire is a must, though underfloor central heating is provided strictly for use out of opening hours.

MAM: I like a fire. A fire's company.

DAD: This fire, can I spit into it?

HARMAN: At will and never accurately.

MAM: That means I shall have to blacklead.

HARMAN: Constantly.

MAM: What will I cook?

HARMAN: Tripe, cowheel, trotters, breast of mutton. The traditional food of your class.

MAM: I hope you've got an understanding butcher. And I can bake. Bake like I did when I was first married.

DAD: You never baked. My mother baked. You never did.

MAM: I did, I'm sure I did. Quiches are the in thing now, aren't they? All the young marrieds go in for quiches. I keep reading about it in these magazines. I imagine you have quiches, Kim? You have done well.

MS CRAIG: It'll be exactly like it was when I was little.

MAM: I can't remember what I was like when you were little.

MS CRAIG: Don't worry. I can.

MAM: Was I a good mother? A capable housewife?

MS CRAIG: Down to the last detail.

MAM: I never let you go short?

MS CRAIG: With you self-sacrifice always came first.

MAM: I sound to have been a perfect mother.

MS CRAIG: You were.

HARMAN: And shall be again. And people coming round will watch you work and skimp and save and remember the labour their mothers had and all for nothing and will go away contented and assured of the future. And if you do forget, don't worry; it simply tells another story.

DAD: What's in it for you?

HARMAN: We're a young team. We do it for love.

DAD: Love! I'm paralysed.

MAM: Has it not gone off yet? It will, I'm sure. Try to look on the bright side.

DAD: I don't want to go.

MAM: I do.

HARMAN: Perfect. The woman clings to the past, the man holds out for the future. You were right, Kim. They are ideal.

DAD: I want our Linda.

MAM: It doesn't sound to me in Linda's line. Ask her.

DAD: How can I ask her? She's in Saudi Arabia.

MAM: She's not in Saudi Arabia. She's upstairs.

MS CRAIG: Linda can come if she wants.

DAD: I'm not going anywhere without Linda. Me and Linda are inseparable.

HARMAN: I must go. Dear lady. Put one or two things together, but only the barest essentials. Packing is unnecessary as these trained staff will shortly transfer your home and its contents to its new setting. Nothing will change.

MAM: That's ideal.

HARMAN: The only difference, unavoidable in the circumstances, is that your windows will have a distant prospect of green fields. That apart, no expense has been spared to convince you that you are still living in the depths of the slums.

MAM: It sounds a work of art. I'm so excited. I've always felt the past was over and that I'd somehow missed it. Now it's starting all over again.

(HARMAN *kisses* MAM *on both cheeks.*)

That's the classy way of kissing, isn't it? Do you kiss like that, Kim? Oh, love, I'm so proud! (*She goes upstairs.*)

DAD: I'm not coming. I refuse to move.

HARMAN: Warm. Familiar. A genuine community where misfortune brings not isolation but a spate of visitors. Neighbours (with broth, possibly). A family doctor, your name at his fingertips, a vicar of stout faith to whom consolation is second nature. A place, Dad. *Roots. Home.* It's such a powerful image I'm loath to lose him.

MS CRAIG: He embarrasses me.

HARMAN: Of course.

DAD: Young man. Young man, I've something to tell you, something that will change your ideas. That's not a woman. I'm ashamed to say that's my son. He's a lad dressed up. Or something.

HARMAN: (*Whispering*) I *know*. (*He goes back to* MS CRAIG *and the others*.) We must have him.

DAD: I shall write personally to the Town Hall.

HARMAN: Bless you. Kim's a big feather in their cap. We're very proud of Kim, aren't we?

DAD: I feel sick.

(HARMAN *kisses* MS CRAIG.)

HARMAN: Do your best. (*To* DAD.) Goodbye. And don't change.

(HARMAN *goes*. GREGORY, ADRIAN, ROWLAND *and* CHARLES *remain*.)

MS CRAIG *looks at the magazine that has the pictures of* LINDA *in it*.)

DAD: That's mine. Put it away. Don't let her see it.

(MS CRAIG *goes on looking at it*.)

You'd never get into a magazine like that. *Kim*. Magazines like that . . . they go into thousands of homes. They're distributed in every part of the English-speaking world. She's famous is our Linda. She's a known face. She'll get correspondence from all over. Be asked to open precincts, supermarkets, betting-shops. You can't despise fame.

(MS CRAIG *puts the magazine away*. LINDA *comes in*.)

That's your brother, Linda.

LINDA: I had a feeling it might be. Hi. Long time no see.

DAD: Doesn't he disgust you?

LINDA: Should he?

DAD: He disgusts me.

LINDA: I find him not unattractive.

DAD: It's unnatural.

LINDA: Dad. This is the twentieth century. Mam was telling me about the museum. I won't come if it's all the same to you. Quite frankly I don't feel part of this environment any more.

(LINDA *and* MS CRAIG *are smiling at one another*.)

We've both of us had to break out. In our different ways.

DAD: Don't bracket yourself with him, Linda. You're a personal secretary. He's bent.

LINDA: I knew that years ago. I knew it as soon as I saw the photographs in his room.

DAD: Male nudes?

LINDA: Judy Garland.

DAD: Don't leave me, Linda. I don't fancy being in a glass case. I want my declining years to be spent with you.

LINDA: Be practical. You can't be with me.

DAD: Why?

LINDA: I work late; I often bring work home.

DAD: I find the sound of typing soothing.

LINDA: Typing! (*She laughs*.) Sid was telling me upstairs he has a brother-in-law with a string of launderettes all over the Channel Islands. He thinks I may be qualified for an executive post.

DAD: Could there be a position for me?

LINDA: Dad, you're paralysed from the neck downwards.

DAD: It sounds a large organization, there might just be a niche.

LINDA: Oh Dad.

DAD: I blame you. She'd have stayed if it hadn't been for you. What did you want to come back for?

MS CRAIG: I wanted to refresh my memory. It's my job.

DAD: Your job to stir things up. Your job to provoke. Your job to sit there, casting an educated eye. We were a more or less united family on the threshold of a nice modern flat. Now Linda's leaving and your Mam and me are stuck in a museum the rest of our lives. Stay the same? It's a revolution.

MS CRAIG: Some degree of interference in the social processes is inevitable. The trained observer makes allowances for that. (MS CRAIG *gives* LINDA *the magazine*.)

DAD: No. Don't look, Linda. Take no notice. You, you're a passive observer. You're not supposed to take a hand.

MS CRAIG: I'm your son, Dad.

DAD: You want me killed.

LINDA: (*To* MS CRAIG) Is this yours?

326

MS CRAIG: No. It's our Dad's.

LINDA: But you thought I was a personal secretary.

DAD: Not altogether.

LINDA: You thought I was a typist.

DAD: I always had an inkling.

LINDA: You never let on?

DAD: Out of love, Linda. Out of consideration. Out of tact.

LINDA: Your only daughter drifts into prostitution and you don't lift a finger.

DAD: It's not prostitution, Linda. It's art. Fame. Those magazines go all over. People will know you who've never seen you. In Denmark or West Germany! I just wanted you to get on.

LINDA: You disgust me.

DAD: We were always such pals.

LINDA: He interfered with me, that's what he means.

(*She shows* MS CRAIG *the magazine.*)

Nice wallpaper, don't you think. To look at him you'd never dream he'd got a degree in philosophy would you. Some daughters would have reported you. You could be had up. Sent to prison.

DAD: Don't say such things. You're hurting me.

LINDA: They gave me that candlestick. It's upstairs.

DAD: I've still got feelings.

LINDA: I was supposed to be the apple of your eye. That's one of them continental quilts. She's from Birmingham. You can tell as soon as she opens her mouth.

DAD: I love you, Linda.

LINDA: Too late. I'm not a personal secretary. I'm a slag.

DAD: We could still be together. I could be standing by.

LINDA: Do you mean watching?

DAD: Some people like being watched. Being watched improves it for some people. Alters it. Makes it different.

LINDA: You can hardly see.

DAD: They won't know that. You've got to adapt to changing circumstances. I've been slow to adapt. Looking back I can see that's been my problem all the way through. Come on, Linda. We could make an enterprising duo and we'd be together.

LINDA: Dad!

DAD: I've still a bit of a future left. If you leave me I shall be on my own.

LINDA: You won't. You'll be in the park with Mam. There'll be people traipsing round every day, looking at you. They'll be watching you all the time. You won't be lonely. You'll never have a moment to yourself. And there'll always be Kim to pop in and keep an eye on you. I'm telling you, you'll be in clover. Bye-bye, chick.

(LINDA *kisses* DAD *on the top of his head.* MAM *comes in looking very smart.*)

MAM: Are you off, love? Where is it this time? Winnipeg? Santa Fe?

LINDA: Actually I'm just popping across to Jersey.

DAD: Jersey! Show her. Show your Mam that magazine. Go on. See whether that's Jersey. Look. That's not Jersey. It's filth.

(MAM *looks at the magazine.*)

MAM: Well, times change. You've got to keep up with the times.

DAD: It's our Linda.

MAM: Top secretaries, they do get their pictures in magazines.

DAD: She's no clothes on.

MAM: They use nudes to sell office furniture now. It's the modern world. Bye-bye, love. Spare us a thought when you're coming through the duty free. Say goodbye to Kim.

DAD: Don't let him touch you, Linda. He may be successful, but he's still a nancy.

LINDA: He obviously fancies me. How can he be a nancy?

DAD: He's wearing a frock so it's still wrong.

MAM: It's clear you could have had a lovely brother-and-sister relationship. What a pity you're going now we're all together.

LINDA: (*Shouts upstairs*) Sid.

DAD: Kiss me, Linda. Just give me a kiss.

MAM: Now Dad, don't spoil it.

(SID *appears.*)

LINDA: I hope these launderettes aren't a figment of your imagination.

SID: Thank you for letting me see your lovely home.

MAM: It's been a pleasure. Off you go.

(SID *and* LINDA *depart.*)

DAD: Linda!

(MAM *stands, a bit lost.*)

MAM: Now, I'm all dressed up and I know we're going somewhere but I've forgotten where it is. Are we going to London, Kim?

DAD: She's getting worse. You don't know what you're taking on. She'll drive you mad. We're going into cold storage, you dozy cow. We're headed for a glass case.

MAM: We're not going into a home?

MS CRAIG: No, Mam. It's not a home.

DAD: It's worse than a home.

MAM: It can't be. There's nowhere worse than a home. My mother went into a home. I've never forgiven myself.

DAD: Now it's our turn.

MS CRAIG: Listen, it's your life as it used to be, down to the last detail. But it's not a home. It's this home, for ever and ever. I promise.

(*At this point* GREGORY, ADRIAN, ROWLAND *and* CHARLES *begin to dismantle the house. Large sections of the room are removed, walls, furniture, the lot.*)

MAM: If Kim says it isn't a home, Dad, I think we should believe her. So let's get you dressed and ready. She's been educated and (MAM *watches as a wall is silently and smoothly removed.*) they seem to know exactly what they're doing.

DAD: He tried to kill me.

MAM: When? With the car? She probably doesn't even drive. Oh, Dad.

DAD: What's matter?

MAM: You're all wet. Why didn't you say you wanted to go?

DAD: I didn't know. I've told you, I can't feel anything.

MAM: I've just put my best frock on.

DAD: It's not my fault.

MAM: Where's your clean pants?

(MAM *manages to rescue a pair from a piece of furniture which is on one of the sections being removed. She does this as if it is the most natural thing in the world.*)

329

This puts a different complexion on things. If he's going to be like this, Kim, he'll want tip-top nursing. I'm not sure I'm up to that.

DAD: You are, Mam, you are.

MAM: In the absence of any labour-saving devices I shall have quite enough to do without you wetting all up and down.

MS CRAIG: We're basically a museum. We haven't the facilities to cope with incontinence.

MAM: Whereas a hospital would have all that at their fingertips. What do you think?

MS CRAIG: You must decide. It must be your decision.

MAM: You are a comfort. I've never had such support from your father.

MS CRAIG: Maybe when we've got you settled in we could look round for somebody else. A nice lodger, perhaps. That's a traditional situation, ideal for a model community.

MAM: He'd have to be clean. A widower perhaps. Someone retired. Gents' outfitters have always seemed to me a nice class of person.

DAD: What are you whispering about? I want to go with you. I want to be preserved too.

MAM: Say if he didn't go, we could advertise for some sort of attendant. A young person wanting to pull their weight in society might just jump at a genuine invalid.

MS CRAIG: That's true.

MAM: Opportunities calling for devoted self-sacrifice don't turn up every day of the week.

MS CRAIG: Quite. Any really first-rate chance of improving the soul gets snapped up by the social services department. (MAM *has been stood with a bowl and towel and now just manages to park them on the next piece of the room that is on its way out.*)

MAM: Another thing, Dad, is now that Kim's come back, Terry as was, I can see how little you and me have got in common. Even memories. Husband and wife you'd think we'd have the same memories, but we don't. My memory's bad, I know that. I take after my mother, but the memories I do have I share with Kim. And she's interested. You're not.

You've never been bothered about the past at all. You couldn't wait to get to the future.

DAD: I only want to get into the flat. All this'll be different when we get into the flat.

MAM: No, love. You'll be better off in the new wing at the Infirmary. It's the last word in architecture as well as treatment. It was opened by the Duchess of Kent.

DAD: I won't wet myself again, I promise.

MAM: It doesn't matter if you do, love. It'll all be catered for by the nurses, it's part of their training. We'll be able to bob in and see you any time: they're very liberal about visiting hours now. It's this new dispensation: you can pop in any time provided you don't actually see the patients being treated. (*She goes out, calling.*) Don't take away the scullery till I've washed my hands.

(*The scullery is removed.* DAD *and* MS CRAIG *are now left on a completely open stage.*)

DAD: Don't leave me, Terry. You've been educated, you can't abandon me. I love you. I know I loved Linda more but you can't always love your children fifty-fifty.

MS CRAIG: Don't worry about it, Dad.

DAD: Take me with you. I'll even use your name. I'd call you . . . Kim.

MS CRAIG: You wouldn't enjoy it.

DAD: I would. I'd enjoy anywhere. I enjoy life. I just need the right circumstances. Given the proper environment I'd be a different person.

MS CRAIG: No.

DAD: Then kill me. Don't leave me. Kill me.

MS CRAIG: I don't want to kill you.

DAD: You always wanted to kill me. So go on. Get it over with.
(*In the scullery* MAM *starts singing* '*We'll Gather Lilacs*' (*Novello*, Perchance to Dream).)

MS CRAIG: No.

DAD: What are you doing?

MS CRAIG: I'm going to kiss you.

DAD: I'd rather you killed me than kissed me. I don't want kissing. Men don't kiss.

MS CRAIG: I'm not a man.

DAD: Get away.

MS CRAIG: Go on, Dad. Just a hug.

(*He takes* DAD *and holds* DAD's *face against his chest as* DAD *struggles briefly, then stops.*
MAM *comes back.*)

MAM: Where is it we're bound for? Are we off to London?

MS CRAIG: *No.* The park. Your old life. Remember.

MAM: I don't, love, but you can explain as we go. (*Pause*) You know you remind me of somebody and I've forgotten who it is.

MS CRAIG: Terry, Mam.

MAM: It *is* Terry. I *am* sorry. I shan't forget like this love, once I get settled. There's courses you can take to improve your memory, you see them advertised. I'm going to send up. Your Dad's asleep. Never mind. I knew he wouldn't be interested. Anything that bit unusual you could never get him interested, bless him. I could have had a promising singing career but for him, and he'd never have let you stop on at school. That was all me. I was the one. You get it all from me.

(GREGORY, *having worn a brown coat for the removals, now enters in a white one with a wheelchair.*)

What a spanking wheelchair. Light as a feather. Bye-bye, Wilf. (*Kisses* DAD.) Oh, I've lipsticked you. (*She takes out a hanky and wipes it off.*) We've never really got on. You could tell by our names. Connie and Wilf . . . it doesn't sound right somehow. Not to me anyway. Peggy and Frank, Madge and Perce, Duggie and Maureen . . . they all sound like couples. But Connie and Wilf—that never sounded like anybody to me.

(DAD *is wheeled off by* GREGORY.)

He'll be better off in hospital. Waited on hand and foot.

MS CRAIG: Naturally.

MAM: They're very good that way now. It's wonderful what they do for you. We never had services like that when we were young.

(ADRIAN *takes her arm to the music of 'Did You Not Hear My*

332

Lady' (Handel) sung by MAM *on tape.*)
Oh, are you my escort? This takes me back to when I was
first married. I don't know where we're going but I'm
looking forward to it.
I forget everything but never songs. What does that mean?
(MAM *continues singing as she is escorted away, leaving*
MS CRAIG *alone.*)

MS CRAIG: That's a load off my mind, seeing them both settled
. . . my father didn't die: he'd just swooned from distaste at
that physical contact with his ex-son. I shan't stay around
long. I've got my sights set on New York. You can be
yourself there and nobody turns a hair. Meanwhile I seem
to be coming round to my Dad. When I go to see him they
wheel him out on to the balcony and we talk. We talk a lot
now.
(DAD *and* MAM *appear on either side of the stage,* DAD *in a
wheelchair. All three characters remain isolated.*)

DAD: They showed this view to Princess Alexandra when she
came round and she said 'This view is as good as any
medicine.' You can see the whole of Leeds. I wish I'd
branched out a bit now, Terry. I should have been more
like you. Do you still wear that stuff?

MS CRAIG: Sometimes.

DAD: You want to blame your Mam.

MAM: I have a young woman comes to see me. I think she must
be a social worker. She's quite pleasant but then, that's
what she's paid for. She gets cross if I say it's a home. But
if it's not a home, what is it?

MS CRAIG: Home for me at the moment is a little place on the
edge of the moors, a farmhouse I've done up. It's only forty
minutes but it's another world. I look down on everything.
Leeds . . . it's just a glow in the sky. I feel I'm ready to
start now.

The Faber contemporary Classics series
aims to provide a body of work, in collected form,
for all the Faber playwrights.

April de Angelis
Alan Ayckbourn
Alan Bennett
Steven Berkoff
Marina Carr
Martin Crimp
Nick Dear
Brian Friel
Athol Fugard
Trevor Griffiths
Christopher Hampton
David Hare
Tony Harrison
Ronald Harwood
Hanif Kureishi
Sharman Macdonald
Frank McGuinness
Richard Nelson
Sean O'Casey
John Osborne
Harold Pinter
Wallace Shawn
Sam Shepard
Tom Stoppard
Nick Ward
Timberlake Wertenbaker